PRINCE REGENT

The Scandalous Private Life of George IV

HARRY EDGINGTON

Hamlyn Paperbacks

For Margaret

PRINCE REGENT
ISBN 0 600 20007 8

First published
in Great Britain 1979
by Hamlyn Paperbacks
Copyright © 1979 by Harry Edgington

Hamlyn Paperbacks are published by
The Hamlyn Publishing Group Ltd,
Astronaut House,
Feltham,
Middlesex, England

Set, printed and bound in Great Britain by
Cox & Wyman Ltd, Reading

PRINCE REGENT

One thinks of Regency England as a time of unequalled elegance and taste, of Nash terraces, the Brighton Pavilion, Beau Brummell and antique silverware.

But the man who gave his title to the time was a libertine whose entire life was spent in pursuit of pleasure. From an early age he began a career of seduction and debauchery.

Harry Edgington chronicles George IV's misspent life with comprehensive skill revealing the story behind a royal rake's progress through a life of gambling, drink and unfettered sexual greed.

The portrait of the Prince Regent shown on the cover is reproduced by permission of the National Portrait Gallery, London.

CONTENTS

I

CHILDHOOD

As the summer of 1762 passed, every member of the English Court – not to mention millions of interested subjects – strained for news from the royal grapevine of the pregnancy of their eighteen-year-old Queen, Charlotte of Mecklenburg-Strelitz.

Her husband, the young George III, was, understandably, beside himself with excitement when he heard late on the afternoon of August 12 that Queen Charlotte's labour had started. For the child, their first, would also be the first born to a reigning English monarch in three-quarters of a century.

He spent the day of nervous waiting in his private apartments at St James's Palace, while progress reports from the Queen's bedchamber were relayed to him by couriers. This was by no means a sign of indifference on his part. In fact, he was so enthralled by the events a few rooms away that he passed the word around that he would pay a £500 reward to the person who brought him news of a daughter. If the announcement was of a son, the bounty would be doubled. The King's open-handed generosity reflected the extravagance engendered by the period. That very day a rich load of plunder from Spanish galleons had passed the Palace en route to storage at the Bank of England.

The birth was to be a most public event, in vivid contrast to the seemingly miraculous arrival of James II's son in 1688, which was so secretive that it led to claims of fraud. That son, James, was obliged to live his life out in exile in France as the Old Pretender.

When word spread that the birth was imminent,

dignitaries from the government, the Court, and the Church hurried to wait in the Queen's ante-chamber. Ladies of the Bedchamber and Charlotte's German women attendants had to make room for the Archbishop of Canterbury, the First Lord of the Treasury, two Secretaries of State, and the officers of the Privy Council and the Royal Household.

Prince George entered this royal world at precisely 7.24 PM. The task of relaying the news to the waiting King should have fallen to Lord Cantelupe, Vice-Chamberlain to the Queen, who had been ordered to hold himself ready for this duty. But an over-anxious Earl of Huntingdon, Master of the King's Horse, eager to claim the reward, could not contain himself. He rushed through the Palace to break the first news of the birth to the King. However, the hapless Earl lost his bounty because in his unseemly haste he confused the sex of the newborn child. He announced the arrival of a daughter.

King George, who had clearly been praying earnestly for a son, haughtily declared to Huntingdon that he did not care what sex the child was, so long as the Queen was safe. He strode along the corridors of St James's Palace to her bed-chamber, entering by a rear door to avoid the crowd packed into the ante-chamber.

There he was shown his healthy, lusty, and fine-looking son. King George, at twenty-four, and within a year of his marriage to Charlotte, the youngest daughter of a German duke, had seen the royal line secured. His happiness was mirrored by a nation which had allowed the monarchy to be restored just over a century before, following the Cromwellian Commonwealth.

The boy was automatically Duke of Cornwall, Duke of Rothesay, Earl of Carrick, and Baron of Renfrew. Before he was two weeks old, he was christened George Augustus Frederick and created Prince of Wales and Earl of Cromer. He was to be known to history as the Prince Regent, George IV, or just Prinny.

Within minutes of his birth, the Prince was displayed to the gathered dignitaries, and greeted them with lusty cries. The gathering cheered, and the birth was celebrated in porter and wine up and down the country. London enjoyed a day-long scene of dancing and gaiety.

At the age of two weeks, he was given an infant lying-in-state when he was put on show in his cradle at St James's Palace for two hours on six successive afternoons. So many members of the nobility were drawn to the spectacle of the baby Prince, heir to the thrones of England, Scotland, Ireland and Hanover, sleeping behind a lattice-work partition that £500 worth of cake was consumed, along with a daily intake of eight gallons of spiced and sweetened warm wine.

An ostentatious christening by the Archbishop of Canterbury followed in the midst of the ornate carvings, the gold-trimmed satin and velvet, of the Queen's drawing-room at St James's Palace. Prince George was brought in on a white satin pillow, attended by a procession led by the Lord Chamberlain, the Duke of Devonshire, and sponsored by venerable members of the royal family. His father shed a tear of happiness as the boy, true to tradition of all babies, bellowed throughout the ceremony.

George was given a large infantine establishment, which consisted of a wet nurse, a dry nurse, a necessary woman, a seamstress, and two rockers of the royal cradle, under the jurisdiction of the royal governess, Lady Charlotte Finch, and her chief deputy.

When he was pushed in his perambulator to take the air in Hyde Park, crowds gathered to watch him and cheer. One recorded cry was, 'God bless him, he is a lusty, jolly young dog, truly!'

His popularity with the population at large was to last during his youth, but, sadly, when people became appalled at his gross self-indulgence, his appeal drained away.

His mother idolised her first-born son. She commissioned a painting of him lying in her arms, countless miniature portraits, and a model of him in wax which she displayed on a velvet cushion in her room.

A roundly precocious child, George astonished a charity gathering when, at two years of age, he made an eloquent and faultless reply to a group who presented a hundred-pound gift. When he was four he was obliged to stay in bed in a darkened room following a smallpox inoculation; his mother's Keeper of the Robes asked him if he was upset at the enforced confinement, and he replied in a most serious tone, 'Not at all. I lie and make reflections.'

George III was, however, determined not to spoil his son or, for that matter, any of his other children. He ordered a rigid and strictly administered upbringing and education for George and the fourteen brothers and sisters who were to arrive in the following twenty-one years. The King's intentions were doubtless admirable, but the effect of his instructions on George's mind was to prove disastrous.

The Prince's early school lessons lasted from just after breakfast at 7 AM until dinner at 3 PM. By the time he was five, he was well on his way to mastering English grammar and had learned the art of handwriting from the Royal Writing Master. He was healthy and intelligent, if somewhat short on temper and determination. It took just a couple of spills when he was learning to skate to convince him to give up the effort. Any flaws in his character, the King hoped, would be ironed out by the rigorous training he was undergoing.

King George and his wife disdained the regal opulence of St James's Palace and preferred a scene of domestic simplicity. Prince George's first years were spent in the secluded privacy of Buckingham House, then a cosy red-brick building in St James's Park. Later his parents chose for him the rural isolation offered by Richmond Lodge in Kew, a small house which was part of the Queen's marriage settlement.

Queen Charlotte was obsessive about her children's health, and had two doctors permanently on hand to look after them, with orders in particular to watch for signs of the fearful scrofula disease, a tendency to tuberculosis inherited from their father. She supervised their bathing at six each morning, watched the girls in their schoolroom, and took a deep interest in their mode of dress.

However, by the time Queen Charlotte had mothered eight other children – Prince Frederick, Prince William, Princess Charlotte, Prince Edward, Princess Augusta, Princess Elizabeth and Prince Ernest – the family, attended by a veritable army of servants, was feeling cramped in

Richmond Lodge, which had previously been the Keeper's Lodge of Richmond Park. So George and his oldest brother, Prince Frederick, a year younger, were boarded out in a nearby house.

On the explicit orders of the King, their shared education became even more exacting, lasting from early morning till eight o'clock at night. The Princes were taught Latin, Greek, French, German, and Italian. Inseparable for years, they learned the arts of riding and fencing together. They also shared floggings, meted out with a long whip by their teachers to remind them sharply of the impropriety of lying and laziness.

Overlord of the intensified education was a stolid disciplinarian, Robert D'Arcy, Earl of Holdernesse, who was employed as their governor. Sub-governor was Leonard Smelt, a Royal Engineers officer who had a surprising penchant for literature and art. Their main tutor was the arrogant William Markham, a former Headmaster of Westminster School, Dean of Christ Church, Bishop of Chester, and later Archbishop of York.

Under their watchful eyes, George learned the languages, though he attained fluency only in French. Greek epigrams he learned parrot-fashion. But his adeptness at letter-writing was commended by those members of his family he corresponded with.

A different facet of his education centred on a strip of ground which he and his brother cultivated at Kew. They sowed wheat, reaped and harvested the crop, using the resultant flour to bake their own loaves of bread.

A musical interest was encouraged by visits of the astounding child prodigy, the nine-year-old Wolfgang Mozart, to the royal household at the invitation of King George. Johann Christian Bach, youngest son of the composer, Johann Sebastian, was appointed Music Master of the Queen's Household, and also gave regular concerts.

Moral guidance was heaped on Prince George from every direction. His father urged him to truth, warning that God was watching his every move. The Earl of Holdernesse also advocated truth, and warned him of the dangers of his growing appetite for food and flattery. The Queen advised him similarly of the dangers of enjoying flattery, and urged him to keep clear of all vice.

The King's love for his younger children was clearly displayed to visitors who grew used to seeing him rolling on the floor with them in the royal apartments, playing mock rough-and-tumble games. But as the children grew older, his affection for them appeared to wane correspondingly. As if wanting to imprison his son in babyhood, the King made George wear frocks with lace hems and cuffs long after he should have progressed to adult clothes. Indeed, the young but growing Prince could hardly help but notice that his contemporaries had long since abandoned the frilly clothes of their infant childhood. On one occasion, he showed his anger and frustration at this. He snatched at his collar and complained to a servant, 'See how I am treated!'

The public was admitted to the gardens surrounding the royal home at Kew on two days a week and river parties travelled up the Thames, accompanied by bands, to moor near Prince George's house. The King arranged birthday entertainments, dances, and firework displays. Prince George and his elder brother were permitted to attend evening parties at St James's Palace and Buckingham House, to which two or three hundred people would be invited to play cards and listen to music. George was also allowed to visit Covent Garden to see a performance of Bach's children's operetta *The Fairy Favour*, given specially for him, and a subsequent staging of the opera *Caratacco*. The artists John Zoffany and Thomas Gainsborough came to the royal houses to paint his portrait.

All this offered a scene of a royal family living in the bosom of their subjects. But these events were rare, and provided Prince George with his only glimpses of life beyond his own personal stockade, which lay within the garden walls of Buckingham House and Richmond Lodge. The only other child of his own age he could have as a companion was his brother Frederick. Their father could foresee no problem inherent in this. He compounded the crime by ensuring that George was kept well clear of any adults who might be expected to fill out his extremely limited knowledge of the exciting and exotic world outside the royal confines. The King even ordained that it was the duty of those surrounding the young Prince to throw a veil over the outside world, as if any comprehension of it would endanger him.

Prince George was some months over the threshold of his teens when his father sacked Dr Markham as his tutor. The King reasoned that Prince and educator had become too friendly, and consequently the whip could not be cracked sharply enough. So he paid Markham off with an engraved copy of the *Odes of Pindar* and the post of Archbishop of York.

Absolutely determined to subdue his son, King George recruited Dr Richard Hurd, Bishop of Lichfield and Coventry, as replacement for Markham. He made it crystal clear that he expected the new man to impose a regime more rigorous than the one his sons had grown accustomed to. Even at that very early age, the King seemed jealous of his eldest son and filled with apprehension about him as he grew towards maturity. His solution to both problems was more discipline, in an unfeeling and cruel attempt to break the boy's spirit.

Dr Hurd promptly prepared his precise and demanding Plans of Study for the Princes. The programme encompassed religion, morals, history, government, laws, mathematics, philosophy, and literature. His history lessons warned the Princes of the despotic and popish intentions of the Stuart royal line, potent propaganda in a time when Britain was alive with fears that Catholicism might attempt to reinstate Papal power over the realm. Civil government lessons preached against flattery, which, Dr Hurd asserted, 'degrades subjects to slaves, in order that it may lift princes into the ranks of Gods'. The classics were ingrained in the two boys, with a special feature of the week provided by Dr Hurd's orders for Sundays, when they were expected to read constantly from the Greek Testament.

George's education under Dr Hurd was broadened to include playing the cello, singing, fencing, boxing, and drawing. But he was reminded of the strictures of the process when he received a New Year present from Dr Hurd. It was a set of prayers.

The seclusion gave him a synthetic boyhood. Though schooled efficiently in the classics, he probably knew less of the world than any boy of his age in the whole country. His boyhood remained strangely artificial, as empty of character as the listless family portraits which adorned the royal homes, and convey a somewhat lifeless message to us through the ages.

The King, however, achieved what he had aimed for. An heir to the throne whose education was apparently all-pervading.

It amounted to a tragic error.

True, Prince George had absorbed a mountain of useful knowledge, and every day had been taken up learning languages and the arts. He was a classics scholar, a musician of some ability, a fencer of considerable skill.

Yet no one had even attempted to interest his mind in the art of government or the mechanics of politics or the profound lessons of history.

His knowledge of social conditions, of the type of poverty which was soon to light the fuse of the French Revolution, was nil. The high walls and the narrow mind of King George had seen to that.

To leave in such ignorance a Prince destined to rule a thrusting empire amounted to gross irresponsibility.

Despite the oppression of his childhood days, George managed to become a likeable and charming young man, and an entertaining conversationalist. One of the Queen's attendants was to recall that at the age of sixteen, 'His countenance was of a sweetness and intelligence quite irresistible. He had an elegant person, engaging and distinguished manners, added to an affectionate disposition and the cheerfulness of youth.'

As he strode confidently towards manhood, George displayed a distressing weakness for the flattery and over-eating he had been repeatedly warned about. The result was reflected in the gentle rounding of his physique.

He was a fine-looking teenager, with clear blue eyes, intelligent and full of life, and flowing blond hair. In a letter to a sister's attendant he made mention, immodestly, of his delightful personality, but he conceded he had ugly ears and was rather too fond of wine and women. He was tolling out an anticipatory message for the future.

He was also a devastating mimic, an ability he developed through having virtually nothing to entertain and brighten his barren existence. His imitations of the King and members of the Court reduced his brothers and sisters to tears.

Another trait was a somewhat dubious sense of humour, demonstrated by his liking for the practical joke. Once he invited a celebrated musician to a meal following a concert, assuring the guest that a delectable meal was being prepared for him. When they sat at the dining-table, George lifted a cover and a live rabbit sprang up to leap across the room. The distraught musician, nervous enough without such entertainment, saw to it that he avoided any further invitations from the impish Prince.

George's father, hovering glowering and disapproving in the background, considered him vain and capricious. The King informed the tutors that he was disturbed about George's duplicity, evasiveness, and what he quaintly described as the boy's bad habit of not speaking the truth.

The King was also appalled that the heir to his throne had only a fragile grasp of the constitutional, legal, financial, and commercial history of Europe and of the German language when one day, as Elector of Hanover, he would occupy a leading post in the Germanic empire.

Somehow, the King could not grasp that so many of these shortcomings were of his own design.

George seemed untroubled by his father's cold and distant attitude towards him. But the King's carefully planned education of the young Prince was a recipe for disaster. The result was predictable. The restrictions of his youth made him a natural rebel and, when he was finally released from the bonds of his royal prison, he burst out with an insatiable desire to avenge himself on his father.

2

FIRST LOVES

George's first break out from the confinement imposed by his father was triggered by his fancy for the slender and pretty wife of a groom who worked in the royal stables. She was no lady of refinement, as members of the Court noted, but George, who had not yet reached the age of discernment, was determined to get her, come what may. He arranged for her husband, a coarse stableman, to be dressed in incongruous style and given a job in his own apartments. Thus, the wife could be seen around the Prince's rooms with no comment made or suspicion being aroused by it.

The King was mightily alarmed about the quality and nature of the company his heir was falling in with, and feared that their influence on him would be disastrous. Most galling to the King was the fact that the worst influence on George came from two of his own brothers, the Dukes of Gloucester and Cumberland. The Duke of Gloucester, eldest brother of the King, had scandalised and outraged his kinfolk when in 1766 he entered into a clandestine marriage with the Dowager Countess Waldegrave, illegitimate daughter of a radical politician and widow of a much reviled former Court official. The Duke had been banished from Court when news of his marriage leaked out. He spent the next few years of his life on the Continent, mainly in Italy, but his frequent visits to England and his numerous encounters with a string of young lovelies provided the newspaper gossip writers of the day with a wealth of much welcomed items. The Duke of Cumberland had determined to emulate his brother, and applied himself diligently to the task. He had an affair with the wife of the Earl of Grosvenor and the impending charges had to be smothered with an inducement of £10,000. All the brothers were required to chip in a share of this bribe to preserve the honour of the family name. The highly moral King seethed with anger, partly because of the lack of control his younger brother displayed, and partly because he had to pay for it out of his own pocket. Undeterred by this familial fury, Cumberland plunged into an affair with a lady named Olivia Wilmot. A daughter was produced from this liaison and, adamant that her parents had, in fact, married, she proceeded to call herself Princess Olive of Cumberland. As if this was not sufficient abuse of the royal patience, Cumberland then married Mrs Anne Horton, a widow who, though of noble birth, always managed to freeze gatherings to which she had been unwittingly invited with crude jokes told in a very loud voice.

Writhing in the embarrassment caused by all this unbecoming behaviour, King George concocted the Royal Marriage Act of 1772, which laid down that no members of the royal family would be allowed to marry without consent from the sovereign, unless they were over twenty-five and the Privy Council had seen fit to grant the necessary approval.

The King could not bring himself to mend the rift with his brothers for many years, and even then relations between them were to remain cool and distant.

Young George, however, viewed his uncles in a very different light. He was an ardent and unmitigated admirer of their sexual adventures and excesses. He eagerly followed their example, slipping out of the royal home for clandestine escapades when his parents thought he had retired to bed for the night. The King was aghast when he heard the open talk going round the household staff of the fifteen-year-old Prince seducing one of the Queen's maids of honour, who clearly found it impossible to live up to the title of her job. More distressing was the news relayed to him that among his early conquests, George numbered the Duchess of Cumberland – his uncle's wife.

On Prince George's sixteenth birthday, the King felt constrained to send a scolding letter to his son, having a courier take it from one wing of Buckingham House to the other. The King warned George about the wantonness of his behaviour, pointing out what he considered to be the boy's defects of character, and the error of his ways. He made a pious plea for his son to pay more attention to religion and its strictures. He groaned about the publicity surrounding his son's more outlandish exploits, complaining that for months past, even at his tender age, the newspapers had enjoyed field days writing about the debauchery and dissipation he was engaging in. This behaviour, the King asserted, was a terribly bad example for the heir to the throne to set his people, and such an example could not fail to have a detrimental effect on the private conduct of citizens. He urged George to take greater care over his selection of companions and to try to spend his time with worthier people whose very presence was an asset to the country.

Unfortunately, the contrast between the domestic and conventional King and his impulsive and adventurous son could not have been more clearly marked. The King, though amorous by nature, had felt constrained by a sense of duty to be faithful to a plain wife, whose appearance when they first met hours before their arranged marriage had shocked and disappointed him. He felt aggrieved – and perhaps a little envious? – that his son should show such abandon in enjoying spontaneous love affairs.

Prince George was introduced to the Court as having reached his majority on New Year's Day of 1781, when he was eighteen. This meant he was considered old enough to rule on his own if he were to ascend to the throne. The King's ruminations on this prospect are unrecorded, but easily imaginable. For he saw to it that, though considered old enough to rule the country, the Prince was not going to have unfettered control over his own life. King George had spent many years firmly tied to his mother's apron strings and he was adamant that his errant heir was going to remain living under the same roof as his parents. He was facing monumental difficulties in controlling his son, and determined to maintain some check on his behaviour.

The King, let it be said, was motivated by the best of intentions. His heavy-handed approach he hoped would make his son a sober and God-fearing English gentleman. But, imprisoned by his own past, his stubborn and rigid attitude to his son worked only to produce the very opposite effect. The full-blooded young George was all pent-up energy, like an imprisoned eagle straining for its flight into the outside world.

The King granted him a small allowance and his own horses, but insisted that his tutorial instruction should continue and that he still lived in his Buckingham House apartments. He was still well and truly tethered. It was frustrating for him, because he knew that not far away young men of like mind and wanton appetites were waiting to welcome him into their gregarious company. George thought he spied the opportunity to circumvent his restriction when he was invited to a number of country homes. He planned an itinerary which made use of all invitations, but the King, fearing a rake's progress around the country and attendant adverse publicity, vetoed the journey. Instead, he took his son on a visit to Chatham, where they inspected the dockyard and fortifications. Which was not exactly the sort of recreation Prince George had envisaged.

Back at Buckingham House, George had to content himself with the tedious musical parties, to which he contributed playing on the piano and cello and, occasionally, singing. More to his style, when he could slip away, was revelry at the notorious Noblemen's and Gentlemen's Catch and Glee Club, held in the Thatched House Tavern. More restrained were his visits to the boat parties, held on the river at Richmond, which George was allowed to attend only in the restrictive company of his governor and sub-governor, who saw to it that he returned home in time for the Queen's evening parties. If he went to the theatre or the opera, he was instructed by the King always to use the royal box under the watchful eyes of a group of attendants.

The royal straightjacket was firmly in place still, but his father's imposed limitations and remonstrances had no effect on George. On the surface, he appeared calmly to accede to the domestic round. Underneath he nursed a fire which was screaming hungrily for human experience.

Because his only close-up views of the fairer sex were of

ladies about Court, it was only natural that his earliest adolescent romantic fancies would centre on them. He fell in love with Mary Hamilton, great-granddaughter of the Duke of Hamilton, who was one of his sister's attendants, and several years his senior. One evening he confided to her that he was desperately, irrevocably in love, but declined to identify the lady who was the object of his affections. Next morning the bewildered Miss Hamilton received a letter from George in which he declared that she was the lady in question. He had found himself incapable of declaring this to her face to face but, bold behind the modesty-shield of his pen, he pronounced his opinion that she was head and shoulders above any other woman of his acquaintance, and proclaimed that his love for her was above and beyond the expression of mere words.

The besotted Prince inundated Miss Hamilton with presents and a letter every day over the course of the next weeks and months. The letters were passionate, if very juvenile, and filled with protestations of undying love. He openly declared that he would certainly have married her if only he were not trapped by his exalted station in life. The letters which have survived echo the overpowering passion that had clearly engulfed the young man.

He sent her a lock of his light brown hair and begged her to let him have a locket with her date of birth inscribed on the outside and containing some of her hair. On the front he wanted her to engrave a declaration of her eternal love. His response to this, he offered, was to be a bracelet marked with his date of birth and a similar protestation of love.

Miss Hamilton did not really take George's adolescent tirade seriously, a fact which only tended to intensify his efforts to win her. However, she humoured him, which was the only way she knew to take the sting out of the embarrassment of her position. She commended a relationship between them of friendship alone and said that, regretfully, she could offer him no more, for her virtue was the most prized possession of her life. She implored him to stop showering her with presents, which were arriving with an overbearing regularity.

There was no real encouragement from Miss Hamilton, who, after receiving one particularly inflamed and amorous letter, responded with a plea to the Prince to beware of his own impetuosity. After this, George agreed to address her as a sister rather than as a prospective lover. He took to this gleefully, and begged her to give him her direct assessments of his behaviour. She promptly rebuked him for his poor choice of friends, and for his swearing. He apologised for his faults, which he said were induced by his desire to appear manly, and asked for her comments on his dress, a matter which was starting to attract a lot of interest. Eager to meet with Miss Hamilton's approval, he sent her swabs of cloth and silk, together with patterns. Those she favoured, he requested, should be marked with pins.

His frenetic pursuit of Miss Hamilton was abruptly abandoned – no doubt to her profound relief – when he attended a performance of *The Winter's Tale* at the Drury Lane theatre.

Captivating in the role of Perdita in Garrick's modified version of the Shakespearean play was the stunningly beautiful, blonde-haired and willowy Mary Robinson, a stylish if exhibitionist actress whose clothes were designed to display her body at its provocative best.

George was spellbound, and fell in love with her on sight. Throughout the play, staged by royal command, he could not take his eyes off her. He was unable to resist making outlandish laudatory remarks about her whenever her role obliged her to move to the section of the stage below his box. At one point, this made her temporarily forget her lines. Whenever their eyes met – for she could not fail to notice his fixed stare – he gently inclined his head in greeting. The concentrated attention caused her to blush beneath the stage make-up.

Mary Robinson, at twenty-one some three years older than the Prince, was the daughter of an Irish whaling skipper who had abandoned his family. At an early age she married an articled clerk named Thomas Robinson, in the mistaken belief that he was a man of property. This marriage temporarily halted a promising stage career, but a life of extravagance led to the couple being imprisoned for debt, along with their baby daughter. When they were released, she persuaded the renowned actor-impresario David Garrick to cast her as Juliet in a Drury Lane production. From that moment she could not put a foot wrong and quickly became one of the leading actresses of her day. Her reputation as an extrovert offstage was enhanced by an emblem on her carriage door which from a distance appeared to be a coronet. She was always accompanied by her husband and a group of adoring males, each of whom lived in hope that he would be her next lover. A larger-than-life, dreamlike personality, she was the sensation of the London season that year.

Within hours of the last curtain, George's emissary, Lord Malden, had arrived at her Covent Garden house with a letter from the Prince. It was addressed to Perdita and signed Florizel, the heroine's distracted lover. The bemused Mrs Robinson read the letter and frowned at Malden, whom she supposed to be its author. He was not, he said, and announced who had sent it. This was the Prince at his melo-dramatic peak.

Next day a second letter, also conveyed by Malden, asked her to attend an oratorio at which George and the other members of the Royal Family were to be guests of honour. Naturally intrigued by this princely interest, Mrs Robinson went along. Once again, George was totally entranced by her presence. Ostentatiously he called for an attendant to bring a glass of water, which he drank while all the time staring intently at Mrs Robinson in her balcony box. The rest of the audience could not fail to notice the gesture, and many turned to stare at the strikingly beautiful, if suddenly self-conscious, lady.

After this demonstration, he bombarded Mrs Robinson with letters in a campaign which continued for weeks. Lord Malden was kept busy making the journey from Buckingham House to Covent Garden almost every day. Every letter was addressed to Perdita and signed Florizel.

The Prince also used the lock of hair ploy with her. One of the letters contained a cutting from his head, and on the envelope were the words, 'To be redeemed.'

On another occasion, George sent a Jeremiah Meyer miniature portrait of himself along with a heart-shaped piece of paper on which he had written, 'Unalterable to my Perdita through life.'

Mary Hamilton, though so abruptly discarded from George's affections, a fact confirmed by a dramatic and flowery letter from the Prince in which he told of his new love, felt it her duty to warn him of the dangers of associating with Mrs Robinson. She had found out about the actress's earlier lovers and told him of her trickery, which, she said, would plunge him headlong into vice. In a letter which remained unanswered, Mrs Hamilton urged him to 'conquer this unhappy infatuation'.

George ignored the entreaty and was totally undeterred, even though up to that time he had not managed even to meet Mrs Robinson. The messenger Lord Malden was obliged to put to her a preposterous plan of the Prince's, whereby she was to visit George in his rooms at Buckingham House dressed as a boy. Mrs Robinson was trying to keep George at arm's length because she feared incurring the anger of his parents. When she heard the madness of this latest suggestion, she envisaged the storm she would face if she were discovered in the royal house in disguise. She turned it down.

But, apart from his obvious royal allure, George had a number of other points in his favour. He had a gracefulness of manner, was good-looking, and carried himself with dignity. Mrs Robinson felt tempted, but resisted, more out of trepidation than inclination.

These reservations were swept aside with the help of a relentlessly unfaithful husband, who was incautious enough to suffer the misfortune of her coming home unexpectedly early from theatre rehearsals to find him sharing their bed with her maid.

So Mrs Robinson agreed to a highly complicated subterfuge, with Lord Malden called in this time to fill the role of decoy, to meet George for a few minutes in the gardens of the royal home at Kew. But she only agreed to the short rendezvous on the condition that his brother, Frederick, was also present. Lord Malden dined with Mrs Robinson on a river island near the house. A handkerchief waved from the shore was the signal for them to board a boat to be rowed to the landing place at the river gates of the house. Everything went according to plan and an ecstatic George, with Frederick in tow as chaperon, appeared out of the darkness. The long-awaited encounter set George's pulse racing, but they had time to exchange only a few hurried words in the moonlight before she was scared off by people approaching from the house. Mrs Robinson and Lord Malden were obliged to scamper back to the boat, while a frustrated George had to hide in the bushes.

The stream of letters from Florizel continued unabated, but Mrs Robinson continued to resist his repeated pleadings. George's passion for her increased correspondingly. He was so much in love with her that he confided to friends he would do anything to persuade her into his arms. Finally he promised, once again through his messenger, Malden, that if she would agree to become his mistress he would give her the then breathtaking fortune of £20,000, to be paid to her when he was twenty-one and had inherited his royal properties. This kind of allure was too much for Mrs Robinson, and she found it no longer possible to keep up her resistance, though she convinced herself that she had been suddenly overwhelmed by 'the irresistible sweetness of his smile, the tenderness of his melodious yet manly voice'. George committed the promise to a written and solemn bond and Mrs Robinson jettisoned both her stage career and husband to become George's first official mistress.

He made no attempt to be discreet about their relationship, and in no time it was common gossip around London. Helped, no doubt, by the fact that Mrs Robinson took to wearing George's miniature portrait around her neck. Cartoons depicting Perdita and Florizel in the unmistakable likeness of George and Mrs Robinson appeared in shop windows. Gawping crowds gathered round the embarrassed Mrs Robinson in the street, followed her into shops, and the prospect of hundreds of staring faces frequently drove her from her box at the theatre, where she now appeared only as a spectator. Mrs Robinson had herself partly to blame for adding to this surge of public interest, for she applied herself readily to the role of the Prince's mistress, riding around town in a carriage pulled by four horses, and with two servants behind her.

Within a few months, however, the fickle Prince's passion for Mrs Robinson had cooled. His roving eye had alighted on Mrs Grace Dalrymple Elliott, a lady who was divorced from her husband, a noted and wealthy physician. George wanted to put Mrs Robinson out of his life, but he had no real excuse for abandoning her. So he manufactured one. He claimed that she had been publicly rude to a friend of his, and said this was the sort of behaviour he could not possibly tolerate. In a letter – a far cry from his earlier passionate and compromising epistles – he curtly dismissed her, asserting that they must meet each other no more.

But Mrs Robinson was extremely reluctant to make such an accommodating exit. She shamed George into another meeting, at which she believed they had resolved their differences. They talked for some hours and the Prince seemed amiable enough. The encounter was so friendly that Mrs Robinson was convinced they would continue as before. A comforting illusion which left her shocked and speechless at George's behaviour when they came across each other while strolling in Hyde Park the next day. George looked around, pretended he had not seen her, and acted as if he did not know her. It was a terrible blow to her pride but she determined to win back her place.

Now it was George's turn to receive a flood of impassioned letters. Mrs Robinson angrily accused him of making false promises which had induced her to destroy her career. The only remaining legacy of their love, she wrote, was a pile of debts amounting to thousands of pounds.

Like so many high-flying romances, theirs deteriorated into accusations, recriminations, and finally into a subtle but very effective form of blackmail. For there was still the outstanding bond for £20,000, and the written evidence of their affair was detailed, blow by blow, in his rash and irresponsible correspondence, which was still in Mrs Robinson's possession. Before long George, in talks with his closest confidants, was to refer to this matter as 'the old infernal cause Robinson'. It was a sad and shameful episode.

Mrs Robinson called in the faithful Lord Malden as her representative in the delicate negotiations which were to take place over the question of the bond and the letters. George deputed a Colonel Hotham from his staff as his go-between. Mrs Robinson took great pains to remind George that he had made grandiose promises of future favours, and that her belief in him had led her inexorably into her present indebted condition. On the direction of George, Colonel Hotham offered her £5,000 for all the letters. Mrs Robinson rejected this, snorting that she considered such a paltry amount an insult. She said she had resolved to leave the country, would not accept a penny piece from the Prince, and certainly would not part with her valuable papers. The Prince's treatment of her had been disgraceful, she said, and she hoped he was happy enough about that.

This breakdown in negotiations was repaired and the discussions continued. The £5,000 was offered again. By now, she had come to realise that there was no possible way she could regain her position as the Prince's favourite, so she got down to straight financial bargaining. £5,000 was a laughable offer, she said, because she had contrived to run up debts which amounted to £600 more than that. She also wanted a solemn and binding promise from George that when he was able to he would pay her money over and above that which was about to change hands.

Now it was George's turn to react angrily. No such commitment could be made without the agreement of the King. This was all too much, he said, and declared that he wanted to wash his hands of the whole sordid and tasteless business. That was when Mrs Robinson played her trump card. Appalled at his attitude and infuriated by yet another dismissive gesture, she retorted that she now considered herself free to take any step she thought necessary to overcome her financial predicament. This could only mean selling the letters to a perhaps more interested party, and George understood. He capitulated and ended the unsavoury barter by agreeing not only to pay over the sum of £5,000, but to grant Mrs Robinson a yearly sum of £500 until her death, when her daughter would take over the annuity, reduced to £250 per year. Mrs Robinson accepted the deal, but tried to hide the reality of her threats behind the protestation that her true motive was to restore George's peace of mind. Displaying mock horror at the very suggestion that the letters had been handed over for financial reward, she demanded, and got, a written acknowledgment that the papers had not been sold.

There was one problem outstanding for George. He didn't have the money to pay Mrs Robinson off. He approached the King, with whom he was still on the worst of terms, to get him off the hook. Predictably, his father flew into a rage which lasted for hours. He was furious not only because the Prince, who should have been setting a good example to the nation, had got himself into such a mess, but also because he too would have difficulty in raising the cash, which clearly had to be found if a throne-rocking scandal of the worst kind was to be avoided. The invidious nature of his position was compounded when the King had to go cap in hand to the Prime Minister, Lord North, who had unresolved problems enough of his own struggling against the successful revolution in America. The King persuaded North to embezzle £5,000 out of the Secret Service fund to raise the cash to buy back the reckless letters and settle the bond. The King, however, drew the line at meeting the cost of the annuity. He directed that it should be paid from the Prince's own funds, and as far as he was concerned that was the end of what he termed 'this shameful scrape'.

The name Mrs M. Robinson duly appeared regularly alongside 'pensions and annual donations' in the Prince's accounts, and Mrs Robinson lived on the pay-off for the rest of her life. Those few months of her life, though they ended in such acrimony, had been exceedingly well spent. She did leave the country soon after the lump sum was delivered to her and went to live in Paris. When she returned to England, her social life was far from over. She became the mistress of a prominent Member of Parliament. In later years, the

Prince and Mrs Robinson remained friends, each finding it possible to forgive the other the behaviour which brought so much trauma into their lives. A rheumatic disorder left her paralysed from the waist down and, reclining on a sofa, she regularly entertained George at her house in St James's. Some twenty years after their affair had run its course she died, but her last request was that a lock of hair from her head should be sent to the Prince, as a sign of her respect and affection. George saw to it that the half-rate annuity was paid to her daughter.

After the shock waves radiated by the Mrs Robinson episode had subsided, the King tried to pull George into line, but he might as well have tried to cage a whirlwind.

A cordon of equerries was thrown around George, and they were given strict instructions to report any examples of unprincely behaviour.

Another scorching letter, vibrant with the King's disapproval of his son, was carried through the corridors of Buckingham House to the Prince's quarters. It pointedly told George that he was falling a very long way short of the standards expected from the heir to the throne, and spelled out a series of limitations he was in future to be subjected to. He would be allowed to give a dinner for his attendants in his own apartments twice a week, but only when the King was in town. He could go to the theatre or opera with his companions, provided he used the royal box and gave the King advance notice, and also provided that the King was in London. If he wanted to attend a dance, then his parents would arrange a ball for him. He would not be permitted to go to dances or parties held in private houses, and, most important of all as far as the King was concerned, there should be absolutely no question of George attending a masquerade, wherever it might be held. The King's final directives centred on his insistence that George should attend church with his family and take morning horse-rides with him. All this, the King claimed, was to help mould his character for the very special role in life George was destined to fulfil. He offered to enlarge on the various subjects in a private conversation if the Prince so wished, and ended with a flourish, assuring his son that he wanted to be regarded more as a friend than as a parent.

It was naïve of the King to expect a young man possessed of such a naturally rebellious spirit to conform to a lifestyle as rigid as the one he laid down, and, inevitably, the strictures were soon battered down.

Any resolve the Prince might have harboured to improve his behaviour was not helped by the rapid disappearance from his life shortly after of two of the amenable influences on him: his brother Frederick and Lieutenant-Colonel Gerard Lake, George's First Equerry who was also his best friend. Frederick was despatched to Hanover, where he was to perfect his German, complete his military training, and secure his place in derisive folk legend as the Grand Old Duke of York. Thus, George lost the sole companion of his boyhood and the one person in the family with whom he felt a close rapport. He was so distressed when the time came to say goodbye that he could not speak. The parting from Lieutenant-Colonel Lake, a man eighteen years his senior, whom George respected and admired, was almost as traumatic. Lake, a notable exception to the baser friends George passed his time with, distinguished himself fighting in North America and later became Commander-in-Chief in India.

When they had gone, George resumed his pleasure-seeking with renewed vigour, as if to signal to his father that the restrictive measures were going to be of no avail. He struck up close friendships with Lord Chesterfield, Colonel Anthony St Leger, and Charles William Windham, three well-known rakes whose behaviour had gained for them a special form of notoriety. He went on heavy drinking sprees with these doubtful gentlemen, and on a particularly drunken evening at Lord Chesterfield's house at Blackheath – an occasion the King had expressly forbidden George to attend – the host fell downstairs and a footman was savaged by a guard dog. At the end of this session, George was too drunk to drive home and had to pass the reins of his carriage over to his roué uncle, the Duke of Cumberland.

Almost every day there were newspaper reports recounting details of George's rakish existence. They told of his affairs, his drunken brawls, his astonishing behaviour at clubs, and his nightmarish horse-rides through Hyde Park, scattering a nervous citizenry before him. The publicity surrounding him reached the level where his father grew scared to pick up the newspapers in the morning, for fear of what he would hear about the Prince's goings-on. Letters, alternating from threats to pleas, coursed across Buckingham House. None seemed to have any effect on the headstrong Prince.

So the King induced Frederick, who was certainly his favourite son, and the one he would have liked to see succeed to the throne, to write to George. An impassioned plea from a loving brother implored George to slow up his riotous living. Frederick apologised for appearing to preach to his elder brother, but urged him to try to get on better with their parents, pointing out that the King, in particular, already had enough on his plate without the added worry of a wild and reckless son. In a further letter, Frederick warned George that if he carried on living the way he was, his health would be sure to suffer, as he could not possibly stand that kind of life. George took little heed of the warning from Frederick, perhaps because he found out that his apparently flawless brother had got himself enmeshed in a torrid affair with Letitia Smith, a lady of undoubted talents and nonexistent virtue who was infamous around London as the mistress of a highwayman boasting the amazing name of Sixteen-String Jack. When he responded to his brother's letter, George made deliberate mention of an encounter with the lady at one of the masquerades their father had so vehemently forbidden him to attend. He related that they slipped up to a concealed gallery together and had talked for nearly an hour. And the only subject Letitia had wanted to dwell upon was Frederick, declaring that he was the only man for her, that she found living without him an unbearable hell, and was determined to make her way to Hanover to rejoin him. The prospect of this last offering must have set Frederick's nerve-ends jangling. George concluded that he considered Letitia more besotted with his brother than any woman had ever been with a man, for a large part of her conversation had been conducted through sobs. Frederick was doubtless mightily relieved when he heard that the unpredictable Letitia had shortly after this meeting managed to forget her feelings for him and marry Sir John Lade.

George's next correspondent in line, also called in at the behest of the King, was the redoubtable Lieutenant-Colonel Lake, who declared that the trouble the Prince had got himself into over the letters sent to Mrs Robinson should serve as a warning for the future. He urged him, 'Do not write any more letters to a certain sort of lady,' and warned that people who seemed to his young mind both entertaining and gregarious might be helping to lead him astray, and were happy to use his presence in their company to their own advantage. These people, Lake said, would leave him to shoulder the blame when the public condemned conduct he was being led into.

These entreaties to steer clear of dissipation and abuse of his system went unheeded. But the effects were there for all to see. The tall and striking frame of the Prince was showing signs of the tubbiness which was to be a trademark of his later years. And George must have thought about the warnings concerning his health when he shortly fell seriously ill for two days. His face erupted in red blotches and his doctor, Sir Richard Jebb, was highly concerned. The distraught George, not knowing what had brought on the hideous attack, was firmly convinced that his death was imminent. However, two weeks in bed was enough to put the sparkle back in his eyes and a bounce back into his step.

George was particularly enraged when his mother started rebuking him about his extravagance and loose living. The King, he knew, was ever inclined to be bad tempered and mean, but the added weight of his mother's disapprobation seemed all too much. He admitted to answering her back in a loud and vulgar way which would reduce her to silence. He felt no guilt about this, he said, because from the manner of her talks with him, he felt his father was the puppet master pulling the strings behind the scenes.

One would have expected the long-drawn-out drama over the affair with Mrs Robinson and the undignified tussle over the letters to have dampened George's ardour or, at least, to have inclined him towards a degree of discretion. Not a bit of it. In the midst of his habitual drunkenness, he plunged headlong into a series of affairs. Most of the women were older than he, and almost invariably married. There was Lady Augusta Campbell, unhappily married and beautiful daughter of the Duke of Argyll, whose allure had been sufficient to attract George's interest even when he was enraptured by the charms of the redoubtable Mrs Robinson. Another lucky woman to find herself burdened with his charms was Lady Melbourne. Her fourth son was certainly the Prince's and not her husband's. Lady Melbourne was typical of the women who attracted and excited the interest of the Prince. Enjoying the afterglow which followed the last flush of youth, she had a commanding figure, an animated and intelligent face, and captivating manners and conversation. In all, a creature of grace and dignity.

Once George had started casting his eyes outside the limited range of females among the ladies-in-waiting at Court, referred to somewhat disparagingly as the circle of old tabbies, he appeared to be searching for women who reminded him of his mother. Not that he sought women of her age. But he certainly showed a distinct partiality for the conventional maternal figure, and he needed women who could impose a degree of dominance over him. Many of his earliest liaisons showed this trait and the later, more enduring ones were to reflect it too.

George was also attracted by the theatrical flamboyance and vital energy of his mistresses. His yearning for the dangerous woman and his virility were to provide a continuing source of distress and concern for his family.

Demonstrative of the flamboyant type was Elizabeth Billington, a singer at Covent Garden and Drury Lane, who was married to a theatre's double bass player. She elbowed the competition and her morals aside at the prospect of sharing the dashing young Prince's bed. George careered through a spate of short-lived affairs with a long line of very available ladies of this sort. Then he returned to the ennobled fold to claim for himself the delectable Maria Amelia,

Countess of Salisbury, who was twelve years his senior. But he received a double rebuff from the two beautiful daughters of Earl Spencer, Henrietta, Countess of Bessborough, and Georgina, Duchess of Devonshire. Both appreciated his handsomeness, his wit, and striking presence, but, as the Duchess later recalled, she thought he looked a little like a woman in men's clothes and was a trifle fat.

He was to fare better in his encounter with the Countess von Hardenburg, an opportunist, vivacious, predatory lady whose voracious sexual appetite was a match for the Prince's. Formerly the Countess of Reventlow, she was currently married to Count Karl von August von Hardenburg. The couple had come to London from Hanover because the Count entertained a fanciful hope of being appointed the Hanoverian ambassador to the British Court.

George first met the Countess von Hardenburg at a concert given in his mother's apartments at Buckingham House. He could not fail to notice her somewhat extrovert presence, and later told his brother Frederick that her intelligent, agreeable personality was immediately self-evident. She found it easy to fluctuate between the extremes of demeanour, one moment being aloof, the next flirtatious. She was obviously just the unpredictable sort of lady bound to attract him.

However, he contented himself with a view from a distance and he disdained to make any advance until they next happened into each other's company at one of the tedious card parties the Queen was so fond of holding at Windsor. At one stage the Countess was obliged to play a hand with one of George's sisters, a chore which she clearly groaned at inwardly. When she affected to have difficulty in understanding the rules of the game, her companion patiently and diligently laid out the cards face upwards so as to explain the secrets to her. George, seated at a table nearby, was equally uninterested in the domesticity of the parlour games. If they had been games of chance, played for wagers, he would have joined in enthusiastically. As he was later to find out, such gambling games would also have been much more to the liking of the Countess. He passed the time playing listlessly and gazing round the room. Their eyes met and for the rest of the evening the Countess, while feigning interest in the cards, spent the whole time looking past her partner at the hovering George.

Once again, he fell instantly in love. He found her beauty angelic and confided to Frederick that from that very moment he felt the irresistible, if delightful, and certainly familiar, passion arising in him. He adored the Countess, he confessed, and declared that he would sacrifice every earthly thing for her. His flowery language was striking a very familiar note.

His opportunity to pursue the new object of his heart's desire came not very long afterwards when the King invited the Hardenburgs to be his house guests at Windsor for a fortnight. The Count accepted with alacrity, though he had spotted the glaringly obvious signs of electrifying attraction between his wife and the Prince. He was prepared to turn a blind eye to it, happy that any link with the Royal Family would possibly assist his ambitious scheme.

George was gallantry itself during these two weeks, and whenever the Countess raised her eyes, there he was by her side. He had decided to devote himself wholeheartedly to securing her loving and undiluted attentions for himself. Finally, he gathered up the courage to make a direct approach. How sad it was, he said to her, that they could spend so much time in pleasant company there in the country, yet they scarcely ever saw each other in London. Would it not be an eminently good idea for him to come round to her house for a visit when her husband was out? The Countess's immediate reaction was a pose of outraged innocence. How could he make such a bold and, really, improper suggestion? George was forced into some nimble verbal footwork to explain that he had in no way intended to be insulting and had certainly not meant to offend her. Would she forgive him? he begged. Of course she would. The Countess was engaging in the age-old game of playing hard to get. A most adept turn-around, after she had radiated so many 'come hither' signals.

It was all too much for the emotional and distracted

Prince. He could not eat for pondering on his yearning for the Countess. The continuing stress made him ill. His doctor was called in again to attend to the ailing young man, who was coughing so ferociously that he was bringing up blood.

It is difficult to tell whether George was making more of his illness than it really was in an effort to gain the sympathy and affection of the Countess. Whatever the truth is, it seemed to have aided his campaign. For when he shortly after called unannounced at her home – first making sure that her husband was suitably distracted elsewhere – she was very warm towards him. He started by moaning that her reluctance had injured him, and was startled when she turned to confess, 'I do love you most sincerely.' While the Prince stood transfixed and open-mouthed, she told of her very strong attachment to him. His feelings for her, she said, gave her great happiness. There was, however, one matter which she felt she should warn him about. Once in her life, and only once, she had encompassed similar feelings of love for someone else. If the Prince felt that it was possible for a person to love but one other human being in such a way during a whole lifetime, he should let her know there and then so they could end their relationship before it got off the ground and part as friends. George, who had already entertained such emotion on a number of occasions in his short existence, was not going to let this stand remotely in the way of consummating their liaison. He told the Countess he loved her more than ever and that he would allow nothing to stand between them. He promptly wrote to Frederick in Hanover, telling him of his ecstatic delight in finally winning the Countess. The exact details of the consummation he left to Frederick's imagination, quaintly telling of how their connection had gone forward in the most delightful manner.

Prince George had finally mastered at least some of the art of discretion, and his romance with the Countess remained secret, at least from his parents and the hungry gossip writers of the newspapers.

The comfort of this anonymity was shattered, however, by a curious act of fate. The *Morning Herald* carried a story claiming that George's carriage was every day parked outside the Mayfair house of a well-known, but unnamed, German baroness. This was, in fact, not true, and was possibly libellous. The truth, which had become garbled in transmission, was somewhat different. The Countess in question was Polish and the carriage belonged to George's ubiquitous uncle, the Duke of Gloucester. It was, indeed, at the lady's door almost every day, but the journalist had mistakenly identified the carriage as belonging to the Prince of Wales.

Count von Hardenburg could tolerate suspecting a relationship between his wife and the Prince. For it to be blazened in the newspapers – and he was alerted by a servant who read the article – was another matter entirely. He confronted the shattered Countess, who protested her innocence while secretly cursing the slip of the pen which had triggered the storm.

The Count insisted that his wife should write to George forthwith to tell him that their affair was over and that they could never meet again. Refusal on her part, he said, would be confirmation that she had been unfaithful. The Countess said that she would do nothing of the sort, but eventually she had to agree, however reluctantly, to write the letter to the Prince.

A package with two letters arrived for George the next day. The first was from the Countess, dutifully writing as her husband had instructed her; voicing the sentiments he had ordered. The second was from von Hardenburg himself, saying how upset he had been about the newspaper report, the sequel, and the strain it had imposed on his marriage.

George's reaction was apoplectic. His Equerry, Lieutenant-Colonel Samuel Hulse, thought he was going to pass out. For George had been certain that the care with which he conducted the affair was sufficient to maintain its secrecy. Now it was uncovered, not by his own errors, but by the incredibly careless indiscretion of his uncle, the old campaigner who should have known better.

He slumped into a chair, the letters in his hand, and gently wept. When he had recovered sufficiently to act rationally the Prince sat down at his writing desk to answer both letters. The cat may have been out of the bag, but George was determined to calm the storm and emerge as unaffected as possible. Thus far, his father had not been brought openly into the matter, and this he wanted to avoid at all costs. His letter to Count von Hardenburg conceded that he did feel a strong attachment to the Countess, but stressed most gallantly that she consistently reacted to his interest with the utmost coolness. There was no truth whatsoever in the story of a relationship between them, he added, and he was outraged that the newspaper in question should make such a suggestion. The second letter, to Madame von Hardenburg, was couched in the most intimate and passionate terms, reassuring her that his love was as strong as it ever was, and that he would resist any pressure to keep them apart. His avowals went on and on, offering up a dreamlike existence where their love would be allowed to flower without fear of discovery, and unassailed by the threats now offered to it. It was a fanciful piece of imagination, as George realised. He knew there was no way the liaison could continue. Dramaticas ever, George penned a request to Lord Southampton, chief official of his Establishment, asking him to approach the King to request permission for the Prince to go abroad to live for a while to help him get over the abject misery of recent events. The King, who was growing wearily used to his son's amorous adventures, promptly guessed the reason for his request, and turned it down. He felt unable to grant such permission, he wrote to George, especially as the country was at war with the American colonies and the presence of the Prince of Wales on British soil was in that event essential.

Within hours the distraught George received a second letter from the Countess. She made it plain that her love for him was as burning as ever, and reminded him of his vows of undying affection. She also suggested that they should run away together that very night. George was thrown into a maelstrom of confusion. Part of him was electrified at the prospect of elopement, at the opportunity for the romantic adventure. He fantasised about the two of them fleeing in the middle of the night in a carriage, locked in each other's tumultuous embrace. He completely lost touch with reality and agreed that he would run off with her.

As soon as he made the decision, the doubts started to creep in. A little warning voice inside told him it would result in a disastrous scandal. His melodramatic daydream developed. He envisaged being cut off by the King, and a life in exile as a disgraced and dishonourable member of royalty. The picture of a blissful future degenerated into one of a penniless couple living, scorned and reviled, through an impoverished purgatory on the Continent.

He was trapped between the quicksands and the woods. Rationalising that his father would never forgive him for taking such a step, he resolved to find a way of backing out of his hasty and mad commitment. Though he professed Madame von Hardenburg to be the object of all his tenderness and love, he convinced himself that he would be taking the honourable course by not pushing her into a situation where she would exist in misery and perish in want.

His dour, responsible father would clearly be of no help to him in a situation of this kind. So, in a fit of juvenile distress, George, who was just short of his nineteenth birthday, went to speak to his mother. He told her every sordid detail of the story before fainting at her feet. Overcome by her son's obvious distress, the Queen was soothingly maternal. She cradled George's head in her arms, and shed floods of tears. Then, exactly as the Prince had hoped, she showed the more steely practical side of her nature and stepped in to make his decisions for him. She summoned the Equerry, Lieutenant-Colonel Hulse, and instructed him to take a personal message to the Countess, explaining that George would be unable to take part in the agreed flight because of an accident. The next part, to explain the affair to the King, was a little more tricky. This she managed by obliquely suggesting that their son had been ensnared by an ambitious and wanton woman. The King also knew how to deal with such episodes. He called von Hardenburg to an audience at Buckingham House, where he peremptorily ordered him back to Hanover. The Countess, of course, had to accompany her husband, and the young George was in the clear.

Frederick later wrote to George to tell him what a narrow escape he had managed. The Countess, he said, was notorious for her easy virtue, and had even tried to seduce him at their first meeting, during a dance. George responded that he could not believe the Countess would behave in such a way. He still proclaimed his strong love and regard for her. He was thoroughly miserable about the whole business, and his despair was not lightened when he heard that their affair had so damaged her husband's reputation that he was dismissed from the Hanoverian government service. Their marriage was clearly shattered, and her ensuing behaviour forced the Count to divorce her.

George didn't allow his misery over the shattered Hardenburg romance to keep him low for too long. Soon he was behaving notoriously in the company of men the King was aghast to know were in his realm, let alone hobnobbing with his son.

The gulf between George III and his heir widened, partly because of the King's exasperation at the Prince's continued wild behaviour, and partly because this was a time of burgeoning political rivalry and discontent within the governing circle. In the first twenty years of the reign, while his eldest son was growing to manhood, the King exercised almost absolute control over the choice of ministers. It was he who had chosen his tutor, Lord Bute, and Lord North, as a childhood friend, as Prime Ministers, and Parliament had obediently gone along with his wishes. In the autumn of 1781 the disastrous news that the Commander-in-Chief in America, Lord Cornwallis, had surrendered at Yorktown to the colonists and their French allies changed this mode of government for ever. The Whig parliamentarians, for so long locked in opposition, smelled blood and prepared for a return to power. They adopted the accepted practice of unashamedly gathering around the heir to the throne, scheming to use his future influence to hold on to power. George had been warned by his former principal equerry and friend, Colonel Gerard Lake, that party politicians would seek him out to use his comradeship for their own ends. But when, through no effort of his own, George found himself the darling of the Opposition, he discarded Lake's cautious advice and accepted the position with alacrity. It was an honorary status George was to revel in for the next thirty years without making a single serious attempt to have any part in controlling the parties or understanding the secrets of politics. He also found the unsolicited attentions of the charming if dissolute Whig politicians, Charles James Fox and Richard Sheridan, flattering in the extreme.

For his part, George III was depressed by the Whigs sniping at his position, and was dispirited by the continuous gloomy news from America. Shortly after hearing of the surrender at Yorktown, the King wrote out a message of abdication. However, when he examined the prospect of the irresolute Prince of Wales taking over the leadership of the nation, he tore it up. Within months he was obliged to agree to a new Whig parliamentary administration under the Marquess of Rockingham, which ousted his Tory appointees.

When George absented himself without permission from a Buckingham House reception to go hunting with Anthony St Leger, the King fired off a letter of stern rebuke. George III was appalled that his son should let the family down to spend time in such company. But it was the Prince's nascent friendships with the Whigs which were most repugnant to his father.

Of these, the most painful thorn in the King's side was George's obvious liking for Charles Fox, who had developed from almost a child-prodigy parliamentarian into a masterly critic of the government. He had reached a position of national prominence through his incessant criticism of the conduct of the American war under the King's favourite, Lord North. Fox described the King as a despot who had squandered his subjects' blood and treasure in a mad lust for revenge. It is easy to imagine the King's fury when Fox became first a secretary of state in Lord Rockingham's government and later Foreign Secretary in a subsequent coalition. When, on this later appointment, Fox was obliged to kiss the King's hand, it is recorded that George III reacted like a man who had just been embraced by a viper.

A more unsuitable friend for his son the King could not possibly have imagined. Fox's father had suspiciously multiplied his wealth while serving as Paymaster-General of the armed forces, and Charles Fox ploughed his way through the dubious inheritance, indulging in his passion for gambling. Known to lose thousands of pounds in a night at cards, he would rise from the gambling table to take a part in a parliamentary debate, then return hours later to continue playing. If he wasn't gambling he was spending the nights drinking. His debauchery led him into debts which plagued him for the rest of his life. He took up with Mary Robinson, the most famous of George's cast-off mistresses, and followed this by a long association with Mrs Elizabeth Armistead, a noted courtesan who had enjoyed a brief flurry with the Prince of Wales. He was a hard-drinking gambler of brilliant intellect and entrancing conversation, possessed of extraordinary charm and good nature. An unmitigated rogue, he had unlimited style. Prince George, thirteen years his junior, absolutely idolised him.

Richard Sheridan was himself an incredibly heavy drinker, and George enjoyed many drunken revels with him. The Prince also greatly admired Sheridan who, after assuring his place in the immortal scroll of literature with offerings like *The School for Scandal*, had followed Charles Fox into Parliament to become Secretary of the Treasury.

Another bosom friend was Richard Cosway, a gentleman who was reputed to have turned his house into a brothel. The Prince did not fail to delight his friends in turn. He was a formidable raconteur and astounded everybody with his genius for mimicry. The supreme dandy, George 'Beau' Brummell, destined to become George's best friend, offered the considered opinion that if the Prince had belonged to a different section of society he could have become the best comic actor in Europe. His mimicking of his father's ministers always collapsed his companions in howls of laughter, as did his imitation of the harsh guttural German accent of his elderly great-aunt Amelia. The politician George

Canning, who had heard the tales of the Prince's ribaldry and approached a meeting with him with considerable trepidation, reported afterwards that he was astonished to find him a gentleman of rare finesse with a surfeit of charm. For George's charm was fascinating to men and almost irresistible to women.

Unfortunately, this inherent personal appeal was swamped when he had too much to drink. He would become incoherent and bore everybody to tears with his attempts to remember some classical quotations which usually eluded him.

And the drinking was definitely gaining an upper hand. There were times, after sessions which lasted for days, that George would collapse into his bed with high fever. To bring the fever down, his doctors would bleed him, a barbarous medical treatment still much favoured. As if the damage the physicians did was not enough, George would often follow their ministerings by using his own lance to reopen the veins and continue the flow of blood.

Word of his extravagant drunkenness spread. Prince Frederick again wrote to him from Hanover, repeating the assertion that a life of this kind could only put his health in further jeopardy. Even the old roustabout uncle, the Duke of Gloucester, felt he should chip in his comments in a remonstratory letter. He knew his nephew was enjoying himself, he wrote, because he could read every week in the newspapers about the young man's hedonistic and frenetic pursuit of pleasure. His correspondents were wasting their efforts. The gourmandising and drunkenness continued at an unabated pace.

His friends were watching the wasting of a potentially very worthwhile life. Lord Charlemont considered that if only George would slow up on the drinking he could become a blessing to his country, and others believed that self-imposed shackles on his behaviour could lead to him becoming a truly great king.

George's father openly pleaded with him to devote more of his time to open-air and healthy pursuits, instead of leading a life of such debauchery in London. His ever more frequent letters all contained oppressive reprobation about his extravagance and dissipated mode of life. None, however, contained a whisper of parental kindness or affection.

Not once did the King seriously propose to George that his time might be well spent applying himself to duties which would prepare him for his future role as king of a growing Empire. Instead, the King, as if jealous of his son and heir, a not unknown sin of rulers, seemed to be intent upon keeping him away from any position which might offer him the opportunity to exercise power or influence. As the Bishop of Llandaff observed, 'He was a man occupied in trifles, because he had no opportunity of displaying his talents in the conduct of great concerns.' The Prince's own response to a particularly ferocious reproach from his father about lying in bed and occupying himself with trivia, was that he always found the day long enough for doing nothing.

Perhaps part of the reason for George's lack of interest in anything the King considered 'of great concern' lay in the limitations of his education, which had struck a balance between the liberal arts and a strict, Germanic regime. Excellent ground for a would-be dilettante it certainly was, but it offered little to someone destined to practise the art of kingship.

George III must surely have been aware that he was depriving his heir of the all-important training he should have been getting. His motive seems to have been a deep, ineradicable dislike. It is a familiar trait for a man to resent his eldest child for dividing his wife's affections. It is also far from unknown for a king to resent the heir who will eventually take over the throne from him. Among the members of the House of Hanover this had become a sad tradition. George III made no attempt to understand the son who was so vastly different from himself, and made no secret of the fact that Frederick, Duke of York, was his favourite. With considerable justification, Prince George bemoaned to his friends the fact that his father hated him, and had done ever since he was seven years old. After an education which did little to enlighten him about the world, the attempt to impose a spartan discipline magnified his quest for pleasure.

The gulf between the King and his son also explained George's apparent political leanings. Because his father was staunchly Tory, George supported the Whigs merely to oppose the King. He underlined this antipathy when he danced at a fête given at Devonshire House to celebrate the resignation of the King's favourite, Lord North.

As George's twenty-first birthday approached, the King knew that he would have to allow him to move out of Buckingham House and into a London home of his own. George III had taken up hunting at a late age to try to give his heir an interest outside the licentious existence he was leading, but the young man had shown no inclination to join him. So the King was well aware by now that, whether his son lived under the same roof or not, he was going to have the greatest difficulty in influencing his behaviour.

There was also the matter of his yearly allowance, which would be the subject of careful negotiation with the Government. Charles Fox and his friends, though fully conscious of their own Whig principles which called for economy and retrenchment, pledged themselves to obtaining for the Prince a position of financial independence recognised by Parliament.

While the North administration held office, the Prince had been informed that when he set up his own separate establishment, awaiting him would be a £100,000 a year income. Two months before George became of age, the Cabinet which included Fox suggested that he should reasonably expect to receive the annual £100,000. Of the total, £12,000 was to be drawn from the Duchy of Cornwall revenues, and the rest from a Parliamentary grant. The Cabinet also agreed that the King would be asked to settle George's outstanding debts, which then stood at £30,000 because of his incessant extravagance. When the King heard about these proposals he was astounded. He indignantly called it a shameful squandering of public money. He could see no reason why already highly-taxed subjects should be further imposed on to allow George to satiate his passions. He told Colonel George Hotham, the Treasurer of the Prince's Household, that he wanted to see George settled in comfort, but pointed out that the proposed sum was equal to the annual income of his grandfather, who had a wife and nine children to support. A revised proposal offered up the still very handsome figure of £50,000, plus the £12,000 Duchy of Cornwall revenue. The King still baulked at the amount, protesting that it was more than double the annual income he had received under similar circumstances. Then in a letter to Colonel Hotham, he launched into an all-too-familiar tirade against the Prince, complaining about his notorious conduct, his lack of civility to his family, and how he flagrantly disobeyed every instruction given to him.

Whether George's reaction to the vast income being offered to his son was coloured by the fact that it was being offered by an administration to which he was opposed is something we cannot know. But the storm he raised over it did rock the coalition and threaten to bring down the government. The King would have shed no tears over this outcome, but when the crisis reached its peak he suddenly relented. He devised a compromise which would leave him still firmly in control of the Prince's purse-strings. George was to get the £62,000 a year, but £50,000 of it was to come out of the Civil List, which was paid to the King. The rest was the Duchy of Cornwall revenue. A blistering row had developed within the royal family over the finances and the King called in the Duke of Portland, then Prime Minister, to resolve the problem. Portland in turn induced Fox to persuade George to accept the new arrangements. He did, but only on condition that Parliament agreed to pay £30,000 to settle the Prince's debts, and an equal amount to furnish and decorate the house George moved into. This was agreed, and the government was saved. But from then the acid relations between the King and his ministers were even worse than before. George III, exhausted by the continuing running battle with his son, declared that every morning he woke up he wished he were eight, or ninety, or dead.

There was a lot of family discussion about the house to be provided for George. There were no suitable country homes available, and the King, still trying to keep his errant son within range, offered that his apartments at Windsor would be available if he wanted them. The Prince laughed this offer out of court and finally the King agreed he could take over Carlton House, a rambling if dilapidated Pall Mall mansion almost in the shadow of St James's Palace. The house, which had been empty and neglected since the death of its last occupant, George's aunt, eleven years before, boasted extensive and beautiful gardens which stretched down to the Mall.

King George, while optimistically stating that the house could be made ready for occupancy with the judicious application of a few touches of paint, was astute enough to make sure that part of the agreement was that the Prince would be responsible for its restoration and redecoration.

Though the house was not a complete wreck, it could not be made habitable without substantial expense. An economic restoration may have been possible. But that was something George would never be content with, as the King must have known. To the impulsive, artistic young man just released from the captivity of his family, the abandoned mansion offered a breathtaking opportunity to create his own new world, which would reflect his taste, his dignity, his love of pleasure and splendour. Here, for the first time in his life, the Prince felt he could create a work of art around him. He prided himself on being a connoisseur of elegant living, and schemed a building of solid assurance and exquisite detail.

The fêted architect Henry Holland, former partner of Capability Brown, was called in to mastermind the renaissance of Carlton House. Work began in the early autumn of 1783 and by November Prince George had insisted on moving into a set of completed rooms and lived there while the work went on around him.

The expenses of building and furnishing were to be enormous, as the Prince confessed. The work was to continue intermittently over the next thirty years.

A marked feature of the transformed mansion was the influence on Henry Holland's style of Louis XVI's Paris. His inspiration encompassed Corinthian porticos, a hall decorated with Ionic columns of brown Siena marble, balustraded wings looked out on a garden containing a cascade, a temple paved in Italian marble, and disciplined lawns stretching beneath elms to the line of chestnuts along the Mall. Later additions included a Chinese salon hung with yellow silk, and a vast Gothic conservatory opening on to the gardens. The bill for the drapes and lanterns in the salon amounted to nearly £7,000. Soon there was no halting the Prince in his grandiose ambitions for his house. Ignoring the ever-rising astronomical costs, splendour after splendour was added. Adjoining houses were bought and demolished to make way for new wings. The best of English craftsmen were joined by their counterparts from Europe to work on the Prince's extravaganza, which the novelist Robert Plumer Ward considered a rival to the Palace of Versailles. Others considered that it was a bit overdone and that its opulence amounted to vulgarity. Expensive paintings adorned the walls, and the furniture, china, and tapestries were the finest money could buy.

A few days after he moved into Carlton House, George took his seat in the House of Lords, dressed in the unexampled finery of black velvet with gold embroidery and shoes with pink heels. His hair was especially frizzed and curled for the occasion. This was an age of grace and elegance, and George was seated among the best-dressed gentlemen of that age, yet he managed to stand out. Later the same day the Prince sat in the gallery of the House of Commons to listen to his hero, Charles Fox, give a speech on treaties signed with the United States, France, and Spain. It was hailed as a magnificent speech, but Fox's time in power was limited. A month later the ambitious politician tried to introduce a Bill aimed at reforming the government of India, bringing it effectively under his control. The Bill failed, and the coalition toppled with it. William Pitt moved into the supreme position of Parliamentary power as Prime Minister, a post he was to hold for the rest of the century.

Not that this meant the end for the irrepressible Fox. In the new elections occasioned by the collapse of the coalition, he was returned as Member of Parliament for Westminster. And when the triumphant candidate was escorted through London in a chair bedecked with the laurels of victory, the

Prince of Wales rode in his carriage in a prominent position. George invited Fox and the other members of the procession to a gargantuan breakfast at Carlton House which developed so well that the guests were still there at six o'clock the next morning. At a second day-long banquet given a few days later, the Prince himself waited on the guests. But the celebrations for Fox's victory got out of hand when the Prince, at yet another party, consumed so much wine that, in the middle of a dance, he fell flat on his face and was violently sick.

George himself topped all the celebrations when he considered the restoration work at Carlton House was sufficiently advanced to hold a ball and garden fête. Nine mammoth marquees were laid out on the lawns and four bands entertained the guests, who stayed from breakfast till late in the evening. When George III rode by down the Mall after opening the new Parliamentary session, he could not fail to see the buff and blue flags – the electoral colours of the Whigs – fluttering atop poles in the gardens.

The lavish entertainments of Carlton House were typical of the Prince's open-handed generosity. But he was also to distribute his largesse in a different direction: as the most prolific patron of the arts of his generation. He commissioned Gainsborough to paint a picture of his three eldest sisters and hung it in the state room at Carlton House. He also sat for a Gainsborough portrait himself. This painting was shown at the Royal Academy, and so pleased was George with the result that he also commissioned Gainsborough to paint a picture of himself in hussar uniform.

George loved owning painted likenesses of himself or his friends, and often gave them as gifts. His accounts included details of paintings ordered from Joshua Reynolds, John Hoppner, and George Stubbs, amongst many others. However, a leopard cannot change its spots. When Gainsborough died in 1788 George owed him in excess of a thousand pounds. Many of the other painters were kept waiting for their royal fees, though in the end all were eventually paid.

3

MRS FITZHERBERT

The stream of mistresses, by their very number, showed that
George quickly tired of superficial relationships. On the
other hand, his devotion to his mother, his brother Frederick
and his sisters, as well as his wholehearted friendships, bore
witness to his affectionate nature. Clearly the Prince needed
love, an all-absorbing love based on mutal respect as well as
passion. Like so many people in exalted positions, he yearned
for the constant, strong devotion of a woman who wanted
him solely for himself. If only he could find such a woman,
he confided to his closest companions, all the unhappy lega-
cies of his youth would be forgotten, his excesses readily
abandoned.

As he progressed with apparent wild delight through his
twenty-second year, an event at once momentous and devastating was awaiting George. He was about to meet a gentle,
maternal, and eminently lovable lady who was to envelop
him in a profound and disinterested affection. He was to fall
irretrievably in love with her. Their love, if not the association, was to survive over forty years to his death.

Maria Fitzherbert was a lady of twenty-eight whose likeable personality was enhanced by a good figure and fine dark
eyes. The fact that she was a commoner was the least of the
obstacles which were to stand between them. She was twice
widowed and a Catholic, which represented political anath-
ema in a country where the government remained convinced
that the Pope sat in the Vatican harbouring dreams of an
international conspiracy to reinstate the power of the Catholic Church over the realm.

Mrs Fitzherbert's arrival in London for the season of 1784

was trumpeted by the *Morning Herald*. Not long after, George caught his first sight of her seated, resplendent in a white hood, in a friend's box at the opera. When the performance was finished, George took the friend, Lady Sefton, aside to inquire who was the idyllic, angelic creature seated beside her. He had fallen instantly and madly in love.

Born Maria Smythe to a north of England Roman Catholic family, Mrs Fitzherbert was educated at a convent in Paris. When she was seventeen she married a widower, Edward Weld, of Lulworth Castle in Dorset, who was twenty-six years older than herself. Within the year, Weld had died, leaving his will unsigned and his widow dependent on the generosity of his younger brother. Three years later she became the bride of Thomas Fitzherbert, of Swynnerton in Staffordshire. Mr Fitzherbert died prematurely of tuberculosis and, at twenty-four, Maria was a widow for the second time. Her second husband had, fortunately, remembered to sign his will, and she inherited a sizeable income, together with a small house in Park Street, close to Hyde Park.

Since Mr Fitzherbert's death she had resided in the South of France and later in Paris, before arriving in London to move into a magnificent Palladian house at Twickenham which George II had built for a favoured mistress. Later she moved into the Mayfair house, where at first she lived a quiet, almost reclusive existence, rarely meeting people outside the confines of her family. Then she burst out, favouring driving her carriage in Hyde Park and going to the opera.

Charming and graceful, though not exceptionally good-looking, she was a vibrant success in London society. Her gentle expression correctly proclaimed her gentle nature. Everybody who saw her felt constrained to comment, privately, on her fine bosom, her clear skin, and golden hair, which a teenager would have been proud of. She made up for her lack of flair as a conversationalist by being a good listener. A slight arrogance of nature and a shortish fuse on her temper did not prevent anybody who met her from liking her.

George contrived meetings with her through the assistance of his legion of friends. His interest in her was glaringly obvious and he pursued her with a frenzy which flattered Mrs Fitzherbert to the extreme.

But she was no Mary Robinson, prepared to drop her scruples at the drop of a hat. She was a devout Roman Catholic, possessed of a firm and unassailable morality.

Wealthy and able to live comfortably on the proceeds of her second husband's estate, she could also resist George's financial blandishments.

She adamantly refused to become his mistress and with each rebuttal he felt his desire for her grow. She said she would not share his bed unless they were married. And a marriage, she pointed out, was outlawed by two Acts of Parliament. The Act of Settlement prevented any heir to the throne marrying a Catholic. The Royal Marriage Act – passed twelve years before when the Duke of Gloucester disgraced the family with a poor choice of nuptial partner – prohibited royal marriages without the monarch's consent.

Unused to resistance to his amorous advances, the Prince was driven to distraction and regularly threw childish tantrums in futile attempts to circumvent her virtue. But Mrs Fitzherbert stood firm.

George protested that he could not live without her. He regularly burst into tears. He would throw himself on to his bed in a rage of pent-up frustration. He threatened to do away with himself.

It was all very wearing on his family and friends, who had never observed such violent passion even in the passionate Prince. This lady, he repeated again and again to anyone who had the patience to listen, was more important to him than anybody else in the world, meant more to him than anybody past or present. He vowed he would do anything for her, and would give up anything for her, even the throne itself.

Mrs Fitzherbert had been told of the fate of the earlier royal favourites and had no intention of seeing the same thing happen to her. She held a deep affection for the Prince, but knew that it was not in her to be a party to separating the heir to the throne from his royal duty.

With marriage most certainly out of the question, she resolved to cut the knot by going abroad to live.

George was devastated when he heard the news, and devised a devilish ploy to stop her going.

Four Gentlemen of his Household, including his surgeon, Thomas Keate, took a carriage to Mrs Fitzherbert's house to deliver some terrifying news about the Prince. They told her that George had stabbed himself at Carlton House and that his life was in imminent danger. Only her immediate presence could possibly save him.

Though the four men were obviously distressed, Mrs Fitzherbert at first refused to go. She suspected it was a trick and was adamant that she would not pass the portals of Carlton House. Once she took that step, unaccompanied, she knew her reputation would be in tatters. Such was the accepted level of morality at the time.

The messengers persisted, pleading with her, and finally she succumbed to their importunings. She agreed to go to Carlton House provided that a lady of high and impeccable character attended her. On the way, the party stopped at the Duchess of Devonshire's house, snatched the Duchess from her supper-table, and proceeded to the Prince's mansion in Pall Mall.

They found George lying on a couch in a room overlooking St James's Park. He was pale, had blood all over his shirt and chest, and a glass of brandy on the floor nearby.

Saying that he had stabbed himself with a sword, he declared he had no desire to go on living if Mrs Fitzherbert would not marry him.

Whether he had, in fact, injured himself is open to conjecture. There have been various stories that he had stabbed himself, but with a dagger; that he tried to shoot himself, missed, then tried to kill himself with a table knife. The most likely explanation is that after the surgeon Keate had bled him to relieve the tension from which the Prince was suffering, George ripped away the bandages to reopen the wound and smeared the flowing blood over his chest. Whatever was the truth, the episode affected Mrs Fitzherbert in the way

George hoped it would. He was a ghastly sight, and Mrs Fitzherbert was so overcome that she almost fainted.

George, speaking in a fading voice, told Mrs Fitzherbert that nothing could save him, that he wanted to die, unless she immediately promised to become his wife and allowed him to put a ring on her finger.

Mrs Fitzherbert believed that the Prince was about to expire unless she did exactly as he asked. She had the Duchess of Devonshire take a ring off one of her fingers and hand it to the ailing Prince. He then placed it on Mrs Fitzherbert's wedding finger.

The macabre ceremony over, Mrs Fitzherbert went home and, pondering what had passed, suddenly regained her senses. Had she been tricked? Had George really been on the point of death? Later she was to declare that it had all been in earnest and that she herself had seen the wound George was bleeding from. All the same, she felt the Prince's Household quartet were culpable for allowing her to succumb to the shock of the occasion and go through with the rite. One of the men, Lord Southampton, received a chastising letter complaining about his behaviour. Then she and the Duchess of Devonshire signed a statement of events, declaring that 'promises obtained in such a manner are entirely void'.

The statement, however, did not seem guarantee enough to avoid problems in future. So the next day she left England, intent upon staying abroad until George was safely married. Together with a loyal friend, Lady Anne Lindsay, she sailed for France, later travelling on to Belgium, Holland, and finally Switzerland.

George, who had made a sensationally rapid and remarkable recovery, exploded when he heard about this, and determined to follow Mrs Fitzherbert to Europe. He still needed permission from his father for such a venture and accordingly wrote to him, explaining that the very embarrassed state of his affairs made it necessary for him to go abroad immediately. The King refused, taking the opportunity to complain yet again about his son's reprehensible behaviour, which had grown worse since he moved to Carlton House. He also chipped in a remonstration about the amount of money George was spending on the furnishing of Carlton House, which was running at a staggering £1,000 a month. So George wrote again, pleading that the purpose of his trip was solely because of his mounting expenses and debts. He made no mention of the real reason for his wish to leave England but it was not long before the King heard about the amazing episode, which had become the high spot of drawing-room chatter around London. The prospect of the heir to the British throne marrying in a Catholic cathedral on the Continent must have sent a shiver down his spine. No, he told George in final rejection, there was absolutely no question at all of him being allowed to travel to Europe, and no point in raising the matter any more. When George received the letter which so clearly marked the King's intransigence, he threw himself on the floor in a rage.

George's spies swiftly located Mrs Fitzherbert and he started another letter campaign. All were passionate in the extreme, pouring out his love for her on page after page. The letters, which ran to ten, twenty, even forty pages, addressed her as his beloved wife. He stated resolutely that from the moment she had promised to wed him at Carlton House, he had regarded himself as married to her. She was his 'ever beloved Maria', 'adored wife', 'dearest wife', and he pleaded with her not to marry anyone else. He tried everything. All his links with other women had been severed, he declared. The King would see to it that they could marry. She was everything in his life. He signed his letters 'lover' and 'husband', and so many of them were there that the French government became suspicious of the number of British couriers moving backwards and forward across the country. Three of them ended up in prison before they were able to explain away the romantic innocence of their missions.

Friends of the Prince despaired for his continued good health. He cried for hours every day, hit his head against the wall, tore his hair out, had hysterics. When he was calm enough to discuss his future plans, he swore he would give up the Crown, sell his possessions, and flee with Mrs Fitzherbert to America.

He did none of these things, and was obliged to stay in England, driving himself to distraction thinking of the love of his life separated from him by hundreds of miles.

Mrs Fitzherbert, for her part, was also in a quandary. One day she would resolve to return to the Prince. The next she would decide it was impossible. In the mornings she would write letters to him. In the afternoons she would tear them up.

Her stay abroad stretched beyond a year, which seemed like a lifetime to George. He took to drinking even more than before, and on one infamous occasion he got totally inebriated with three friends and they proceeded to make an exhibition of themselves in his box at the opera.

However, upset as George might be, he was unable to control his libido completely. He went to a race meeting at Salisbury and stayed at a friend's house in the company of Lady Bamfylde, wife of Sir Charles Bamfylde. He was her escort at a ball held in the town. They rode around together in a carriage, and caused a flood of gossip by sharing the same apartments. Connoisseurs of the female form made sure to comment on the appearance of Lady Bamfylde, who was advancing in years, overweight, and bordering on the ugly. George seemed not to mind.

A matter of equal concern to George III was the amount of money the Prince was burning his way through, and the debts he was accumulating. In one of his blistering letters, the King complained to him about the fortune he was squandering on Carlton House. He pointed out that, far from having a bit of painting done and furniture installed where necessary, his son had run amuck, reshaping and enlarging the house as well as holding fêtes and banquets which continued for days. The King urged his son that if he were truly interested in doing something about his debts, it could be easily accomplished by cutting down on the vast expenditures of his home. He ended by advising him that the nation was constantly watching the behaviour of the heir to the throne. Once he lost their respect and admiration, he would never get it back.

Relations between George and his father had never been

worse. When they encountered each other at Court, the King would either ignore his son, while chatting amiably with someone not a couple of feet away, or would address him in the most cutting tones. Not unnaturally, George believed that they would never be reconciled.

The King, as much for his own peace of mind as George's, did agree to investigate the situation and try to help his son climb out of his financial abyss. Lord Southampton, head of George's Household, was instructed to draw up a summary of the debts, and the task was in turn passed over to Colonel George Hotham, the Prince's Treasurer and Secretary.

Hotham's findings were alarming, and he reported that the Prince's affairs were in a wretched and disgraceful state. His debts had shot up to £147,293. An army of tradesmen, led by his builder, upholsterer, jeweller and tailor, had supplied goods and services on demand without once questioning whether George would be able to raise the money to pay their accounts. £25,000 had been spent in a way that Hotham could not uncover and stabling costs alone were running at £31,000 a year. The Treasurer concluded that, with rising costs, the only prospect he could hold out was that the torrent of expenses and debts would increase rather than diminish.

Shortly after this investigation, George entertained a diplomat and friend, Sir James Harris, at Carlton House and showed him some of the correspondence which had passed between himself and his father. Sir James noted how stilted and deferential were the words of George, and that the King's responses were invariably harsh and severe, void of any hint of parental affection. George wailed that his father detested him, and Sir James was forced to conclude that the Prince's opinion was correct.

Sir James, and others close to George, suggested to him that a suitable royal marriage, which would please his father greatly, might be the solution to his problems. A favourite candidate put forward by his family was Princess Louisa of Orange. But George reacted angrily to such suggestions, asserting vehemently that he would never marry.

George had, indeed, spelled out his intentions to Frederick

in his letters. Because he could not marry Mrs Fitzherbert, he wrote, he would never marry anyone; Frederick would make a suitable dynastic match, and the royal line would continue through his children. Sir James Harris sagely advised George, 'Till you are married and have children you will have no hold on the affections of the people.'

His fascination for Mrs Fitzherbert was developing into a personal tragedy of epic dimensions. He told the Duchess of Devonshire how he admired Mrs Fitzherbert's strength of mind and natural nobility; his respect for her was equal to his passion. He was not going to allow her to slip from his life, he said, for he knew that she had fled only because she feared their emotions, and their longing for each other.

For sixteen months Mrs Fitzherbert remained abroad and out of reach, until November, 1785, when George wrote her a flowery proposal of marriage. Where all the other entreaties had failed, this one succeeded, and Mrs Fitzherbert packed her belongings to come back to England.

The electrifying news that Mrs Fitzherbert had decided to abandon her self-exile could not pass unnoticed. When Charles Fox was told about it, he rushed a letter out to Prince George, begging him not to take the very desperate step of entering into matrimony with the widow. He intoned the inherent danger to his succession to the throne, and reminded him of the country's prejudice against Roman Catholics. A marriage to the lady in question, he underlined, would be ruled illegal by the Royal Marriage Act, and if there were offspring the children would be considered illegitimate. A union, he concluded, would bring them not happiness, but misery and mischief.

The devious George promptly sat down to answer Fox's letter, reassuring his friend that he had no intention whatsoever of entering into the marriage. He thanked Fox for his concern, and declared that any rumours circulating on the subject were malevolent and groundless.

His next task, which he applied himself to diligently, was to search out a clergyman prepared to break the law and risk imprisonment by performing the marriage ceremony.

The marriage would be invalid under the Royal Marriage

Act because George was under twenty-five and had not obtained the King's consent. Mrs Fitzherbert was a Catholic, which would lose him the crown under the Act of Settlement. But his overpowering desire for her brushed aside rational thinking. Mrs Fitzherbert well knew that a marriage would be invalid in law, thought the whole business nonsense, and told George so. In fact, she said, it would all be as unreal as the melodramatic betrothal at Carlton House. But she knew the man she loved needed her and steeled herself to go through with the ceremony. She would have been content to live with the Prince without benefit of matrimony of any sort. George, however, insisted that they must have a wedding, and she bent the knee to his wishes.

George's quest for an Anglican minister got under way. An emissary approached the Reverend Philip Rosenhagen, an army chaplain of dubious reputation. But, shady as he may have been, Rosenhagen did not possess the nerve to be a party to the proposed wedding. Next in line was a promising candidate, the Reverend Johnes Knight, rector of Welwyn, a childhood friend of the Prince, who enjoying the same sporting, drinking and eating interests. George discussed the matter with Knight at Carlton House and showed him the scar caused by his falling on to a sword during the betrothal drama. Knight saw that George was very distressed, yet at the same time firmly determined to be married. If Knight would not perform the ceremony, he said, he would have to find someone else. This made the rector fear that George might be so desperate that he could fall into the trap of finding a less reliable man of the cloth who would sell his secret for a bribe. So, flattered that George remembered their friendship and overpowered by his persuasive manner, Knight agreed to go to Mrs Fitzherbert's house at a date set a few days hence. George thanked him profusely and the rector stepped out into Pall Mall, to have his resolve drain immediately away. As soon as he arrived home he wrote to the Prince to tell him that warnings offered by friends had led him to realise he could not fulfil his part of the arrangement. To his credit, George answered Knight's letter in a friendly tone and released him from his pledge.

The search continued in lower and lower circles until an agent of the Prince discovered a young and troubled curate, who had ambitions to be released from his Fleet Prison cell, in which he had been imprisoned for debt. The Reverend John Burt was offered three inducements to officiate at the wedding: £500 to pay off his debts; an appointment as chaplain to the Prince; and elevation to the post of bishop when George became King. Burt, reasoning that he had little to lose, accepted the triple bribe.

The understandably limited number of people at the wedding ceremony were sworn to lifelong secrecy. They gathered furtively, one at a time, at Mrs Fitzherbert's house in Park Street in the late afternoon of December 15, 1785. Mrs Fitzherbert's uncle and guardian, Henry Errington, who at first opposed the marriage, but dropped his objection when he realised it would not change the course of events, agreed to give the bride away. A second witness was her younger brother, John Smythe. When the Prince arrived, Mrs Fitzherbert and John Burt were already waiting in the drawing-room. The doors to the room were locked and the ceremony proceeded, with a guard standing outside to protect against any possible interruption. Afterwards, George wrote out a marriage certificate, which everyone present signed. Then he handed it to his 'wife' for her safekeeping. In legal terms, the document was not worth the paper it was written on, and Mrs Fitzherbert was to say later that she set no value on the ceremony. Of more tangible benefit was the £6,000 annual allowance George made out to her.

The Reverend John Burt was made a chaplain and may have gone on to gain the remainder of his reward by being made a bishop if he had not died before George succeeded to the throne.

In exultant spirits, George and Mrs Fitzherbert rode off in a carriage for a week's honeymoon at Richmond.

Before Christmas they returned to London, which was already alive with tales of the secret marriage. In fact, in many circles it was the only topic of conversation. For the incredibly naïve George had confided in two or three friends and members of his Household. And, as a secret is something passed on to one person at a time, the hottest gossip in Europe spread with the speed of a forest fire.

There was, of course, a certain garbling of the narrative as it passed from mouth to mouth. One story related that the couple had been married by a Roman Catholic priest, another that Mrs Fitzherbert would shortly be created a Duchess. Even the Reverend Johnes Knight's name was mentioned and he had, truthfully, to deny that he had performed the ceremony.

Politicians and leading members of the nobility shuddered. They feared that the marriage would be construed as a royal attack on the constitution and might jeopardise the future of the throne. The King must have heard the rumours, but chose prudently to ignore them.

On the surface, the stories appeared to be groundless. The couple continued to live in separate houses, though Mrs Fitzherbert moved to a rented St James's Square mansion to be closer to Carlton House.

They were seen out in each other's company, but George was always so polite and courteous that no knowledgeable person believed they could possibly be married. If they left a party or the theatre together he would bow gracefully and ask to be allowed the honour of seeing Mrs Fitzherbert home in his carriage. However, George took to always refusing invitations that did not include the woman he considered his wife. At banquets the rules of social precedence had to be suspended so they could be seated at the same table. Her courteous nature and the fact that she was never known to use her influence improperly ensured that Mrs Fitzherbert was welcomed wherever she went. George was wildly proud of her.

Their relationship survived a tirade of satirical political cartoons depicting the wedding, which were sold in London in considerable numbers. One of them showed Charles Fox giving the bride away, for Fox was strongly suspected at the time of having connived at the marriage, or even to have actually attended the ceremony.

Shortly after the 'wedding' the King's accountants reported to him that George's debts up to the end of 1785 were a staggering £269,878. The Prince requested help to clear them, but his father refused until George gave him a full explanation of how he had got into such a position and also gave a solid assurance that he would be more frugal in future. George haughtily refused, and said he would not raise the matter again as it was clear to him the King had no intention of helping him out of his dilemma. The King's retort was that, in that event, he washed his hands of the matter and would leave his son to resolve it in his own way.

The King did, however, see to it that broad hints were dropped to George on the lines that a marriage to a suitable foreign princess would so delight him and the nation that a way might be found to loosen the purse strings and raise the money to clear the debts. George's response was a typical display of anger. No, no, no, he would never marry, he stormed.

Instead, the Prince suggested that he might help his financial situation by closing up Carlton House, selling his carriages and horses, and dismissing most of his staff. Of course, he said, with his diminished retinue and possessions, he could not possibly appear in public again until he was able to do so with dignity and splendour. George III immediately spotted this as a device to gain public sympathy by making the King himself look mean, and refused to allow him to take such a step. Charles Fox stepped in with the eminently sensible suggestion that up to £40,000 a year of George's allowance from the Civil List should be handled by trustees, who would pay off the creditors by instalments, thereby avoiding public displeasure.

George felt he had somehow to put these problems behind him, so he decided to hide himself away in Brighton, the Sussex coastal town which was to become his favourite bolt-hole and the site of his most memorable extravaganza, the Marine Pavilion.

He had first visited the little town some two years earlier, when it was sometimes still known by its earlier name of Brighthelmstone. In those days it was little more than a fishing village, where mackerel boats were pulled up on the shingle and nets were hung up to dry outside the low-beamed fishermen's cottages.

Its claim to a very limited amount of fame had recently been laid by the noted physician Dr Richard Russell, who believed the combination of bracing fresh air and sea bathing was a panacea for all ills.

George had been introduced to the town when he accompanied his uncle, the Duke of Cumberland, for a short recuperative course of sea bathing to cure the swollen neck glands he was suffering from. The following year, 1784, he leased Grove House, a pleasant red-brick building within half a mile of the sea, and revelled in a simple, though somewhat boisterous, existence. He rode on the Downs, shot partridge, and swam in the sea under the watchful eye of a bathing-machine attendant. The little flint-cobbled town was a delight to be in, with racing and shooting parties, long hours of drinking, heady flirtations, and the night air heavy with gambling fever.

The Prince liked Brighton, and the town liked him. His patronage was destined eventually to transform the overgrown village into a thriving town with a European reputation.

He had clearly enjoyed good fortune with some of the more mature ladies there for, as the *Morning Post* observed, 'The visit of a certain gay, illustrious character at Brighton has frightened away a number of old maids, who used constantly to frequent the place. The old tabbies shake in their boots when his R— H— is mentioned.'

George decided he must have his own house in the delightful little town, with its very special air of grace, tranquillity, and fun. So he set Louis Weltje, his Comptroller and Clerk of the Kitchen and Cellars, to find one for him. Weltje, whose title belied his true worth to the Prince, was a financial expert and steely negotiator. He selected a farmhouse which boasted a panoramic view of the sea front.

It was to this comfortingly respectable two-storey house that George went in the summer of 1786. Mrs Fitzherbert followed shortly after and he settled her into a villa which was far enough away for respectability and close enough not to strain his legs.

For the next few months, George was happier than he had ever been in his life. He and Mrs Fitzherbert passed carefree days devoted to the relaxed living in a country town, strolling along the sea front. Passers-by would greet them with friendly respect as they drank tea in public at the local inn.

Away from the searchlight gaze of London society, their love blossomed. George gambled and drank much less than usual and seemed not to miss the flurry of London life.

By all his normal standards, George lived frugally, and hoped his good behaviour would persuade the King to look favourably on the troublesome matter of his finances. Such restraint on spending was totally alien to him, and to keep costs down when the couple moved on from Brighton that autumn he took to using houses borrowed from the Duke of Gloucester and Lord North.

Mrs Fitzherbert, brightly optimistic, reassured George that his father would surely help him. The Prince was by no means as hopeful and planned to try to borrow the money he needed from bankers in France. If that failed, he told his political associates, he would try to have the matter raised in Parliament. His friends took George quietly aside to warn him that this could be extremely dangerous. For if the question of his finances were raised there, so might be the matter of his marriage.

Their bliss had already been sniped at by the open talk of their 'wedding', and political pamphleteers – the *Private Eyes* of their day – had made a meal of it. Most notorious of these was one entitled *Reported Marriage of the Prince of Wales*, published by the politician and former clergyman, John Tooke. His account stated that 'a most amiable and justly valued female character' was 'legally, really, worthily, and happily for this country, her Royal Highness the Princess of Wales'.

The potential danger telegraphed itself to George. But he had no choice. He was desperate for money and had to do something. He found an independent Member of Parliament, Alderman Nathanial Newnham, a wealthy merchant who held the seat for the City of London.

Newnham introduced a motion into the House of Commons which he said was designed to rescue the Prince from his present embarrassed position. When this produced no reaction, he rose again a few days later to ask if the King proposed to help his son. The response from the Tory benches was delivered by John Rolle, a Church of England squire from Devon. Rolle said the implications were serious because the matter Newnham was referring to affected the Church and the Constitution. He was clearly alluding to the secret marriage.

The loyal Richard Sheridan rose to the rescue, first by pretending that he did not understand what Rolle was talking about. William Pitt, the Tory Prime Minister, rose to warn that if Newnham persisted with the motion he might be driven 'though with infinite reluctance, to the disclosure of circumstances which he should otherwise think it his duty to conceal'. Sheridan retorted baldly that the insinuations thrown out about the Prince of Wales made it impossible for his friends to withdraw the motion. The gauntlet was down, and Pitt decided that he had gone too far. He stressed that he had been referring only to the financial embarrassment of the Prince of Wales and that these were in no way connected with any outside circumstances.

But George knew he was not clear of trouble yet. He and Sheridan met for a conference that night at Carlton House to review what had so far happened, what was likely to happen in the future, and what they could do about it. Both agreed that the parliamentary pressure would be kept up, though William Pitt had obliquely apologised, through Lord Southampton, for his indiscretion in the House. When the matter came up again they would not be able to get off the hook so easily. George believed that next time there might have to be an outright denial of the marriage. It was an odious prospect for him, for he was ecstatically happy with Mrs Fitzherbert. But it was by far the lesser of two evils. For, if rumours of the wedding were to appear confirmed, it would have meant ruin and disgrace for both of them.

George wanted to warn Mrs Fitzherbert that their marriage might have to be denied in Parliament, but he could not bring himself to tell her. So he got the dutiful Sheridan, who was very friendly with Mrs Fitzherbert, to do it for him.

Even Sheridan found it impossible to say baldly that he could be obliged to deny the marriage outright. He did, however, impress on her that she and the Prince were facing a great danger and that both could be ruined if she were to admit to a hidden secret in their relationship. Mrs Fitzherbert assured Sheridan that he and the Prince could rely on her. She would never say anything, for she was aware of the potential danger. Sheridan was content with this. He felt extremely sorry for the lady, and determined to protect her. She had, he recorded later, the look of a dog with a log tied round its neck.

George's second parliamentary stooge, called in to protect him from the Tory barrage, was Charles Fox. Their friendship had cooled somewhat since Mrs Fitzherbert came on the scene. Fox had, in fact, suggested that George should make Mrs Fitzherbert his mistress instead of marrying her. When she heard about it, Mrs Fitzherbert was very angry, and her anger had simmered. George, helpless under her spell, had mirrored her coolness. But Fox determined to tread the dangerous ground of lying to Parliament, partly to help his old friend, and partly for the pleasure of annoying his Tory opponents. He was also eager to stifle the accusations, voiced in newspaper columns and cartoons, that he had attended the wedding. Fox could justifiably disclaim the marriage. Prince George had, after all, written a letter denying it, and discounting continuing rumours as nonsense. George's rationale seemed to be that as the wedding was illegal, and therefore in the eyes of the law there had been no marriage, he could deny it with impunity.

As expected, the subject was again raised in Parliament. Fox rose to address a packed and expectant house. The story, he claimed, was a 'low malicious falsehood' for which there was not 'the shadow of anything like reality'. It was a monstrous report, without the smallest degree of foundation. Citing his direct authority from Prince George, Fox said the wedding could not have taken place legally, and had not been conducted, even outside the limits of the law.

Parliament was obliged to accept his statement, but Fox was reminded of the thin ice he was walking on when later at

Brooks's Club he was approached by a man who said, 'I hear that you have denied in the House the Prince's marriage to Mrs Fitzherbert. You have been misinformed. I was at the marriage.' The man was the one who had stood guard at Mrs Fitzherbert's locked drawing-room door. Fox did not want to be told such things when he knew that as the one who had conveyed the lie to Parliament he was in a very delicate position. He avoided saying anything more about the marriage, and also studiously avoided George.

Fox's courageous action had certainly saved the situation for George and Mrs Fitzherbert. Yet, within a day, George visited Mrs Fitzherbert to tell her angrily that Fox had denied they were man and wife. Mrs Fitzherbert paled at the news, and George's incredible duplicity ensured that her antipathy towards Fox increased. According to George's own account later, Mrs Fitzherbert was reduced to tears by Fox's statement. She told a friend, 'Fox rolled me in the kennel like a street-walker when he knew every word was a lie.' In the end, she built up such a torrent of anger that she threatened to sever her relationship with the Prince permanently. She told George not to come round to see her.

Now it was the Prince's turn to be furious. He told a friend of Fox, 'Charles certainly went too far last night.' Somehow the statement would have to be modified to pacify Mrs Fitzherbert. Then, incredibly, he confessed that the wedding had taken place.

George turned again to Sheridan, who agreed to undertake the tricky task of salvaging Mrs Fitzherbert's name while still protecting the secrecy surrounding the wedding. He acquitted himself well. While avoiding mention of Mrs Fitzherbert's name, he acclaimed her as truly respectable and above reproach.

Mrs Fitzherbert was partially mollified but still refused to see George. He worked himself into another frenzy, including violent fevers for which his doctors bled him. He started drinking heavily again, first wine, then any liqueur he could lay his hands on. He turned up at one party extremely drunk and flopped into a corner. More wine revived him and he started grabbing at the women guests and threatening the men. Finally, the friends he had arrived with called a carriage and managed to persuade him to leave.

Even when George resorted to his favourite ploy of threatening to kill himself, Mrs Fitzherbert would not relent. She felt he had let her down in the interests of increasing his allowance, and was very hurt by that.

However, the calumny of George's political friends had the desired effect. George was granted an extra £10,000 a year from the Civil List, £161,000 to pay off his debts, and £60,000 to complete the work on Carlton House.

Cartoonists were less kind to him. Gillray published one showing Mrs Fitzherbert clasping a crucifix and forlornly sitting on a rock. George, Fox and Sheridan were sailing away in a boat called *Honour,* with the Prince swearing, 'I never saw her in my life.'

Had George not been a King's son, he and Mrs Fitzherbert would have married and probably spent the rest of their lives in enviable domestic happiness. But his birth barred him from his chosen wife. For years this fact was to cause both the Prince and Mrs Fitzherbert much distress. Both were fond of children and Mrs Fitzherbert told friends that she would like to have had a dozen of her own.

As it was, they had to make do with what happiness they could snatch together. Mrs Fitzherbert eventually forgot her fury over the denials and the couple drifted back into society as a pair once again.

George even affected a reconciliation with his father, and was once again openly welcomed at Windsor. He assured the King that he intended to incur no further debts. Unfortunately, this was to be a promise he could not keep.

In the summer of 1787 the Prince and Mrs Fitzherbert slipped off to Brighton, where a hundred and fifty workmen were busy transforming the farmhouse under the expert direction of Henry Holland. Gone was the plain façade, and in its place were Ionic columns, bow-fronted rooms, and classical statues.

The couple stayed in the town for the rest of the year, and the Prince seemed in better health and spirits than for quite some time. He lost some of the weight he had piled up during his split from Mrs Fitzherbert, when it had risen to over sixteen stone.

Their time was taken up with walking, swimming, and visits to the theatre. George also played cricket in the grounds of his house. He treated his staff well and generously and the tradesmen of the town were thankful for the prosperity his presence there was bringing them, though he could still not bring himself to pay his accounts promptly. Even the normally vitriolic *Morning Post* appreciated the new Prince, reporting him more sober, behaving better, and winning friends by his affability and good humour. Mrs Fitzherbert was certainly responsible for this improvement in him. He showed his gratitude by lavishing presents on her, including £50,000 worth of jewellery. Back in London, George rented Mrs Fitzherbert a new and beautifully furnished Pall Mall house, which was also in the shadow of Carlton House. She lived there surrounded by the trappings of a princess, with a full-length portrait of the Prince staring down at her from a drawing-room wall.

The highlight of the year for George was the return of his brother Frederick after six years spent in Hanover. When they met, they hugged each other and cried. George took him down to Brighton to introduce him to Mrs Fitzherbert. The Prince's lady and Frederick liked each other instantly and became firm friends.

George's life must have seemed as happy as it could be, but just over the horizon a storm was brewing which would shake him out of the complacency of his idyllic existence.

4

THE REGENCY CRISIS

In contrast to the exuberance of his son, George III slipped into depression and low spirits. His physicians, finding themselves unable to draw him out of his despair, sent him in the spring of 1788 for a rare holiday in Cheltenham. They hoped the spa waters would revive him and cure him of the bilious disorder he also appeared to be suffering from.

The King seemed to regain his strength, but as the year passed he displayed signs of mildly eccentric behaviour. The Dean of Worcester could not help noticing this when he was woken to accompany the King to watch the dawn light fill his cathedral nave. By the autumn the King, apparently refreshed, returned to London.

Within weeks it was clear he was heading for a serious illness.

His chief physician, Sir George Baker, received an early-morning summons to attend the King, who was reported to be having convulsions and suffering great pain. The doctor found the King suffering from shooting pains in his back and sides, and having difficulty breathing. At first Sir George believed the King's problems were caused by a soaking he got when he went riding in the rain. He prescribed a purgative.

The first person to realise the illness was going to be the cause of great concern was a member of the Court to whom the King sombrely handed a sheet of paper bearing nothing more than his signature at the bottom.

The King became feverish, the whites of his eyes turned yellow and his urine brown. His feet swelled and his stomach gave him such pain he could not sit up. He tried to drag himself up by writing a letter to his Prime Minister, William Pitt. The effort was too much for him. He kept wandering and his hand shook. He concluded the letter by apologising that he could see he was in no condition to write it.

Sir George Baker was recalled, to be met by a very belligerent King, who cursed him and his treatment. Stating that he wanted to reassure his subjects as to his continued good health, the King insisted on attending a gathering at St James's. His untidy dress and slurred speech only served to convince everyone that he was not at all well.

Newspapers speculated that he was suffering from dropsy or gout, but those who came into contact with the King feared it was something far worse. He chattered incessantly and once in the middle of a service in Windsor Chapel he jumped from his seat, clasped his arms around the Queen and asked in a loud voice, 'You know what it is to be nervous, but was you ever as bad as this?' His hearing started to fade and he had hallucinations.

The King himself seems to have been the first to realise he was losing his grip on sanity. One morning he laid his head on Prince Frederick's shoulder, burst into tears, and said, 'I wish to God I may die, for I am going mad.'

It was during these days that the famous Oak Tree incident is alleged to have occurred. A page who had been dismissed from the royal service claimed that King George had walked over to the tree, taken one of the drooping branches in his hand, and addressed it as the King of Prussia.

Prince George went to Windsor to see his father, and wept when he realised how ill he was. A few days later he returned to join his parents at dinner. The King grew more and more agitated until the table talk turned to murder. In a delirious rage, his lifelong dislike of his eldest son burst out. He grabbed George by the collar, dragged him out of his chair, and threw him against a wall. The Prince was so distressed by this that he insisted he must be bled.

Sir George Baker, called in haste, found the King had a pounding pulse and was showing signs of derangement. His eyes were so bloodshot they looked like currant jelly, the veins on his face were distended, and he foamed at the mouth.

For two nights George and Frederick sat up all night outside the King's bedroom. On the second night the King babbled on inconsequentially for sixteen hours, then suddenly leaped up to walk into his ante-room, where his two sons and many of his Court were seated. He demanded to know what they were doing there. Sir George Baker, by now in permanent attendance at the castle, tried to lead him back to bed, but the King thrust him aside, saying, 'You are nothing but an old woman.'

The King's condition deteriorated progressively. He became more violent and his doctors feared that, in a paroxysm, he might burst the solid mahogany doors of his rooms. So they were strengthened. The convulsions continued and he sweated profusely. He either talked to himself or issued orders to people who did not exist. He became convinced that London was flooded and that he could view Hanover through a telescope. He dictated letters to foreign courts on subjects which were pure figments of his imagination. Any attendant who came near him was likely to be instantly awarded some noble honour. He would not bath and, after refusing for a fortnight to allow himself to be shaved, he relented, but only long enough to allow the barber to shave one side of his face.

News of the King's illness, and wild speculation about what he was suffering from, spread around the country, and prayers were offered for his recovery. Bulletins were purposely innocuous. A pall of silence fell over Windsor. No bells were rung, attendants changed places noiselessly, the park gates were locked, and no stranger was allowed to enter.

In the heart of this nightmarish world, the King talked on and on. When Prince George produced a case of his best Madeira wines, he refused them ungraciously. The illness had stripped him of all pretence of affection for his son.

Sir George Baker was bewildered by the illness and decided to seek other opinions, a difficult chore because the King was well known to be suspicious of doctors from outside his own circle. Dr William Herberden, a retired physician living near by, could offer no help. Prince George asked a doctor of his own acquaintance, Dr Richard Warren, to come to Windsor. He did, and was ordered out of the room by the King, who greeted him with a fury, foaming at the mouth. Dr Warren took his verdict to George. The King, he said, had suffered a violent brain seizure and his life was in imminent danger.

The Queen summoned two other doctors, but they were also at a loss. They could offer neither explanation nor cure for the illness. William Pitt was called to a conference at Windsor by Prince George. He returned to London with the worrying news that the most likely diagnosis was insanity, and that the King was unlikely to recover.

Crowds waiting in the street for news of the King offered up prayers for his recovery. Rumours of his death became so consistent that the *Morning Chronicle* printed a formal denial. But this failed to prevent a precipitous drop in the value of stocks.

The King's doctors decided that he should be moved to Kew, where he could be hidden from the public gaze. But the King decided he did not want to go, and threatened to assault Dr Warren when he tried to persuade him. Finally he agreed to go, but on arrival at Kew he found the Queen was not to be allowed to stay there with him. He flew into a rage, attacked three servants, and refused to eat.

Other doctors were called in, and the family finally settled for Dr Francis Willis, the proprietor of a lunatic asylum in Lincoln. Dr Willis was considered an expert in the treatment of madness, utilising lectures, threats, and the strait-jacket. If the King refused food or was restless, his legs were tied to the bed and a band strapped across his chest. Later Willis introduced a special iron chair to restrain his patient. With bitter irony George called this terrible contraption his 'coronation chair'. There were other torments, in the form of poultices of Spanish Fly and mustard being put all over the King's body. The idea was that the painful blisters which resulted would draw out the 'evil humours'. When, not unnaturally, the King became abusive to his tormentor, the attentive Dr Willis would stuff a handkerchief into his mouth.

Back at Windsor, Prince George took control of the Court,

arrogantly ordering his mother about. He was clearly flexing his muscles in preparation for royal command.

The politicians at Westminster were not so eager for the demise of George III. They were appalled at the daunting prospect of rule by the erratic, emotional, and irresponsible young Prince. William Pitt had realised soon after the onset of the King's illness that a Regency would have to be enacted, with the Prince the only realistic candidate as Regent. He also realised that Prince George would probably want to oust him and call his Whig friends to power. So he dragged his feet over enacting the necessary legislation. In fact, Pitt was so certain that the King's disability, and possible death, meant the end of the line for him politically that he made arrangements to resume his legal practice in Lincoln's Inn.

Charles Fox, the politician most likely to gain from the situation, was on holiday in Italy at the time. He received the news from a messenger, and hurried home. He asserted that a void in the royal power caused by madness was the same as a void caused by death. As the King was clearly incapable of carrying out his duties, he claimed, the royal authority should be assumed by the heir to the throne.

Fox's views, weighted with his own interest in mind, were at best dubious. Pitt acknowledged Prince George had a claim to the Regency, but said it was not an incontrovertible one. He proposed that the Regent should be given strictly limited powers.

As there would be no means of obtaining the royal assent, the Bill for the Regency would itself be unconstitutional. So the discussion raged on, both inside and outside Parliament.

Prince George, with his father's shackles removed, and drunk with excitement at the prospect of the Regency, was behaving more wildly than ever. Carlton House banquets took on the air of Roman orgies. London clubs saw a lot of him, and he entertained his friends with tasteless mimicking of his father's ravings.

When Pitt showed signs of resolute resistance to the Regency, George talked openly of mounting a coup d'état to take over full royal power. He also met secretly with groups of Whigs to discuss the crisis and sound out who was likely to allow him the most latitude. To Richard Sheridan he voiced the fear that his marriage to Mrs Fitzherbert might be brought up all over again. Sheridan considered this most unlikely, and chided his friend for being such a worrier. But the Prince's concern showed itself justified when a pamphlet entitled *The Crisis* asked what the mysterious connection was between him and Mrs Fitzherbert. It thundered that the nation was entitled to know if George was married to a Papist or, worse still, was a Papist himself. Other pamphleteers sneered at the carousing and gambling company he kept, and suggested that in the event of a Regency, he should not allow such people to enjoy his friendship.

The debate on the Regency Bill continued for the rest of the year and stretched into 1789. Society was split into two rival camps. Those on one side favoured the Prince. The others favoured fettering his Regency powers, or denying them altogether. The royal family was also divided. Prince Frederick, who had been introduced to the sweet life of wine, women, and gambling by George, supported his brother, as did the King's brothers. The Queen and her daughters were against him. And when the Queen heard of George's cruel impersonations of the King, she barred him from visiting Kew. The Prince was kept informed of his father's condition, but only in bulletins slightly fuller than those posted each day at St James's.

Pamphleteers emphasised the recklessness and immaturity of Prince George, trying to show how unsuitable he would be as Regent. One spotlighted an account of him driving a carriage so wildly through the streets that he had broken several lamps. George's political allies, Fox and Sheridan, were labelled adventurers and desperadoes. A counter-attack mounted by Whig pamphleteers presented Prince George as a true genius and hailed him as 'the first young man in Great Britain'.

By the time Parliament got round to discussing the Regency, some of the King's doctors were able to talk hopefully of his recovery. Most of them now concluded he was delirious, but not insane. Even the arch-torturer Dr Willis thought his health could be restored. The Tories tended to quote the doctors who spoke in this vein. The Whigs favoured those who offered a more gloomy prognosis. The debates were rowdy and acrimonious.

King George was recovering and gradually regaining his reason despite the efforts of his doctors, rather than due to them.

Ever since that time, doctors and historians have argued about the nature of the King's illness. From the symptoms passed down to us it seems that he was suffering from porphyria, a rare hereditary metabolic imbalance which displays all the signs of insanity, and which was not properly understood until recent years.

The resourceful William Pitt eventually got his way. When the Regency Bill was passed by an almost hysterical House of Commons in February, 1789, it ruled that Prince George did not hold an automatic right to take over power. It barred the Regent, if one had to be appointed, from creating peerages or awarding other honours and pensions. The Royal Household would be left under the control of the Queen.

Within days of the vote, the need for a Regency disappeared as reports from the doctors at Kew became increasingly optimistic. These flowered into a report, issued at the end of February, declaring that His Majesty was completely cured.

Prince George suspected a cover-up plot and rode to Kew with Frederick to find out if the King was really as well as the doctors claimed. They were refused admittance on the grounds that their presence might upset the King and cause a relapse. So they wrote a joint letter to the Queen, requesting a visit by appointment. This was set up and the Princes had an emotional meeting with their father, who, though still ill, was clearly on his way to recovery. After the meeting the two young men went to Brooks's Club, where they insisted the King was still out of his mind. Word of this got back to the Queen, and she told her husband. The King was already exasperated with Prince Frederick, who was showing signs, under the playboy influence of George, of becoming as great a rake as his brother. When the two brothers returned to visit him in March, the King refused point-blank to see them. They were reluctantly invited to a Windsor concert given to celebrate the King's recovery, but the Queen's behaviour made them feel like outcasts. The King was polite but distant.

Prince George's growing unpopularity, fuelled by his mad spending and reckless behaviour, was a tragedy. As a young man, he radiated a natural charm which encouraged people to take to him. When he walked through the streets near Carlton House butchers and other tradesmen would gather round to cheer him. Outside London, he was always well received. But his rapport with the man in the street was not to last.

The King's illness had contrived to increase his rating amongst the population, but George's waned because people saw him as an ambitious, opportunist young man, trying to wrest power from a sick father. Crowds lined the streets cheering when a service of thanksgiving was given for the King's recovery in St Paul's Cathedral. By contrast, when George and Frederick drove to the opera one night a mob surrounded their coach, forced the door open, and shouted, 'Pitt for ever!' George yelled 'Fox for ever!' in response, and his coachman was obliged to whip the horses to get clear of the crowd.

Prince George seemed almost to relish the displeasure and to be courting public disapproval. He had attended the St Paul's service given for his father, but spent most of the time making jokes to Frederick and ostentatiously munching biscuits.

That summer the Bastille fell in the first blow of the French Revolution, and the Bourbon dynasty started to crumble in the wake of Louis XVI's unpopularity. Many people in the Court circle in England felt that a similar fate could await the Hanover line if a man with Prince George's character weaknesses succeeded to the British throne.

However, the Prince's behaviour appeared unaffected by events on the other side of the Channel. Frustrated by seeing the prospect of power fade so rapidly, he devoted himself even more diligently to carousing. He took Frederick on a visit to York races, where the predominantly Whig population greeted them rapturously. George was given the freedom of the city and the two brothers plunged into a furious round of balls, concerts, and dinners.

When he returned to London, he found it a study in disapproval. The King believed that, had George become Regent, he would never have relinquished power. Consequently, the Prince was not welcome at Court, and if he visited Windsor he had to dine at an inn. *The Times* condemned him as 'a hard-drinking, swearing, whoring man who at all times would prefer a girl and a bottle to politics and a sermon'. A famous Gillray caricature shows him slumped at a table, huge belly bursting out of his trousers, recovering from a gargantuan meal at Carlton House. The backdrop of the cartoon shows empty wine bottles, a pile of unpaid bills, and cures for venereal disease.

George's response was to live up to his reputation. He was regularly seen drunk in clubs, and had to be dragged bodily out of one because of his obnoxious behaviour.

On his behalf, it must be said he was given little opportunity to excel at anything else. Though the most intelligent of the King's sons he was deliberately excluded from politics. His brothers trained as soldiers and sailors, but he was not allowed to. They were promoted to the highest ranks but he was fobbed off with the honorary rank of Colonel in the 10th Light Dragoons. His brothers had travelled all over Europe but he was confined to York and Newmarket for the races, Bath for the art of living, and Brighton for the pleasure of being himself.

He fell in with a bunch of hell-raising companions and stories of their escapades filled column after column in newspapers. Signposts on the Brighton road were uprooted and stunned householders would answer their doors to find a bunch of young men holding up a coffin, declaring that they had come to collect the family corpse. And one of his friends distinguished himself by riding a horse up the staircase in Mrs Fitzherbert's house.

Hints about George's marriage to Mrs Fitzherbert started to reappear, and his soaring debts were again raising more than a few eyebrows. He promised to keep a tight rein on his finances when Parliament rescued him once more, but his hypocrisy was demonstrated when he immediately started spending more than ever, and built up a huge racing establishment at Newmarket.

Racing was like a drug for the Prince, but it involved him in a devastating scandal when he was believed to have won a lot of money gambling on one of his own horses in a fixed race at Newmarket. A Jockey Club inquiry cleared him, but the stain remained, and he had to sack the jockey concerned. After this incident, George's colours disappeared from racecourses for years.

He tried half-heartedly to set up a political party to rival the Tories. This failed miserably. So he comforted himself with lavish entertaining at Carlton House, which added to his debts and contributed to his bad Press.

The King seems to have felt sorry for his son, and repaired their relationship by holding a ball for him to celebrate his birthday in August, 1791. Even *The Times* – whose editor was clandestinely in the pay of the government – spoke well of Prince George in its coverage of the event.

At Brighton, George personally welcomed parties of French refugees as they arrived on the beach in flight from the 'Reign of Terror'. Many aristocrats who had been butchered in France were friends who had stayed as guests at his homes in London and Brighton during happier times.

He surprised everybody with an apparently spontaneous three-minute maiden speech to the House of Lords in which he supported a proclamation against seditious publications and avowed his devotion to the constitution.

His speech won widespread approval, even in *The Times*. It helped his relations with his parents and he was once again invited to Windsor and, later, to join the Court on holiday in Weymouth.

It is possible that the Prince's actions were not wholly unconnected with the question of his debts, which had risen relentlessly to almost £400,000. His level of spending must have astounded the working man of the day. In his time, a farm hand could expect to earn ten pounds a year, a maid half that amount. A country parson recorded in his auto-biography that on a salary of £300 per year he could live well enough to employ two maids, a footman, a house boy, and a farm hand.

The King affected to be sympathetic about George's financial problems, but he let his son know that, regrettably, there was nothing he could do to help. The matter was mentioned to William Pitt, who said that he had no intention of trying to squeeze more money out of Parliament for the free-spending Prince. George shrugged his shoulders and again announced that he would try to trim his spending by cutting down on his staff.

In 1793 revolutionary France declared war on England and George pleaded to be given a command for the coming fighting. His father refused and appointed Prince Frederick as commander of the expeditionary force sent to the Netherlands for what was to be the start of some twenty years' fighting in Europe. So George wrote to the Austrian Emperor offering his services in the conflict. The offer was politely refused.

George elected to soldier on with the 10th Light Dragoons and rode at the head of his regiment through Lewes to establish a camp at Hove, where, oddly enough, he was as close to the enemy capital as his brother Frederick or any of the other commanders in the field. George conducted military exercises and manoeuvres with his men on the South Downs, but it would be misleading to assume that he suffered the privations of a campaigner. For his tent was a vast marquee emblazoned with the feathers insignia of the Prince of Wales, and containing a huge divan draped in lilac and green chintz. The Light Dragoons also never strayed more than two hours' ride from the Pavilion. However, the Prince did become conversant with the problems of the soldier in the field, though the rains of autumn tended to wash away his enthusiasm for soldiering and he headed back to the warmer comforts of Carlton House.

But he liked the pageantry of the military and for the rest of his life retained an encyclopaedic knowledge of uniforms and decorations and an unfailing eye for incorrect dress. He designed shoe buckles and a lavish frock-coat for himself, and years later he would delight in designing new uniforms for what was then his army.

It was during this time that George got to know George 'Beau' Brummell, a Dragoons officer who was to become known throughout the country as the supreme arbiter of taste, and the Prince's closest friend. Brummell introduced him to cravats and to the art of taking snuff; soon the Prince possessed the finest collection of snuff boxes that money could buy.

But always hovering at George's shoulder was the spectre of his debts. There seemed no way out of the dilemma. Then Prince Frederick set him thinking. His brother solved his own financial problems by marrying Princess Frederica, the eldest daughter of Frederick William II of Prussia. She was plain and had poor teeth, but Frederick liked her. The £70,000 per year that went with the bride made her absolutely irresistible.

George began to think that perhaps he could find a way out of his problems by making a similar match. The improvements to Carlton House were still costing £60,000 a year, his racehorses and stables over £30,000, and there were other monumental expenses. His agents in Britain, France, Holland and Belgium were casting around to try to raise loans, but without much success. A banking firm in The Hague had recently been ruined when neither an earlier loan to George nor the interest was paid. With that sort of track record, moneylenders were not interested in offers of inflated interest. In desperation, George closed up Carlton House and sold his horses. It was not enough. Tradesmen started turning down orders and even confronted him in the street to ask when they could expect to be paid.

Because of his 'marriage' to Mrs Fitzherbert, George had always reacted angrily to the prospect of finding a suitable foreign bride. But their relationship had cooled considerably. Her temper, he complained, was a strain on him. She, for her part, was no doubt put out by his more rakish friends at Brighton, and their annoying habit of turning up at her house drunk. George also kept her waiting for her allowance, which meant she was constantly in debt. This led on one occasion to two bailiffs turning up on the doorstep of her house, in Pall Mall, demanding that she either settle a £2,000 debt or go to prison. She could not raise the money and appealed to George. He was in no position to pay it either, so he had to pawn some jewellery to keep her out of prison. They quarrelled frequently, first about her debts, and later about his interests in other women. For George was over the first flush of his love for Mrs Fitzherbert and was casting his eye around again. A lady named Lucy Howard bore his son. Then he met Mrs Anna Crouch, an actress of extraordinary beauty whose enchanting voice was commented on by all who knew her. Half French and half Welsh, she was living in a *ménage à trois* with her naval officer husband and an Irish opera singer, Michael Kelly, when the Prince came into her life. The longsuffering husband opted out at this stage and George set Mrs Crouch up in a house in Berkeley Square. He showered her with £5,000 worth of jewellery and gave her a post-dated bond for £10,000. When the husband started being troublesome, he was given £400 a year inducement to dissuade him from bringing an action against the Prince. The liaison with this vital and demonstrative lady ended, it was said, after George had made love to her only once. Unfortunately, Mrs Crouch then fell on hard times and pestered George for payment of the bond. £10,000 was too high a price for even him to pay up happily, so he sent a friend to negotiate with her for the return of the bond. The emissary took a bag containing one thousand guineas into the house. Luckily, Mrs Crouch accepted, which meant the friend did not have to call in his footmen, who were waiting outside in his carriage with two bags, each stuffed with a further thousand guineas.

Mrs Fitzherbert found it easy to forgive George his casual indiscretions. Perhaps because, in response to them, she was not above playing about herself. But a much more serious rival came into sight in the form of Frances, the Countess of Jersey. Lady Jersey, whose elderly husband had worked in the King's Household and was known disparagingly as the 'Prince of Maccaronies', was a friend of the Queen. Already a grandmother, she was nine years older than George, who was captivated by her charm as much as by her beauty. She was unprincipled, if not particularly intelligent. Later she was to claim that she had scarcely noticed the Prince, and had certainly not led him on. The truth was that George did not have a chance once she had set her cap at him. He was overwhelmed by her seductive fascination. Though he had known her for years, he only now came to the conclusion that he desired her.

Lady Jersey persuaded George to write a letter to Mrs Fitzherbert, ending their affair. He did, and Mrs Fitzherbert was carelessly tossed aside to make way for his new love. Lady Jersey's evil invective against Mrs Fitzherbert convinced George that their 'wedding' had been unwise and had been the reason for his unpopularity and for the King's reluctance to help him over his financial problems. She even claimed that Mrs Fitzherbert had admitted she was in love with George's rank rather than him.

George separated from Mrs Fitzherbert for some months, but he missed her, though he did not want to give up Lady Jersey. He wanted both women at once, so he wrote to Mrs Fitzherbert, begging her forgiveness. She retorted that his feelings for her could not be very strong if he had kept away for so long. George wrote again and again, and finally she relented.

Lady Jersey's position seemed secured when apartments at the Brighton Pavilion were set aside for her and a secret staircase leading from George's rooms to hers was put in.

When George sent Mrs Fitzherbert another abrupt letter of dismissal, she assumed she had lost him completely to her rival and went abroad. She did not know the real reason was George's decision to marry a royal princess who would represent a suitable dynastic choice, a match which he hoped would cure his financial problems.

In August, 1794, George went to see his father, on holiday at Weymouth, to tell him that he had broken off all connections with Mrs Fitzherbert and wished to marry his cousin, Princess Caroline of Brunswick. The King was delighted, both with his son's decision, and his choice of bride.

5

PRINCESS CAROLINE OF BRUNSWICK

George, as Prince of Wales and heir to the British throne, was the most eligible male of his time. He could have had the pick of all the princesses of Europe's then numerous and flourishing royal families. We can only suppose that as this was strictly a marriage of duty he did mind which one he chose.

He selected Caroline of Brunswick without first setting eyes on her. He did see a miniature painting which depicted the twenty-six-year-old Princess as a pretty, bright-eyed girl. However, these paintings were often notoriously flattering, for the artists who produced them realised their fee depended on the approval of the sitter.

Caroline's mother, Augusta, Duchess of Brunswick, a small German state, was the eldest and last surviving sister of George III, and two of Caroline's brothers were mentally unsound. The King was well known to disapprove of marriages between close relatives, and might reasonably have been expected to oppose this match because of the possibility of genetic madness shown by the brothers. But he was so delighted that his heir had at last decided to settle down that he agreed to it.

As soon as word got out about Prince George's decision, the warning bells started to toll. Travelling diplomats who knew more about the Princess than could be conveyed by a tiny painting started writing to their friends at the British Court. Arthur Paget, the British envoy extraordinary in Berlin, could not bring himself to write down his assessment of her character, but he would say that he believed the marriage, far from ensuring the Prince's happiness, would only guarantee him misery. There was talk of Caroline's stained reputation, of her loose morals and bad manners, and dark tales of affairs with soldiers and others below her station. The Prince's mother was stunned at his choice of bride. She had many links with the German Courts, and had heard all the damaging gossip going round the circuit. In a letter to a brother, the Queen said her husband knew nothing about Caroline's family and that she did not want to talk disparagingly to the King about his niece. But the Queen wanted to do something to prevent her son from falling into such an obviously poor match. She told her brother she had heard from a friend at the Brunswick Court that Caroline was so immoral that at dances she had to be shadowed by a governess, who followed her wherever she went. This had followed a series of indiscretions which, aided by her outrageous and exhibitionist conduct, had disgraced her family.

None of this condemnation reached the King's ears. He wrote to William Pitt announcing that the proposed marriage met with his complete approval.

George seems to have been least concerned of all about finding out about his future wife. Some of his friends believed he had made the choice as a peevish gesture, a protest at being obliged to marry. His selection of Princess Caroline was almost certainly assisted by Lady Jersey, his current favourite mistress. She may have been eager to see him married to a woman of such poor reputation, that her own virtues might shine out by comparison.

Whatever truly lay behind the Prince's reasoning, his confidant Sir James Harris, now created Earl of Malmesbury, was entrusted with the mission to approach the Brunswick Court in November, 1794, to make the formal request for the hand of Princess Caroline. He found the Duke of Brunswick reserved and stiff, but the Duchess, bowled over at the prospect of her daughter marrying Europe's leading prince, was openly flattered.

Even before Malmesbury set eyes on Princess Caroline he must surely have had forebodings of disaster. Perhaps unfortunately for George, he had not been sent to advise on the suitability of the marriage and the choice of bride. His job was simply to deliver the proposal on behalf of George.

Malmesbury's first sight of Caroline certainly shocked him. She was stocky and her head was too large in proportion to her body. Worse, her teeth were bad and she gave off an offensive body odour because she didn't trouble too much about washing. But Malmesbury noted optimistically in his journal that she had good hands and a fine head of hair.

Princess Caroline, though embarrassed at the sudden and unexpected attention, was delighted at the prospect offered by Malmesbury's mission. At her age, she had either been heading for a place on the shelf or as wife of a minor German prince of little discernment.

Malmesbury recorded that Caroline had no acquired morality and no strong notions of its value or necessity, but the more he got to know the Princess the more he liked her. She had a good sense of humour and she enjoyed laughing, and her good nature and generosity were apparent. She also listened most attentively to Malmesbury's proffered advice on how she should behave in England. The Duke of Brunswick had heard, as had all of Europe, of Prince George's madcap and irresponsible behaviour and his voracious appetite for mistresses. He begged Malmesbury to remain a friend and adviser to his daughter in England, for, he said, the Prince's behaviour and fancy for other women was likely to upset her and make her jealous. His daughter, he told Malmesbury, was not stupid, but she did lack judgment. She was impressionable, and easily led.

It was clear that Princess Caroline needed all the advice and guidance that Malmesbury could offer her. Her gaucheness proclaimed itself as she chattered away indiscreetly at the supper table. She was over-friendly with the staff, he noted, and gossiped with them in a manner most unsuitable for a future Queen of England. Malmesbury warned her that behaviour of this type would not under any circumstances be tolerated at the British Court. He held up the dignity and discreet charm of George's mother, the present Queen, as an example for her to follow if she wanted to please her future husband and the Court they were to inherit.

He warned her that she would no doubt feel jealous when she suspected her new husband of being unfaithful to her. She must hide such feelings, he said, because if she showed bad temper about his affairs, it would not stop him. In fact, it would urge the headstrong Prince on to more reprehensible behaviour. Theirs was not a love match. The marriage had been arranged merely to secure the royal line. But she could win her husband over, Malmesbury suggested, by gentle persuasion.

Prince Caroline knew all about the liaison with the Countess of Jersey, for an anonymous letter, believed to have been written by an aggrieved maid-servant, which spelled it all out was delivered to the Brunswick court. The Duchess had shown this letter to her daughter, but it only raised a ripple of idle interest. For every gentleman of any note had at least one mistress. The letter-writer had cheekily ended by offering to find a suitable lover for Princess Caroline. The Princess showed this letter to Malmesbury, who affected to be shocked and incredulous at the news. If Lady Jersey were the Prince's lover, he pointed out, she was guilty of high treason, an offence punishable by death.

A subsequent letter, this time from George III, caused Princess Caroline a little more concern. In it the King expressed the hope that once in England her behaviour would be less vivacious, and that she would soon settle down to a life both sedentary and retired. Reading between the lines, she saw that the King considered her behaviour as reprehensible as his son's, and didn't want to see it continued after the wedding.

Lord Malmesbury's observation of Princess Caroline had confirmed his impression of her good nature and good humour, but it did nothing to dispel his conviction that she was really a totally unacceptable candidate as Britain's future Queen. She lacked judgment, was impulsive, and had no sense of values. He considered that under the influence of a steady and sensible man, she could flower into a strong and reliable personality. But, goaded on by someone whose faults were so much like her own, her character would, he considered, always be suspect.

Prince George had no such reservations about Caroline. The fact that his bride-to-be was coarse and lacked good sense didn't seem to matter to him. Or perhaps the truth was that he was not told about her manifest weaknesses. The Duke of Gloucester had written to him that everyone was very pleased about his choice of bride, that she was graceful and dignified. Even Malmesbury helped to dupe the Prince, by writing flowingly about the Princess, and relating the story of how her face had lit up when she saw his portrait, and had insisted on wearing the miniature round her neck since then.

Unfavourable reports about Caroline did filter into London, but George chose to ignore them. He had made up his mind, and he felt constrained to optimism.

At the beginning of December, George wrote a letter to Malmesbury, reminding him that he was not supposed to exercise any discretion over the desirability of the marriage, but merely to complete the legal formalities. He urged him to speedily wrap up the details, and bring the Princess to England as quickly as possible.

The Marriage Treaty, which George had sent to Malmesbury with his letter, was signed on December 3, 1794. But because of the need to make secure travel arrangements through a Europe largely involved in the Napoleonic wars, the Princess, accompanied by Malmesbury, her mother, and a sizeable retinue, did not set out until the end of the month. A multitude of difficulties meant that George would have to survive three impatient months before he met his bride. A string of French victories in the fighting involved the party in long and tortuous detours in atrocious winter conditions. Even the last seaborne leg was held up by a severe frost which put the British navy escort ships out of action.

Lord Malmesbury used the time to take a close look at the Princess. His opinion of her was not enhanced. She was rude to her mother, rarely washed, and wore her underclothes almost until they rotted. The question of the Princess's personal hygiene was a most embarrassing one for him to raise, but he felt he had to do it.

Malmesbury recorded that the aroma from Caroline was offensive, and that he was amazed her English-born mother seemed to have done nothing to make her pay more attention to personal cleanliness. He took it upon himself to encourage the Princess to wash more, and make sure that her clothes were always clean. He had noticed, he told her, that she always rushed so much to get herself ready in the morning that she often did not wash at all. A few moments with a bowl of water could, he assured her, make a big difference. After one such lecture, she turned out the next morning clearly well washed and with clean clothes. But the transformation did not last. In no time, she had slipped back into her slovenly ways.

When Caroline sent a page to Malmesbury with one of her teeth that had been pulled out, he complained at her indelicacy.

When she loudly described the time when a sea voyage made her violently sick, leaving no detail to the imagination, he shuddered.

Prince George, he told Caroline, was a most fastidious man who paid great attention to personal cleanliness and hated crass manners. Caroline greeted this news in typical fashion. She laughed out loud.

The royal yacht *Augusta* was sent to collect Princess Caroline from the German port of Stade and bring her to England. On April 5, 1795, it sailed up the Thames to Gravesend, where the Princess and her retinue disembarked. The crew had observed how happy she was at the prospect of her coming wedding, but the welcomes she was to receive were dark forebodings of what was waiting for her in the years ahead.

There was nobody to greet her at Gravesend, save some coaching staff who drove her to Greenwich. Once again, there was no sign of George or any member of his Household. Caroline had to make do with the enthusiastic attentions of the crippled pensioners and staff of the Greenwich Hospital, who gathered around to cheer her. 'Why is every

Englishman without an arm or a leg?' she asked. It was her idea of a joke.

For an hour she was forced to cool her heels while the official greeting party made its leisurely way down from London.

When the party did arrive, Caroline was outraged to find that George had not bothered to travel down himself. Instead, he had sent the Princess's newly appointed, and appropriately titled, Lady of the Bedchamber. It was none other than the Countess of Jersey.

Lady Jersey immediately incurred the undying hatred of Princess Caroline by making derogatory remarks about her clothes and insisting that she instead put on a dress brought down for her. She also suggested that the bride-to-be looked pale and should put some rouge on her cheeks. As if this were not enough, Lady Jersey then suggested that she ride next to the Princess on the journey back to London. Lord Malmesbury vetoed this, and the journey passed in an atmosphere of stony contempt, much to everybody's discomfort. The poor Princess Caroline, incensed by the presence of the sophisticated and well-groomed Lady Jersey, distinguished herself by talking in a very loud voice about an affair she had had with a man which had been obliged to end because his station in life was no match for hers. This was just the sort of indiscreet behaviour that Malmesbury had warned the Princess about, and Lady Jersey lost no time in making certain that George heard all about it at the earliest possible opportunity.

Worse was to come when Princess Caroline was taken to St James's Palace for her first meeting with her future husband. George walked into the room and up to her. The Princess took his hand and tried to curtsy. George raised her up, and as he did so he seemed to see her clearly for the first time. He took in the dishevelled clothes and the blackened, rotting teeth. Then he noticed the smell. He backed off, and without saying a word walked over to a far corner of the room. He looked pale and Malmesbury went over to him. 'Harris, I am not well,' George said to his old friend. 'Pray get me a glass of brandy.' Malmesbury suggested that he might prefer a glass of water, but the Prince insisted on the brandy, which he gulped down. Then, without a further glance at the unfortunate Caroline, he walked out of the room, telling Malmesbury that he was going to see the Queen.

Caroline, naturally shocked by George's behaviour, said to Malmesbury, 'Does the Prince always act like this?' She asked him if the Prince were disappointed, adding that she had a couple of matters of complaint. George was nowhere near as good-looking as his portrait, she said, and he was unexpectedly fat.

Malmesbury graciously apologised for George behaviour, and assured her that his manner would be different at dinner that evening.

At that very moment, George was having a loud and acrimonious disagreement with his mother. He felt cheated, he said, because this Princess was nothing like the one he had been led to expect. A sense of humour and a sweet nature were fine. But why had he not been told how gauche and dirty she was?

However, there was no going back on the arrangement. The contract of marriage had been signed, and the wedding would have to go ahead. George wondered how he could possibly survive it.

The King heard of his son's opinion of his bride-to-be and later received Malmesbury. He asked the Earl, 'Is she good-humoured?' Malmesbury said she was. 'Then I am glad of it,' said the King.

Dinner that evening at St James's was a predictable embarrassment. Caroline spent the time making vulgar remarks about Lady Jersey, who was seated a few feet away. The Countess maintained a dignified silence, refusing to be drawn by the baiting from Caroline. George observed the coarse behaviour of his future wife – and just looked miserable.

From this inauspicious opening, their relationship did not have a chance. George, revolted by Caroline's appearance, hated her from the first. The vulgarity she showed at the dinner table that night confirmed his feelings.

Princess Caroline considered herself witty. Her new companions regarded her as unpleasantly sarcastic.

George just ignored her. Not surprisingly, a friend noted in a journal, because he had always been used to ladies of sweetness and delicacy.

Of the royal family, only the King took to her. When they met he wept and greeted her as affectionately as if she were his favourite child.

But Princess Caroline was immediately popular with the public, and was to retain that popularity for the rest of her life.

The day after she reached London, Caroline was enthusiastically greeted by a crowd gathered outside St James's Palace. She spoke to them from a window, praising 'the brave English nation – the best on earth'. The reaction to this was ecstatic until George, pleading that the Princess was tired, ended the adulation by closing the window.

The people's enthusiasm for her was helped by newspaper accounts of a tumultuous reception they claimed was accorded her triumphal entry into London. This had, of course, never happened, and was a fabrication. As was the *London Chronicle* story of her 'teeth as white as ivory, her good complexion'.

To steel himself for the wedding, George drank heavily. The three days between Caroline's arrival and the ceremony on April 8 were obliterated by alcohol.

George also tended to the embers of his relationship with Mrs Fitzherbert, his other 'wife' and the woman he had 'married' almost ten years before. Their separation had not interrupted her allowance, which George ensured was paid regularly. Now he had made arrangements that, even in the event of his death, the allowance should continue to be paid. She was clearly very much on his mind, and on the day before his wedding, he wrote to Mrs Fitzherbert, declaring that she was the only woman he would ever love.

Mrs Fitzherbert lit up her house in honour of the wedding and was to write, 'I shall have the approbation of my own conscience and heart in knowing I have never said or done anything to hurt him.'

As the hours to the wedding ticked past, George confided his feelings towards Mrs Fitzherbert to those around him. He sadly told the Duke of Clarence, the brother whose job was to stay with him every moment up the the ceremony, to deliver a message to her: 'William, tell Mrs Fitzherbert she is the only woman I shall ever love.' And in the coach actually taking him to St James's, he told the Earl of Moira, 'It's no use, I shall never love any woman but Maria Fitzherbert.'

His feelings for Mrs Fitzherbert struck an incongruous note. For Lady Jersey was still seated in glory as the apparent object, in public at any rate, of all his affections.

On the evening of April 8, 1795, Caroline strode confidently down the aisle of the Chapel Royal at St James's Palace on the arms of her uncle, George III, who was to give her away. She almost fell over because of the weight of her wedding gown, but recovered to stand by the altar, talking loudly to some of her ladies-in-waiting.

George came in a few minutes late, delayed because he felt obliged to sink several glasses of brandy to see him through the ordeal. Two friends, the Dukes of Bedford and Roxburghe, walked on each side of the Prince, holding him up. Without their assistance, he would have slumped in the aisle. Everybody in the congregation knew he was drunk, and Lord Melbourne said later, 'It was like Macheath going to an execution.'

Propped up by his friends and with his eyes glazed over, George went through the wedding as if in a trance. He tried desperately not to look at Caroline, and spent the whole of the ceremony gazing dolefully at Lady Jersey. He looked so unhappy the guests thought he was going to burst into tears.

A special anthem of rejoicing was sung and, around the country, church bells pealed the people's happiness. But the Prince looked as if he wished he was not there, which was undeniably the case. So preoccupied was he with thoughts of Mrs Fitzherbert that his mind was elsewhere and he had the greatest difficulty following the proceedings.

In the middle of one prayer, George abruptly stood up and froze the ceremony in mid-sentence. His father leaned over to whisper something to him, the Prince sat down again, and the service continued.

Throughout the wedding, a guest recounted, 'George looked like death and full of confusion, as if he wished to hide himself from the looks of the whole world.' His behaviour does not appear to have troubled Princess Caroline, who smiled and nodded at anyone who caught her eye.

At the point in the service where he was obliged to ask if there were any lawful impediment to the wedding, the Archbishop of Canterbury, Dr John Moore, stared intently at both George and his father, convincing everybody that he, too, was aware of the earlier marriage to Mrs Fitzherbert. When Dr Moore got no response, he continued to the passage referring to married fidelity, intoning it very slowly and repeating it twice while again staring at George. This message got through to the Prince, who started weeping.

A reception was held for the newly-weds in the Queen's apartments at St James's Palace. George's behaviour was no better, and he directed scarcely a word to his wife. He tried to ease his misery by drinking more brandy. It helped calm him down, but he still could not raise a smile.

The thought of sharing a bed with his unappealing bride threw George into a cold panic. Copious glasses of brandy failed to improve the prospect, though he got as drunk as anyone could remember seeing him. Eventually he tottered his way to Caroline's bedroom, where, after staggering about, he slumped face-down in the fireplace. He spent his wedding night there.

This inauspicious beginning to married life was hardly helped by a pamphleteer who took it upon himself to remind Prince George that his wife had the right to demand he give up his 'former attachments'. Nothing was, however, likely to induce George to do that. Lady Jersey still dined at the couple's table, where George flagrantly paid court to her, and she remained in official attendance throughout the honeymoon.

Despite this, the first weeks of the marriage, spent at the Brighton house, actually took on the appearance of happiness. Caroline tried to make friends of her sisters-in-law and told them of her 'present happiness' and of her love for her husband. She offered the hope that she would become a very comfortable wife. George wrote to tell his mother of their happiness, and assure her that Caroline was in the best of health.

That was the surface picture. In fact, the couple lived together as man and wife for only the first two weeks of their marriage. This enforced union had the desired effect, however, and soon the Court was jubilant with the news that Caroline was pregnant.

George displayed much concern about Caroline's health and worried himself into a state of nervous tension over the prospect of fatherhood. He even stayed up the two nights before the birth. It proved a long and difficult labour and at 9.45 AM January 7, 1796, nine months almost to the day after the wedding, Princess Charlotte was born.

Though disappointed he did not have a son, George was delighted with his daughter. His father hoped they would have many more children, and that some of them would be boys. It was a forlorn hope. For, despite outward appearances, the rot had quickly set in. The wedding had been a shambles. The marriage was disastrous. Even if he were guaranteed a dozen sons, George could not have brought himself to go near Caroline again.

Caroline had dropped her mask of happiness, which she had maintained in the hope that George would become reconciled to her. The lively spirit from Brunswick had deteriorated into a miserable lady who could not hide her melancholy from those around her.

Perhaps in response to her unhappiness, Caroline's coarse manners became even worse. George, irritated in the extreme, telegraphed his continuing desire for Lady Jersey at every opportunity. Caroline's repeated sarcastic references to the Countess only tended to inflame their distressing relationship.

After one such display of bad manners and temperament at a Carlton House dinner, George rounded on the Earl of Malmesbury. If the Earl had known Princess Caroline could be so gauche and unpleasant, why had no one one told him, he demanded. Malmesbury said the responsibility could not possibly rest on him. When he had gone to Brunswick as the royal emissary, his orders had centred only on arranging the marriage contract. He had never been asked to offer his opinion on the suitability of the Princess as a bride. This was of course true, but George could not help wishing that his old friend had given him some word of warning.

George hated his wife, and took an instant dislike to anyone who befriended her. To strike at them, he had her dining-room furniture removed. He also retrieved a pair of pearl bracelets which he had given her as part of her wedding gift, and insultingly passed them on to Lady Jersey. His mistress wore the jewels in front of Caroline on every possible occasion, flaunting George's favouring of her. When it entered his head that his ignoring of Caroline might lead her to desiring the company of young men, he ordained that she could not entertain anyone without his permission and approval. So her male companions, when she was allowed them, were taken from the old men of London. She was obliged to ride out alone, and the other members of the royal family avoided her. To a friend in Brunswick she wrote, 'I do not know how I shall be able to bear the loneliness. The Countess is still here. I hate her and I know she feels the same towards me. My husband is wholly given up to her, so you can easily imagine the rest.'

George gallivanted around the country in the company of Lady Jersey, leaving his wife to wither away at Carlton House, a prisoner refused permission to travel anywhere outside London. His relationship with the Countess was by now so open that she had moved her bed into his dressing-room at the Brighton Pavilion.

Ironically, and cruelly, one of the people George allowed his wife to spend time with was Lady Jersey, who still held her post as Lady of the Bedchamber. She was no friend, of course, and delighted in collecting tittle-tattle about the Princess to take back to George and, sometimes, his mother. She even opened letters which Princess Caroline had written and which were destined for friends in Brunswick. Soon the Queen learned that Caroline not only spoke rudely about her royal relatives, but called her mother-in-law 'Old Snuffy'.

Within a few months of the birth of her daughter, Caroline snapped under the pressure.

Her complaints had to be conveyed to George by letter, and the correspondence between them just a year after their marriage bears witness to the terseness of their relationship.

Caroline demanded that she should not be obliged to dine any more with Lady Jersey, on the grounds that she was weary of sharing her table as well as her husband with the redoubtable Lady of the Bedchamber. George, adopting an aura of bland innocence, protested that her suggestions were unwise and groundless. If she were distressed that Lady Jersey was his mistress – a fact which he resolutely denied – then, he said, she should not have agreed to marry him. He protested that Lady Jersey, as one of his oldest friends, had actually encouraged him to marry Caroline. Then he conceded that they were never going to find happiness together, and begged her not to make the situation any worse. She in turn bemoaned his coldness and contempt. He suggested she was obnoxious and added that her strident tones were unlikely to lure him closer. He complained about her behaviour, and she retorted that his behaviour with Lady Jersey and towards his wife was hardly commendable. She suggested he would do well to copy the impeccable behaviour of his father.

George grew tired of the acrimonious correspondence, and tried to terminate it. But Princess Caroline was not yet finished. She wanted an assurance, she added, as they were now man and wife in name only, that even in the event of the death of their daughter, he would not wish to try to produce another heir. He was only too pleased to give her this guarantee.

The couple were clearly beyond any possibility of reconciliation, and both planned to ask the King to sanction a formal separation. His agreement to the inevitable was not forthcoming. George III told his son that the marriage had not been merely a private transaction. The wedding of the heir to the throne was a public act, and could not be put aside so easily. He quietly warned George that the Princess enjoyed a continuing popularity with his subjects, and that they would not be happy to see the Princess treated in an offhand way. Parliament would have to be told the facts and would have to agree to a separation. While the King appreciated that Caroline's natural temperament made her a difficult person to live with, he did not feel his son had done all he could to ensure the success of the match. King George also feared that an open breach in his son's marriage, which had been greeted with such popular acclaim, would reflect upon himself. Caroline, encouraged by her new lover, the politician George Canning, fanned the flames of familial discontent with obvious relish. Prince George, seemingly chained to a wife he despised, hated her more than ever.

All his anger with Caroline seemed to have boiled over when George sat down to write out an extraordinary last will and testament, which rambled on for over three thousand words. He had just passed through one of his theatrical, emotional illnesses, and believed he was about to die. He asked the King to take care of his loyal servants, and begged his parents to forgive him his many faults. His daughter, Princess Charlotte, he commended to their care. He forgave his wife the 'falsehood and treachery of her conduct' but insisted that she must in no way be entrusted with the education or care of their child. For he felt constrained to prevent the child's future being under her improper guidance.

After safeguarding Princess Charlotte, George's chief concern in the will was 'my beloved and adored Maria Fitzherbert'. Mrs Fitzherbert was, he declared, to inherit all his estates, possessions, and money. His avowed adulation of her knew no bounds. Asserting that he never ceased to love her, he addressed her as 'my real and true wife', and the 'wife of my heart and soul'. He requested that he should be buried 'with my constant companion, the picture of my beloved wife, my Maria Fitzherbert, suspended round my neck by a ribbon as I used to wear it when I lived, and placed upon my heart'. He asked that when Mrs Fitzherbert followed him into death, his coffin should be taken to hers so that they could be welded together, then buried together. Always assuming, he added politely, that Mrs Fitzherbert had no objection to such a course. As a postscript, he asked that the jewels he had given to his wife – 'she who is called the Princess of Wales' – should be confiscated from her and given to their daughter. He did not forget Princess Caroline in his ramblings. He bequeathed her one shilling.

His feelings for his wife were not helped when, denied his company, Princess Caroline went alone on two visits to the opera. On each occasion, the audience rose to accord her a standing ovation.

The newspapers started to take Caroline's side and attack George for his mistresses, his incorrigible behaviour, and his contempt for the opinions of the world.

Even his family, who had started out disliking Caroline almost as much as he did, were coming round to the view that George was far from blameless. Public disapproval of royalty was a phenomenon of their time they had grown to fear. Their enforced guests from the former court of the Bourbons in France were witness to its potency. So they tried to persuade George into a public reconciliation with his wife.

Fighting a desperate rearguard defence, Prince George spread the most vindictive lies about Caroline, depicting her as 'a fiend', 'the vilest wretch this world ever was cursed with', unprincipled and wicked. In hysterical letters to his parents, he warned that unless something was done about Caroline, she would ruin the royal family.

The dangers which George ranted about are difficult to ascertain, though Caroline's behaviour was as vulgar and boisterous as ever. We hear of her playing forfeits and enjoying scandalous chatter, which hardly seems to represent a threat to the throne.

The King knew his son a little better than George supposed. He still liked his niece, and believed the evil-doer in the scenario was his heir.

Caroline suggested that their personal problems might be solved and that she and her husband could become reconciled if George evicted Lady Jersey from his life. For, as she told the King in a letter, there could be no peace between her and George as long as she was forced to retain Lady Jersey in her Household.

The Queen leaped at this suggestion, and summarily dismissed George's mistress from her job. He was predictably furious. Caroline invited him to Carlton House to discuss the matter, and to suggest that now Lady Jersey was out of the way, they could resume their married life. George stormed out of this meeting to spend the night with Lady Jersey.

Instead of ending George's association with the Countess, this episode was to throw them even closer together. He took her first as his house guest to an estate he rented in Dorset, then for a short stay in Bognor. When both returned to London, George saw to it that Lady Jersey's husband, the Earl of Jersey, was appointed his Master of the Horse. The couple were installed in a house next door to Carlton House.

Meanwhile, George still made it his business to keep up his harassment of Caroline. He refused her permission to visit friends in the country, and chastised her for holding parties at Carlton House. His friends could not understand why he maintained his vendetta against a wife he cared nothing for. The more charitable considered he was both wrong and foolish. A more despondent view suggested the underlying reason was an inherited madness. If they had separated and George had left her alone, there would have been little or no criticism offered. As it was, no one could fail to notice the glaring hypocrisy of a man whose own behaviour was so notorious.

He helped towards his own humiliation by spreading stories about his wife, and could not understand why the public, satiated with tales which illustrated his own character, considered Caroline a martyr.

Princess Caroline was also not above telling stories about her husband. She recounted his drunkenness on their wedding night, and told of how, when George discovered she was pregnant, he had announced to everybody in the room that he was not the father. When he heard about Caroline's indiscreet talk, George was furious but could do little about it. He declaimed that he would rather see toads and vipers climb all over his food than sit at the same table with her.

George was also convinced that his wife was having a series of affairs with just about any man who came to her door. One of them, he suspected rightly, was George Canning, a leading young light of the Tory party. He could have gone back to live with her and stopped all this, but he felt he would rather die than face up to that prospect. He had to be content with baiting her from a distance.

Caroline appealed to the King to lift some of the restrictions imposed on her by her hated husband. The King answered that he did not feel able to do that, that George was entitled to impose restrictions on his wife.

So Caroline wrote a letter to Prince George, asking for an appointment with him in his quarters in Carlton House. He agreed to meet her, but only on condition that a third person should be present the whole time.

Like everything else in their relationship, the meeting was astonishing. Princess Caroline immediately complained that during their marriage he had not treated her as he should the woman who was his wife, the mother of his child, and the Princess of Wales.

'I give you notice here and now,' she said, 'that I have nothing more to say to you and that I no longer regard myself as subject to your orders or your rules.'

The gauntlet was down, but George was not sure how to respond. He asked her if that was all she had to say. Caroline said it was, George bowed deeply, then left.

The King still refused to allow his son and daughter-in-law a formal separation which might have kept them permanently from each other's throats, but he realised something would have to be done. So, on condition that she maintained her own apartments at Carlton House, thereby keeping up the fiction of marital normality, the Princess was allowed to live elsewhere.

The Old Rectory at the Thames-side village of Charlton was leased and made ready for Caroline and she moved in a few weeks after her stormy interview with George. She stayed there for a while until the King appointed her to the honorary role of Ranger of Greenwich Park, which allowed her to move to the more spacious dignity of Montague

House, a mansion on Blackheath. Occasionally she was allowed up to Carlton House to be put on show during ceremonial events, or to visit her daughter. But most of the time she was kept in exile in her Kentish retreat. She passed the time in learning to play the harp and to paint and in perfecting her English. She had her own vegetable garden at the Blackheath house, and some of her produce was taken up to London to be sold at Covent Garden. She also interested herself in charitable causes, becoming a kindly patron for the orphan boys and girls from dockyard townships along the river.

George must have spent a lot of time at this juncture in his life wondering what he had done to incur such misery.

He had plunged into this disastrous marriage to Caroline only to free himself from his debts. The odious Princess was now effectively removed from his life, but the debts were very much still there. His schemes had not produced the financial rewards he hoped for.

He had been promised an income of £138,000 a year, plus a one-off £52,000 to meet the costs of his wedding and the completion of the work on Carlton House. But when Parliament learned that George's debts had swollen to £630,000 it was clear that a large amount of his income would have to be earmarked to pay off the debts. William Pitt suggested a figure of £38,000 should be deducted, but at that rate the debts would not have been cleared until twenty-seven years had passed.

Members of Parliament expressed outrage that such a burden should be imposed on a country already overtaxed and facing the crippling cost of a war with France, especially when they considered the debts could be attributed to George's reckless living, his drinking, and his womanising.

The King would not support his son against Parliament because the unpopularity George was incurring had already partly rubbed off on himself. Discussions of George's spendthrift ways in Parliament led to an inevitable wave of public hostility, demonstrated when, on its way to the House of Lords, the Prince's carriage was greeted by hurled stones and shouts of abuse.

At one stage it looked as if the government of William Pitt would be forced to resign over the question of George's allowance. It was saved only when George, pressured by his father, agreed that £65,000 of the yearly £138,000 should be set against the debts, and that commissioners should be appointed by Parliament to monitor his financial affairs.

In private, George was outraged, despite the £52,000 of the nation's wealth he was allowed to pay for his wedding and the work on his house. He set about reducing his Household once again, and preached invective against the government, which he felt was depriving him of his birthright.

Another disappointment waited around the corner. His oldest brother Frederick had been made a Field Marshal and many of his other brothers were awarded high military rank. Yet he was still a Colonel of the Dragoons, a rank he had held for a number of years.

He complained to his father, and was not mollified by the response, which pointed out that high military rank was all the brothers could look forward to to fulfil their duty in life. On the other hand, his role as Prince of Wales was, the King felt, sufficiently important to occupy him for the present.

George tried to prove his worth by riding off one night intent on joining his regiment and leading it in the face of a rumoured French attack on the British coast. The French attack never materialised, and the King told his son not to be in such a hurry. If he truly wanted to display his bravery, he would have plenty of opportunity if the French really invaded, and he could do so as commander of his regiment, the 10th Light Dragoons.

6

MRS FITZHERBERT RETURNS

George was tiring of Lady Jersey and desperately wanted
Mrs Fitzherbert back in his life. Though he had not seen her
since shortly before his marriage, when she had gone abroad,
he kept in loose touch with her all the time through mutual
friends who conveyed messages.

Mrs Fitzherbert bore no ill feeling towards George. She
had never considered herself spurned, for she understood the
necessity of the Prince's dynastic marriage to Caroline of
Brunswick.

George had sent his brother, Duke of Cumberland since
his uncle's death, to see Mrs Fitzherbert on his behalf and
sound her out on the possibility of a reunion as early as May,
1796. She rejected this and other approaches, delivered in
letters and by messengers, which bespoke his admiration for
her and his yearning for her return. Not because her
affection for him had dimmed, but because she knew that
while the Countess of Jersey was still around her position
would be in jeopardy. She also suspected that, in any event,
the prospects of a harmonious relationship had been irrevocably destroyed. 'The link once broken could never
be rejoined,' she said, also offering the opinion that if
she and George were reconciled, it would not be for very
long.

As if to prove his intent, George had Lady Jersey evicted
from the Pall Mall house in the summer of 1799, and later
sacked her husband from his job as Master of the Horse,
claiming his hand was forced by the need to make econo-
mies.

Lady Jersey was, however, most reluctant to accept her

dismissal from the position of George's favourite mistress. She turned angrily on the Prince's friends who were entrusted with the embarrassing task of letting her know that he wanted nothing more to do with her.

George sent Mrs Fitzherbert long, rambling, and impassioned letters, pleading with her to come back to him, and assuring her that his affair with Lady Jersey had been terminated. Mrs Fitzherbert's response was to move to a house in the country. She kept away from London and Brighton, so as to avoid meeting the Prince.

Her resistance only served to spur George on to greater effort. The flow of letters became a deluge. He also sent her a series of presents, including a miniature painting of one of his eyes fitted into a locket.

His frantic efforts to retrieve his lost love became obsessive. He declared it was driving him mad, and members of his family believed there was a real danger of him becoming mentally unstable. He could not eat, and lost a vast amount of weight. He looked so ill that worried friends thought he was dying.

A newspaper report that Mrs Fitzherbert had died in Bath stunned him. Numb with grief, he contemplated suicide. Fortunately he did not kill himself, for the story was untrue.

The distraught Prince assured his sisters that he would die if he were not reconciled with Mrs Fitzherbert. Even Queen Charlotte stepped in out of concern for her son and personally wrote to Mrs Fitzherbert, begging her to accept some new arrangement by which she could make the Prince happy.

'If you wish my life, you shall have it,' George wrote in one of his letters. 'You know you are my wife in the presence of God.'

It is perhaps astonishing that Mrs Fitzherbert, who was by now forty-three years old, should for so long have resisted the man she loved. At one stage she agreed to rejoin him, then, after thinking it over again, withdrew her promise.

Finally, in the depths of despair, George sent her an ultimatum. If she did not return to him, he said, he would let out the secret of their marriage, to his father, to Parliament, to the whole world. He wrote, 'I will prove my marriage, relinquish everything for you, rank, situation, birth.' Melodramatic as ever, he added, 'if that is not sufficient, my life shall go also.'

This worked. Mrs Fitzherbert fully realised that if the details of their clandestine marriage were officially announced, George would never become King and might even be hounded into an ignoble exile. Her position, in the face of an outraged population, would also be very precarious.

Mrs Fitzherbert told George they could be reunited, but said that she first wanted to have the facts laid secretly before the Pope, who would rule on the validity of the marriage in the eyes of the Roman Catholic church. George agreed to this proviso, and Mrs Fitzherbert approached her confessor, the Reverend William Nassau, to ask him to lay the case before Pope Pius VI in Rome. If the answer was favourable, she would return to the Prince. If not, she would leave the country for ever.

In the meantime, while awaiting the outcome of the appeal, Mrs Fitzherbert absented herself from London and the Prince's constant badgering by moving to Wales. The unhappy George wanted to get away and try to forget the misery of waiting. He asked for permission to go to Portugal for a rest in the interests of his health. His father, again suspecting that the request had something to do with Mrs Fitzherbert, turned him down.

So George was sentenced to spend months moping around his apartments in Carlton House, for the procedure to secure Papal approval was to take nearly a year. Nassau had speedily laid the facts of the marriage before Pius VI, but the Pope had died shortly afterwards, in August, 1799.

The delay was almost unendurable for the Prince, who was noted drifting around London like a ghost. Once again, friends were convinced the strain might kill him.

The new Pope, Pius VII, was not elected until March, 1800, and only then could the case be laid out again. Pius VII saw that it was a difficult and delicate matter, and took his time over making a decision. In June he gave his private sanction to the marriage, and the interminable waiting was finally over. Mrs Fitzherbert rode back to London for an ecstatic reunion with George.

Mrs Fitzherbert publicly trumpeted the revival of their relationship by giving a grand breakfast for four hundred guests which filled three marquees in the gardens of her new London home in Tilney Street, Mayfair. It continued unabated for fifteen hours.

The couple were inseparable once more. They spent every evening together, and made several journeys to the country to stay with friends. The Prince was often heard to offer the opinion that Roman Catholicism was the only religion for a gentleman.

But they still could not live together openly. Mrs Fitzherbert kept her house, and George stayed in his apartments at Carlton House.

Mrs Fitzherbert believed the trying unpleasantness which marked George's youth had passed and that he had matured into a respectful and considerate man. She also confided to a friend that their relationship had changed in one very important respect. When she agreed to take up with George again she had insisted on laying out the ground rules. One of these stipulated that she would not live with him as wife or mistress. They were not sleeping together any more. George, who would never have tolerated this a few years before, was so pleased to have regained the love of his life that he accepted it without complaint.

George's relatives and friends were relieved to see him happy again after his abject misery of the past months. Only one person felt aggrieved by his happiness. Lady Jersey, who felt her position had been usurped, was most reluctant to accept her dismissal from the Prince's affections. She hoped somehow to win him back and, in the meantime, she tried to disrupt his reforged link with Mrs Fitzherbert by turning up unannounced at gatherings which she knew they were to attend. Mrs Fitzherbert and George haughtily ignored the interloper, but her repeated presence eventually became a strain on him. She kept up the pressure until her trouble-making was finally rewarded with a pension George ordered for her on the sole condition that she keep out of his way. Lady Jersey did keep out of sight, but for years George was to feel her unseen, malevolent presence as she kept society amused with a flood of unseemly and scandalous stories about him. Her vindictive campaign became so bad that George eventually let it be known that he would in no way associate with anybody who remained on good terms with Lady Jersey.

Society, still unwilling to believe a secret marriage which so flagrantly breached the constitution had taken place, was mystified by the continuing hold Mrs Fitzherbert had over George. In her late forties, she was now rather stout, prim, and domesticated. All they seemed to share was a more than ample silhouette. But no one who saw them together, whether they were on a night out at the theatre or relaxing at Brighton, could doubt the mutual contentment with which they greeted the first years of the new century. The gentleness of her manner mellowed his temper, she encouraged him to drastically cut his consumption of alcohol, and she nursed him through his illnesses. Their closer friends saw clearly how much the Prince needed her.

George increased Mrs Fitzherbert's allowance by £1,000 a year and the couple spent a lot of time at Brighton, where, to mark his indelible link with the now fashionable town, his statue was erected. Ensconced in the Pavilion – which his new architect, John Nash, was transforming into an Indian fantasy with onion domes – George was a changed man, relaxed, witty and happy.

Mrs Fitzherbert had a new home built nearby, designed by Robert Adam, and paid for by George. The Prince had an underground passage constructed between it and the Pavilion, so that he could visit her unobserved. They were carefree days. The couple enjoyed entertaining their friends at dinner, when the wine flowed freely. They stayed up late and slept on in the mornings. Soon George, now in his forties, was again putting on weight.

A visitor to the Pavilion at this time recorded the graciousness of the parties and the domestic tranquillity which pervaded the house. The Prince enjoyed instructing his band while footmen distributed sandwiches. Occasionally, some of George's old drinking friends would turn up and, to prevent him from being led astray, Mrs Fitzherbert contrived to find important correspondence which needed his immediate attention and kept him out of their way.

Another frequent and very welcome visitor was George 'Beau' Brummell, the most stylish man of the age. Captain Brummell was an amusing companion whose military career remained undistinguished, perhaps because on parade he could never remember which troops he commanded. He had abruptly resigned his commission when he learned that his regiment was being posted to what he considered the barbaric city of Manchester. For George, Brummell's strictures on sartorial taste were law. He admired Brummell and tried to ape his taste in clothes and presentation. A gentle put-down from him about his clothes would reduce the Prince to a trembling wreck. Theirs was a close friendship which George felt enhanced his life. Mrs Fitzherbert, while tolerating the flighty Brummell, realised his world was artificial and a little empty.

Sadly, money worries were never far away for George. He raised loans to meet his immediate commitments but he was never able to get his finances on an even keel. Staff, who were always being kept waiting for their salaries, had to be laid off. Tradesmen, weary of being fobbed off time and again, struggled to get their accounts paid. The irrepressible George simply raised more loans and proceeded to spend his way deeper into debt.

A jeweller who was owed £89,000 advertised the debt in a newspaper to try to force payment. He didn't succeed. George was still spending thousands of pounds on furnishings for his homes. Over £3,000 was squandered on chandeliers for Carlton House, and £2,000 just on table linen. He spent in excess of £2,000 each year on his own clothes, ordering waistcoats by the dozen. Thousands more went on clothes as presents for his brothers and sisters. Carlton House was crammed with his purchases, which also included an uncountable number of furs, masks, and jackets. He could not buy just one of anything. Tooth-brushes were ordered three dozen at a time, and one day he bought thirty-two walking-sticks. His vast staff which enabled him to run Carlton House and entertain in the grand style cost near to £7,000 a year, and one month's supply of wine could easily cost over £1,000.

Mrs Fitzherbert, it seemed, could persuade George to do anything except curb his spending.

While the happy couple passed their days oblivious to outside problems, George III faced up to dissent amongst his ministers at Westminster. Early in 1801 the hitherto loyal William Pitt, troubled by an Ireland aflame with insurrection, proposed laws which would allow Roman Catholics to stand for Parliament and for executive office. The King, convinced that emancipation of the Catholics entailed a breach of his coronation oath to govern and uphold the Church of England, intervened and Pitt was obliged to resign after holding office for seventeen years.

The strain of this crisis led to a relapse in the King's health and he soon displayed the symptoms of his earlier illness. The uncertainties and intrigues of the Regency Crisis rose once more to the surface.

The King's doctors were called in again and ordered confinement. William Pitt and his successor as Prime Minister, Henry Addington, went to Carlton House to discuss the new crisis with George. The Prince needed no reminding that not long before some members of the House of Commons had drawn up an Exclusion Bill, which would have denied him any right of succession or power of Regency. The newspapers, conversant with his defects, argued forcibly that he should be excluded from the throne. Pitt, who temporarily retained the seals of office which had not yet been handed over to the King, told George that, if the Regency were deemed to be necessary, the Regency powers would be restricted in the same ways as had been proposed during the earlier illness. With so much feeling in Parliament, in the newspapers, and in the country against him, George could only agree to whatever Pitt suggested. However, he started having secret conversations with leading Whig politicians with a view to planning a new government.

He proposed that Ireland should be pacified by laws which would restore Catholic civil rights, a scheme he had outlined in a letter not long before to Pitt when he considered that Ireland was facing a double menace, French invasion and a Catholic rebellion. On that occasion, neither Pitt nor his father had troubled to respond to his interest.

George was not allowed to see the King, but this did not stop him claiming that his father was completely out of his mind. The King was put back into a straitjacket and his mental confusion stretched into weeks. Some days the doctors were optimistic, on others they feared the worst. During one particularly bad night, the whole of the royal family was called to sit outside his bedchamber because the doctors expected the King to die.

When George was permitted to visit his father, he found him pale and thin. They had a long and rambling conversation. The King was far from cured, but he was certainly on his way to recovery, the Prince observed. Unfortunately, the physicians decided otherwise and virtually kidnapped him to take him off to another confinement. Finally, the King managed to free himself from their sometimes violent attentions. Unless he were allowed some freedom, he said, he would not sign any state papers. Shortly after this, the doctors were sent away and the King headed for a convalescence at Weymouth.

George got along well enough with the new Prime Minister, and seized on the opportunity to raise the delicate problem of his finances. He said that he had a right to the revenue from the Duchy of Cornwall which had been withheld from him until he was twenty-one. His lawyers and parliamentary friends held that he was entitled to the arrears, which amounted to £234,000. However, when the request was put to Parliament, it was denied. Addington worked behind the scenes to reach a compromise, so as to re-establish the Prince in 'that splendour which belonged to his rank'. George had to waive his possible rights to the arrears, and in return he would receive £60,000 a year for three years to help him pay off his debts. The law providing for this just squeaked through Parliament, though the Prince came in for more popular criticism for squandering public money at a time of war.

The conflict against Napoleon was not going well, and in 1803 news came through that the French Emperor had occupied Hanover, a fact which was kept from the King, who was about to suffer another bout of illness. In face of the rampant success of Napoleon's army, a broad-based parliamentary coalition was suggested to the King. He turned it down because he could not bear the thought of one of the names on the list being included amongst his ministers. The name was of George's great friend, Charles Fox.

George had given up the idea of obtaining a military command, but the threat of a French invasion later that year provoked him to renew his request, suggesting that this would allow him to set an example to the nation. He wrote to his father, saying, 'I ask to be allowed to display the best energies of my character, to shed the last drop of my blood in support of your Majesty's person, crown, and dignity.' The King let his son know that if the French landed he would be expected to stand at his father's side in the field. But a command before then was out of the question. George, who had been a Colonel for ten years, did not try to disguise his anger. He persisted with his request, so much so that the exasperated King threatened that if the importuning did not stop George would find he had lost command of even the 10th Light Dragoons.

George tried to force his father's hand by publishing their correspondence relating to the military commands. The newspapers enjoyed it, and took another opportunity to poke fun at the Prince, but all it achieved was to further alienate George from his father. For almost a year they studiously avoided each other. The King made regular visits to Blackheath to visit Princess Caroline and his granddaughter, Princess Charlotte, partly because he liked them and partly because it was likely to annoy his son. George retaliated by spreading stories of the King's alarming behaviour on holiday at Weymouth, where he irrationally let fly at people in the street, and openly propositioned some of the ladies of the Court.

7

AN INDELICATE INVESTIGATION

The years of separation from Princess Caroline did nothing
to diminish George's hatred of his wife. He had hoped that
her banishment to Kent would be suitably miserable and
lonely. It was not, for the gregarious and volatile Caroline
soon gathered a court of her own around her. Spencer Perceval, an up-and-coming Tory Member of Parliament, was
a near neighbour and became a friend. George Canning,
who had got to know Caroline when she was welcome in
Carlton House, still called. Her proximity to Greenwich provided her with a diverting cluster of entertaining naval
officers, from young captains up to seventy-year olds like
Admiral Lord Hood. Though the entertainments were occasionally boisterous, they seemed on the surface innocent
enough. Caroline was a chess addict, and would also spend
hours discussing the cultivation of flowers. Some of the male
guests were a little alarmed at her flirtatious manner, but
public opinion, guided by the newspapers, warmed to a Princess left lonely and neglected by a selfish husband. This was
reflected by open abuse of George when he travelled. Conversely, Caroline could count on a good reception from the
people of London whenever she went to town.

When Princess Charlotte, their daughter, reached her
eighth birthday in 1804, George tried to use her to strike at
his wife. She had thus far been brought up by a governess
and was a lively little girl, if possessed of a stubborn temper
and a slight stammer. New arrangements were needed for
her education, and the King suggested that the child, of
whom he was very fond, should be brought to Windsor.
There, he said, her education could be completed under the
watchful eye of the Queen. Princess Charlotte had seen little

enough of her mother, but George saw this as an opportunity to keep Caroline permanently away from her. So he agreed to the King's plan, insisting that the arrangement should be carried out under the sole and exclusive care of his father. This, he believed, would mean the end of any possibility of Princess Caroline influencing their daughter. But the King had other ideas. He invited Caroline down to Kew for a discussion about the granddaughter he called his 'little darling'. It was soon clear that he wanted Caroline to spend more time with her daughter, not less. Caroline, he said, was to visit the royal family and Charlotte frequently at Windsor and Kew, and perhaps during their holidays at Weymouth.

Princess Caroline was overjoyed at the new arrangements. George was, of course, furious. He threatened to keep Charlotte out of the King's family circle altogether. A bitter argument raged over the little girl, conducted through the Lord Chancellor. The King and his son were going through one of their periodic estrangements, and refusing to write letters to each other. A laborious negotiation ensued, and finally it was agreed that Princess Charlotte would live in a Carlton House annexe while the Prince was in London, but go to Windsor or Kew when he was away from the capital. Princess Caroline, who felt further embittered at the offhand treatment, was told that she could see her child occasionally, but only as a visitor.

Not satisfied that he had almost completely excluded Caroline from their daughter's life, George then snatched at a new opportunity to attack his wife. This time he hoped to shatter her reputation beyond repair, and force Parliament into enacting the necessary legislation for a divorce.

For some time, ribald stories about Princess Caroline's behaviour at Blackheath had been peddled around the London gossip circuit. She was reputed to be the archetypal predatory female, bestowing her favours generously on any unsuspecting male who stepped over her threshold. But stories were all they were, with nothing substantial to back them up. Until Lady Charlotte Douglas, a ruthless and vindictive woman who had been a neighbour of Caroline, came forward with information too startling to be ignored.

Lady Douglas, the respected wife of a retired major-general, Sir John Douglas, had become a close friend of Caroline's, and had been taken into her deepest confidence. They were close enough friends for Caroline to be godmother to Lady Douglas's second child. This friendship had, however, ended when Caroline discovered Lady Douglas had been spreading derogatory stories about her conduct.

Most shocking of these stories, which usually centred around Caroline's prolific adultery, was that the Princess had secretly given birth to a son in 1802 and passed the child off as the offspring of a dockyard worker's wife.

George had been informed of such gossip about Caroline's affairs, and of at least one alleged pregnancy. Previously he had had to content himself with complaining about her entertaining young men, and that the cost of her household bills, for which he was responsible, was straining his already overburdened finances.

Now it seemed there was proof, and he wanted an inquiry into his wife's way of life instigated.

The first reaction of the government ministers who were consulted was that any inquiry into the morality of Princess Caroline would be hazardous to Prince George, for it would be certain to raise the question of his mistresses, his marriage to Mrs Fitzherbert, and all his own licentiousness. It was extremely dangerous ground, they stressed, and urged that, on the contrary, everything should be done to avoid an investigation of that type.

However, a different reaction was forthcoming from Lord Thurlow, who as Lord Chancellor was the royal family's leading legal adviser. He told George, 'If you were a common man, she might sleep with the Devil, and I should say, let her alone and hold your tongue. But the Prince of Wales has no right to risk his daughter's crown and his brother's claims. The Princess of Wales should be like Caesar's wife, not even suspected. For both your sakes the accusation, once made, must be examined into.'

Prince George told his father that he felt wounded as a father, as a husband, and a man of honour. King George did not consider his merits high in any of those areas, but he was astute enough to realise that if Caroline had a son he might one day challenge the succession. For, according to Lady Douglas, Caroline said she would claim the Prince was the boy's father.

King George consulted Lord Grenville, Prime Minister of a coalition government, and on his advice a Commission of Inquiry was set up in the summer of 1806. The Commissioners, Grenville himself, the Lord Chancellor, the Lord Chief Justice, the Home Secretary, and the Solicitor-General, were entrusted with what the royal brief called 'This Delicate Investigation'. Their investigation was to prove the most indelicate one ever undertaken by any government.

First witness was Lady Douglas, who said that Princess Caroline had asked to assist at her own confinement. While they were alone, the Princess had revealed to her that she too was expecting a child, and she hinted that it was not her first. According to Lady Douglas, Princess Caroline went on to explain why she had immersed herself in charitable work which gained her a reputation as a lady bountiful. She had informally adopted a number of local children, either foundlings, or from poor families, and helped to take care of them. Many lived for part of the time at her house at Blackheath. But the real motive behind her apparent social conscience was to hide the fact that she had borne children from her many affairs. When visitors saw young children around the house, they would assume they were more of her charity cases. The Princess had disguised her pregnancies by stuffing cushions up her dresses and pretending she had grown fat. When Lady Douglas asked her what would happen if she were found out, Princess Caroline said she was unconcerned, for during that particular pregnancy, she had spent two nights at Carlton House. The child was born in 1802, the Commission of Enquiry was informed, and was registered as William Austin, the son of a labourer, before being 'adopted' by Caroline.

The father of the child, in Lady Douglas's opinion, was Rear-Admiral Sir Sidney Smith, with whom Princess Caroline had an affair and later openly boasted about it, awarding him the highest commendation as a 'bedfellow'.

The Princess had her bedroom next to the staircase leading into an adjoining park so that her visitors could come and go without being observed, said Lady Douglas. She talked of having many men share her bed, observing, 'nothing is more wholesome', and urged Lady Douglas to amuse herself in the same way, offering a recommended list of male companions.

Sir John Douglas said that Princess Caroline often visited his home, but it was clear she came there to meet their old family friend, Sir Sidney Smith. A Page of the Backstairs told of seeing Sir Sidney in the house in the early morning, though at that time no one had yet been let into the house. A housemaid almost caught the Princess and Sir Sidney in bed together. A footman declared the Princess was 'very fond of fucking'. Other servants told of mysterious clandestine visitors, the Princess calling for huge breakfasts in her room, and one declared that a doctor had asked if the Prince ever visited the house, because he believed the Princess was pregnant. A Royal Navy Captain, Thomas Manby, was said to have slept with the Princess, both at Blackheath and during a visit to Southend. A servant told of seeing them kissing. The list of allegations and insinuations went on and on, Caroline was seen nudging Captain Manby's foot with her own at the dinner-table. She was seen being 'too familiar' with various gentlemen at the house, including one occasion when a member of the household staff found her on a sofa draped around Sir Sidney. Selected male dinner guests stayed overnight and had breakfast with Princess Caroline in the morning. Even the name of the respected politician, George Canning, was heard during the investigation. He had in fact been having an affair with Princess Caroline over a long period, but evidence against him was scratched out by Prince George, who did not want to involve him in the scandal. The only references to him in the Commissioners' report were innocuous. Canning breathed a deep sigh of relief about this, for when the investigation began he was convinced that he would be cast in a starring role.

Princess Caroline was also berated in the inquiry for taking men off alone to private drawing-rooms after dinner-parties, and for sitting in bed eating fried onions and potatoes and drinking ale.

Many of the male guests at the house found themselves terrified by Caroline's telegraphed flirtatious attentions. Walter Scott later told his biographer how, during one evening at Blackheath, she had taken him out alone into a conservatory to admire some flowers. She had skipped quickly down the stairs in the darkness, but Scott, who suffered a certain lameness, had hesitated before following her. Caroline had turned around and, in mock indignation, chided him: 'Ah! False and faint-hearted troubadour! You will not trust yourself with me for fear of your neck!'

On the surface, the evidence appeared very damaging. But it was all either circumstantial or unreliable. Many servants from the household came forward to say they had noticed nothing untoward in Caroline's behaviour. Her doctor said he had never offered the opinion that she was pregnant. Both Sir Sidney Smith and Captain Thomas Manby denied any impropriety, and also denied they had slept in the same house as the Princess.

Grave doubts must hang over even the thin hearsay evidence taken by the enquiry, for we now know that money was offered for evidence which would incriminate the Princess. Thomas Manby was offered and angrily refused a bribe of £40,000 to give such evidence. And Lady Douglas for the rest of Prince George's life received from him an unexplained gratuity of £200 a year.

The Commissioners cleared Princess Caroline of the gravest charge against her, for they were convinced that the child in question was born to Samuel and Sophia Austin at the Brownlow Street Hospital in July of 1802. This child was, and remained, under the unofficial care of Princess Caroline, and the inquiry said there was 'no foundation whatever for declaring that the child now with the Princess was the child of her Royal Highness or that she was delivered of any child in the year 1802'.

In other respects, however, they found her behaviour liable to 'very unfavourable interpretations'. There was too much evidence laid in front of them for the Commissioners not to believe she had had some affairs, and they concluded, 'We think the circumstances to which we now refer, particularly those between her Royal Highness and Captain Manby, must be credited until they shall receive some decisive contradiction.' This was a statement demonstrably against the common principle of English justice, which deems everyone innocent until they are proven guilty. Princess Caroline had not been asked to give evidence refuting the allegations, but the Commissioners considered her guilty until she could be proved innocent.

How much of the scandal Princess Caroline brought on herself by her own weakness for senseless gossip is unknown. Friends believed she may have enjoyed teasing Lady Douglas with the most outrageous stories. But it seems to have been common gossip in Blackheath that the Princess did have a child in 1802.

Caroline certainly seems to have gained some macabre pleasure out of assisting the rumours, wickedly leading people on by innuendo. On other occasions, she claimed that the only time she had overstepped the social bounds was when she committed the faux pas of sleeping with Mrs Fitzherbert's husband.

She embroidered the story of young William Austin years later when she asserted he was in fact the son of Prince Louis Ferdinand of Prussia, that he had been brought to this country as a baby and smuggled into the Blackheath house, where he was substituted for Mrs Austin's child.

Whoever William Austin was, he remained under Princess Caroline's care for the rest of her life, travelling wherever she went and living in her household.

The inquiry did nothing to change Princess Caroline. She remained a vulgar exhibitionist, dressing, as companions recalled, like an opera girl, and behaving like a whore. She also devised a special feature for her ribald parties at Blackheath: a mechanical doll which performed obscene antics. A philosophical observer considered that she was the only true friend the Prince of Wales had, because her behaviour did so much to justify the excesses of his own conduct.

George III's fading eyesight would not allow him to read

the report, but such of it as was read to him shocked him. He was offended mainly by the sheer volume of men that Caroline had apparently taken into her bed. In private, he declared, 'If it had been one attachment, or even a child, I would have screened her if it could be done without risk to the Crown'. But he could never bring himself to condone profligacy on such a generous scale. He drafted a royal reprimand, which let Caroline know in no uncertain terms that neither the King nor members of his family had any intention of receiving her at Court. The Queen and the Princesses were told that she could no longer be considered part of the family, as far as visiting her and showing her civility were concerned. However, within a year, Spencer Perceval, who was a genuine friend of Caroline's and never her lover, became Chancellor of the Exchequer and insisted on at least an outward show of reconciliation between the King and Princess Caroline. Although she retained her Blackheath residence, apartments were made available for her in Kensington Palace.

The Delicate Investigation did not, as George had hoped, provide him with such damning evidence of his wife's immorality that he could rid himself of the lady he called 'the fiend from Brunswick'. He felt, however, the findings of the Commission had been too lenient towards her. There was, even he had to concede, insufficient evidence for the Princess to be charged with high treason, but he considered the government ought to have initiated an Act of Parliament aimed at ending the marriage. Lord Grenville and his fellow Commissioners rightly feared that such an attempt would be seen by the public as persecution of Princess Caroline on behalf of the unpopular George. They refused to contemplate the idea, for they knew they had fallen a long way short of establishing the guilt of the Princess.

Far from benefiting George, the episode lowered him still further in the public's esteem. To many it seemed monstrous that, without a chance to speak in her own defence, his wife should be pilloried for lapses which, even if she were guilty of them, were less grave than his own. The Prince came in for another ferocious bout of mockery and lampooning.

Posing as the injured husband, he felt insulted by the attacks on him, and most of all by the ones which brought in his secret wife, Mrs Fitzherbert.

During the months of the Delicate Investigation, George III showed signs of fading into the illness which was going to blot out the last ten years of his life, and George started to come into his own as a figure of major importance in the domestic politics of the country. The Battle of Trafalgar had been won, and though Nelson had died, Britain's seaward flank against Napoleon had been assured. William Pitt had also died shortly after, and the coalition government, known as the 'Ministry of all the Talents', had taken over, with many of George's friends claiming their share of power. Charles Fox became Foreign Secretary and George thought of himself as the spiritual leader of the Whig party.

The thorny problem of Catholic emancipation raised itself again, and the new government hoped the King, now recovered from his most recent spate of illness, would prove less intransigent. But George knew his father well enough, and advised Fox and the other ministers that the issue would have to be shelved until after the King's death. Instead, he advised that the somewhat shaky ministry should apply itself to less fractious reform measures, such as the abolition of the slave trade, rather than risk the fury aroused by mention of Catholic relief. Charles Fox determined to support the move to abolish the slave trade in the British Empire, but the days of this bright political star were numbered. By midsummer of 1806 Fox, his legs grossly swollen from dropsy, looked like a dying man, and was unable to leave his tiny house less than half a mile from Carlton House. Prince George visited him every day that he was in London, and held out to his old friend the promise of recuperation at Brighton. Every bulletin during his last illness was awaited with equal anxiety by both political parties. For all his faults, no public man was ever more loved than Fox for his private qualities. Where other politicians commanded confidence and gratitude, Fox inspired profound affection.

George was in York when he heard of Fox's death, and was shattered by the news. He wrote to a friend, 'Such a loss and such a calamity are almost beyond all suffering.' For George loved and admired Fox as a politician and as an orator. Despite George III's opinion on their friendship, George needed him as a brilliant, original companion, a vital, gifted older man who had increased the Prince's confidence in himself.

George immediately set out for London, intending to pay his final respects to his friend at the funeral in Westminster Abbey. The King, however, still believed that Fox was in part responsible for corrupting his son. Even in death he could not bring himself to forgive him. He curtly refused to allow George to take part in the ceremony. Thus the King took his revenge.

After the death of Fox, the Prince's enthusiasm for politics dropped off again. When Grenville's government was on the verge of collapse, he did nothing to help, for he was piqued that no move had been made to assist him over the matter of his debts. He also considered that Grenville had not done all he could to persuade his colleagues that a Divorce Bill should be prepared to free him from his hated wife. Most important, perhaps, was George's feeling that his parliamentary friends had stopped consulting him about their plans. Fox had known how to flatter the Prince by seeking advice from him; his colleagues did not. But George was not to forget the disillusion he felt at this time in his life, and in later years it was to count heavily against the Whigs.

Princess Caroline was delighted to see George's political links undergo such strain, and made a point of displaying her friendship for the leading members of the Tory party. Men like George Canning and Spencer Perceval backed her over the iniquitous condemnation offered her from the Commission of Enquiry. Perceval declaimed that he considered Caroline a much injured lady, and that, for such a cause, he would face the Tower or even the scaffold. He would never have to, but his theatrical support for her at this time endeared him to her for ever.

An attempt was made to revive the inquiry into her immoral behaviour when a box containing letters written to Captain Manby and a number of personal souvenirs was discovered. An expert claimed that one of the souvenirs, a bunch of woman's hair, could not have come from any woman's head. This evidence was laughed into obscurity when the Lord Chief Justice ruled that the hairs might be admitted if the larger 'record to which they were originally attached was also to be examined and compared'.

The King did not feel Caroline's conduct could be condoned, but he was also not particularly proud of his role in the affair. He finally felt obliged to let the Princess know that her inquisition was at an end, and she promptly tried to get back into the royal family fold. The King persuaded her to keep away from Court for a few months. But when she next turned up, Prince George kept his back to his wife all the time and they didn't look at each other once. George took to arranging his life to avoid any chance encounter with Caroline. It was all most embarrassing for the family, and George said the situation could be resolved if he were given the legal separation he sought. The King refused this, because he feared it would lead to an unpopular divorce.

In public, Princess Caroline was as popular as ever. Whenever she visited a theatre, the audience would clap and cheer her enthusiastically. News of her father's death in a battle on the continent tended to increase sympathy for her. The newspapers sided with her, asserting that she had been harassed by her husband, who had helped concoct a plot to destroy her reputation. The *Morning Post* hailed her as 'a truly virtuous and illustrious female, the object of the most foul and infamous calumny ever advanced by the most unprincipled of men'.

In private, she was soon acting as outrageously as ever, flirting with any man who visited her house, and fuelling the Court gossip. George was outraged, feeling he was coming in for unfair criticism because his wife behaved in such a way. But there was clearly nothing he could do to restrain her.

At the same time, he was about to be called to account for her extravagances. Princess Caroline received a yearly allowance of £12,000 from Prince George, but by 1808 she had managed to run up debts of £49,000. The government adamantly refused to countenance paying them off. That responsibility, they felt strongly, lay with her husband, who received a larger income because he was married. George protested that the thought of paying for her wild and scandalous existence was too much for him to bear. Even if he wanted to do so, he said, he could not afford it. He was quietly advised that if the debts were not paid, the public would learn about it, and their hostility would descend on him, not his wife. Accordingly, an embittered George had to pay her outstanding accounts off at a time when he could not meet his own. At the same time, the government insisted that he raise his wife's allowance to £17,000 so that she might avoid running into debt in the future.

Another scandal besmirched the royal family when Colonel Gwyllym Lloyd Wardle, radical Member of Parliament for Okehampton, laid serious charges against Prince Frederick of corruptly using his position as Commander-in-Chief of the Horse Guards. It was claimed that Frederick's mistress, the actress Mrs Mary Anne Clarke, had been accepting fees for promotion from ambitious officers, that Frederick had instituted the promotions, and the couple had split the bribes. At first, Prince George threw his support behind his brother, but as the evidence became more and more damning he was forced to withdraw in case he became suspect by association. Parliament voted Frederick's innocence, but displayed its true feelings by relieving him of his command.

George consoled himself during these troubled times with frequent trips to Brighton, where his Pavilion was starting to take shape. He had plans drawn up for a Chinese design, then rejected them in favour of one with an Indian flavour. As if to test the idea, he added £55,000 to his debts by having vast Indian-style stables built. The Chinese Room at Carlton House was dismantled and taken down to the Pavilion, which was the only place where he now felt at home. Visitors noticed the change that came over him when he took up residence there, how all his old charm and civility flowed back. There were the occasional drinking bouts, but the gentle influence of Mrs Fitzherbert kept his wild drunkenness a thing of the past. Dinners were as sophisticated and elegant as ever, but the number of guests was usually limited to fifteen. Mrs Fitzherbert had put on a lot of weight, but was still very attractive. Each morning he was in Brighton, George could be seen sitting out on the balcony of her house. The guests at Brighton were varied and scintillating. Richard Sheridan continued to astonish everybody with the nimbleness of his mind, which contrasted with his madcap behaviour. He was known to burst into the drawing-room at the Pavilion dressed as a policeman to 'arrest' unsuspecting house guests for playing some illegal card game. The stylish and original 'Beau' Brummell never failed to entertain with his haughty stories of high fashion. The Prince appreciated Brummell's assertion that two glovers should be employed for one pair of gloves. One to make the thumbs, the other to make the rest. He was also highly amused to hear that Brummell's boots were waxed with champagne and his ties and cravats designed by a portrait painter. Prince George liked to think of himself as the leader of fashion in his world, but he blatantly copied Brummell. He went to the same tailor, Schweitzer and Davidson in Mayfair, and he opened his snuff box in the manner prescribed by Brummell: with one hand only – the left.

Mrs Fitzherbert, unlike many other women in George's life, was maternal by nature. She was extremely fond of children, and confided in her friends that she would like to have a dozen of her own. Her relationship with the Prince precluded this, and for want of children of her own Mrs Fitzherbert delighted in the seven-year-old Mary Seymour, daughter of her friends, Lord Hugh and Lady Horatia Seymour. She was entrusted with the care of the little girl while the parents were abroad. When both parents died within months of each other, Mrs Fitzherbert wanted to keep the child under her guardianship. Mary's mother had, in fact, exacted a promise from Mrs Fitzherbert that she would take care of the child. But Lord Seymour failed to appoint her as guardian in his will, and his relatives called on Mrs Fitzherbert to hand the child back. She could not bear the thought of giving the girl up, and even planned to run away with her. She was as devoted to Mary as if the child were her own.

A long and involved legal dispute followed, in which Lord Seymour's executors objected to Mrs Fitzherbert, ostensibly on the grounds of her religion, and brought a High Court action for the appointment of other guardians. The affair received a vast amount of publicity, including the dubious accolade of satirical prints highlighting the religious prejudice. The executors won the action and a subsequent appeal by Mrs Fitzherbert was rejected. She was about to take her appeal to the House of Lords when Prince George stepped in to persuade the head of the girl's family, Lord Hertford, to agree to a formula which resolved the drama. Lord Hertford announced that he himself would be guardian of the child, but would appoint Mrs Fitzherbert to act for him.

George had himself given written evidence of Mrs Fitzherbert's attachment to Mary Seymour. This was something he had observed from close quarters, because both spent a lot of time with the child, and the Prince was certainly very fond of her. Conversely, he did not seem to be interested in spending much time with his own daughter, Princess Charlotte. This may have been because so many of her extrovert mannerisms reminded him of her mother. Whatever the reasons, Charlotte felt deprived of fatherly devotion, and spoke about this to her governess. George promised to be a more indulgent father, but this proved as empty as all his other promises.

When the case was resolved, George settled a bond of £10,000 on the young Mary, a move which prompted the whisperers to believe that the child was really his. This gossip was reinforced by the fact that he showed the girl more affection than he did his own daughter, always remembering her with presents of jewellery or money. Mary, or Minny as she was affectionately known, wrote to thank George for his many kindnesses, addressing him as 'Dear Prinny'. Political writers heard of this pet name, and it entered the country's folklore as a satirical pseudonym, depicting an ageing prince who still neglected his duties, preferring the constant pursuit of pleasure.

For years, Mrs Fitzherbert had been more of a mother to Minny than had Lady Horatia Seymour. Minny wanted to stay with Mrs Fitzherbert, and was delighted when she was allowed to do so. George was so happy about the outcome that he gave a children's party at the Pavilion to celebrate the victory.

It was a moment of great happiness for Mrs Fitzherbert. So it is sad that this episode was effectively to end her relationship with George. For, in the course of negotiating the compromise which kept Minny Seymour under the care of his secret wife, George spent a lot of time in the company of Lord Hertford and his wife, Isabella, Lady Hertford. She was a refined, elegant, very feminine woman, with a voluptuous figure. Though approaching fifty years of age and a grandmother, she was exactly the sort of woman to whom George was incurably susceptible.

On the thinnest of pretexts, he started appearing with growing regularity at Ragley, the Hertford's Warwickshire country home, and their London mansion in Manchester Square.

It was not long before George's fascination with Isabella was the talk of society, though no one could believe that the formal, almost stately Lady Hertford would become his mistress.

Lady Hertford did indeed resist George's pursuit of her, neatly sidestepping him and on one occasion absenting herself to a family estate in Ireland to try to avoid him.

Her resistance to him only increased his determination. So frantic did his pursuit become that friends once again seriously wondered if he were afflicted by the same malady that was slowly removing his father from public life. One wrote that George expected Lady Hertford to live with him openly, and that he was fretting himself into a fever at her refusal.

Lady Hertford was flattered by George's obvious admiration for her, emphasised by his perpetual presence. He was now in his mid-forties and much of his youthful charm had disappeared with his growing waistline. But he still retained that irresistible aura of a man of power which has swayed women through the ages. She was fascinated at the prospect of manipulating power through him.

George was emotionally as weak as ever, and needed a

dominant woman to take decisions out of his hands. Lady Hertford offered such domination but also something else. Since his childhood, he had never known a family life. She was the first woman in his life who offered him an established family circle. Though the gossips twittered when he dined with the Hertfords, he was not trying to proclaim Lady Hertford's infidelity. He was eagerly joining her family.

But, whatever the explanation of his love for Lady Hertford, his cruelty to Mrs Fitzherbert over the new liaison was unforgiveable. When he paid open attentions to Lady Hertford in Mrs Fitzherbert's presence, he showed the sadistic instinct of a weak man. Clearly, he no longer needed the tranquil domesticity Mrs Fitzherbert offered him. But in the twenty-one years since the marriage which neither of them could acknowledge she had never abused her power, never lost her dignity, and always remained loyal. She did not deserve the treatment he was to mete out to her.

George started avoiding the Pavilion and Mrs Fitzherbert. He needed all his time for his obsessive pursuit of Lady Hertford. He refused to eat and started to shed weight. He repeatedly demanded that his doctors bleed him to relieve the feverish tensions his agitation caused. Once again his disturbed emotions were making him ill. He became so depressed that he would not leave his bedroom in Carlton House. If only Lord and Lady Hertford were there, he said, he would be cured of his distress. He wrote to Lady Hertford, saying that since she had left her country home he had suffered the most incredible pains in the head. 'The agony I suffer is hardly to be credited,' he wrote.

Lady Hertford would not rise to this bait. Playing on an attack of illness was not going to win her over.

His doctors saw that his illness showed all the signs of love-sickness and realised that physical cures were unlikely to do him much good. But he was determined to be bled profusely, and convinced himself that this barbaric treatment was the answer to his problems. When the doctors showed reluctance to bleed him constantly, he duped them by calling three in the course of one night and getting each to bleed him.

Lady Hertford's consistent rejection was driving him into a desperate state of mind, as another society wife testified in a letter to her lover. Lady Bessborough recounted that the Prince had tried to force himself on her, falling on his knees, clutching her, and kissing her before she knew what was happening. 'Such a scene I never went through,' she wrote. 'I screamed with vexation and fright. He continued, sometimes struggling with me, sometimes sobbing and crying.' The Prince vowed eternal love to Lady Bessborough during the struggle, then abused her lover, then promised to break with Mrs Fitzherbert and Lady Hertford for her. He told Lady Bessborough she should make her own terms for their liaison, that she should be his sole confidante and adviser. The mixture of promises and pleadings continued, and Lady Bessborough, seeing how ridiculous it all was, could scarcely stop herself bursting out laughing. She painted a picture of the scene which records George in a pathetic light – 'that immense grotesque figure flouncing about, half on the couch, half on the ground'. Lady Bessborough resisted the Prince, partly because he didn't appeal to her, and partly because she knew that all the time it was Lady Hertford he really wanted.

No one could fail to notice that as surely as Mrs Fitzherbert was being eased into the background, Lady Hertford was slowly moving forward to take her place. The cool and clinical Lady Hertford refused to be a guest at table at Carlton House or the Pavilion if Mrs Fitzherbert were not there too. This served to preserve her own reputation, while at the same time heaping humiliation on Mrs Fitzherbert. George fell in with this intrigue, perhaps because he could not summon up the courage to tell Mrs Fitzherbert openly that after all the years and all the loyalty she had given him he was going to dismiss her. There were evenings at Brighton when he would ignore Mrs Fitzherbert totally, while playing courteous attention to Lady Hertford all the time.

There had been a series of passing affairs over the years, and Mrs Fitzherbert had ignored them, seeing them for what they were. There was the dancer, Louise Hillisberg, and Marie Anne, the French wife of the Earl of Masserene. He

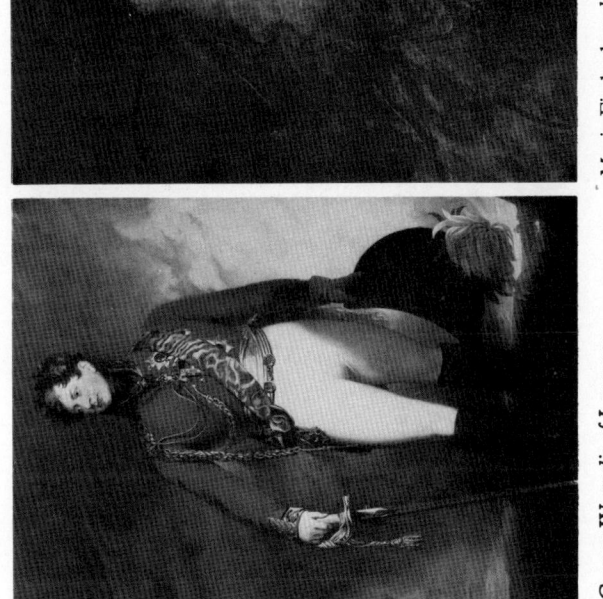

George IV *studio of Lawrence*
(reproduced by permission of the National
Portrait Gallery, London)

Maria Fitzherbert *by Sir Joshua Reynolds*
(Earl of Portarlington; reproduced by permission of the National
Portrait Gallery, London)

The Royal Pavilion, Brighton, before and in 1825
(both reproduced by permission of Borough of Brighton Royal Pavilion, Art Gallery and Museums)

Lady Conyngham by Sir Thomas Lawrence
(by courtesy of the City Museum and Art
Gallery, Birmingham)

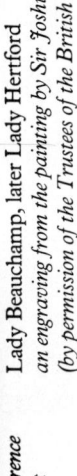

Lady Beauchamp, later Lady Hertford
an engraving from the painting by Sir Joshua Reynolds
(by permission of the Trustees of the British Museum)

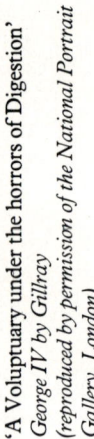

Caroline of Brunswick by Sir Thomas Lawrence
(reproduced by permission of the National Portrait
Gallery, London)

'A Voluptuary under the horrors of Digestion'
George IV by Gillray
(reproduced by permission of the National Portrait
Gallery, London)

had even set up another Frenchwoman, Madame de Meyer, in an elegant Mayfair flat and visited her regularly late at night. His ploy of parking his carriage streets away and trying to disguise himself behind scarf and greatcoat had not hidden him from the gossips.

His obsession with Lady Hertford was far more serious and it was impossible for Mrs Fitzherbert to ignore it, especially when it involved her in so much hurtful embarrassment. On a number of occasions she told George she was going to leave him, but she refrained from making the break because she feared that this might prompt the Hertfords to terminate the arrangement which left Minny Seymour in her care. She still loved George, but wanted to escape from the cruel way he was treating her. Minny was a different matter entirely.

By the summer of 1808 she could take no more, and informed George that their relationship was at an end. He was shattered by the news, and moaned that it was totally unexpected and unjustified. He told her through a friend that if she returned quietly he would ignore what had happened. When this produced no response he wrote a passionately inflamed letter to Mrs Fitzherbert, calling her ' my love, my only love' and telling her he had been unable to sleep for thinking of her. He protested, 'I am a different animal, a different being from any other in the whole creation. Every thought and every idea of my existence and of my life never leave and never quit thee, for the smallest particle of an instant.' He promised he would end his pursuit of Lady Hertford.

Mrs Fitzherbert relented in the face of such heart-rending appeals, and started seeing him again. Amazingly, he still yearned for Lady Hertford and repeatedly made the fact glaringly obvious. Mrs Fitzherbert, unable to tolerate any further insults and embarrassment at his hands, felt driven beyond endurance. She wrote to tell him, 'It has quite destroyed the entire comfort and happiness of both our lives; it has so completely destroyed mine, that neither my health nor my spirits can bear it any longer. What am I to think of the inconsistency of your conduct, when, scarcely three weeks ago, you voluntarily declared to me that this sad affair was quite at an end, and in less than a week afterwards the whole business was begun all over again?' She begged him to make a decision and ended her letter, 'You must decide, and that decision must be done immediately, that I may know what line to pursue. I beg your answer may be a written one, to avoid all unpleasant conversations upon a subject so heart-rending to one whose life has been dedicated to you, and whose affection for you none can surpass.'

George wanted both Mrs Fitzherbert and Lady Hertford in his life, but he was not going to be able to have them. He wrote to Mrs Fitzherbert, begging her indulgence, and hoped they would continue as before. She did, in fact, tolerate the situation for a few months, but with George's longing for Lady Hertford displayed for all to see she could not bear it much longer. Their final break came in December of 1809, when she turned down an invitation to the Pavilion, and wrote to underline her great unhappiness over the 'very great incivilities' and 'indignity' she had suffered. She continued, 'For whatever may be thought of me by some individuals, it is well known your Royal Highness four and twenty years ago placed me in a situation so nearly connected with your own that I have a claim upon your protection. I feel I owe it to myself not to be insulted under your roof with impunity.' In his response, George assured her he would never forget the feelings he held for Mrs Fitzherbert. Neither would forget them, but this was to be the final, irrevocable break. They never set eyes on each other again, though George saw to it that her yearly allowance continued.

George's life, while severely troubled emotionally, continued as glamorous as ever. A dinner at Carlton House for all the Knights of the Garter was unparalleled in splendour.

But while he played, the threat to Britain from Napoleon's armies, sweeping victoriously across Europe, mounted. British troops were being pushed back in Spain and an expeditionary force sent to the Low Countries had met with a catastrophic defeat.

In the autumn of 1810, a problem closer to home raised itself to haunt the government and the country. The news about the King, who for some time had been barely clinging to his reason, was bad. Shortly after his daughter Amelia died of consumption, his attendants noticed he was beginning to let his talk ramble on inconsequentially when he was out riding, and was suffering from delusions.

The new Prime Minister, Spencer Perceval, called to see the King, and found his talk hurried and indiscreet. He came away with the gloomy opinion that another lapse into madness seemed inevitable. The following days confirmed this. The King's conversations with relatives and servants either ran as a series of repetitions or stuck to no common theme. Doctors were called in again, including the keeper of a Kensington madhouse. The King started swearing at his daughters, and showed signs of violence. For a while he was put in a straitjacket again to try to calm his behaviour.

Some days the King showed signs of clarity, and talked rationally about his earlier illnesses. On others, he was worse than ever, ranting and raving and terrifying everybody at Windsor.

The Foreign Secretary, Lord Wellesley, reported hearing a dreadful wailing, and told colleagues, 'The King is as mad as he has ever been in his life.'

The doctors, who were still working with little more than the knowledge of the Dark Ages at their fingertips, were at a loss. There was a split in their ranks. Some believed he would recover from this attack, as he had from the earlier ones. The others saw that the King, who was seventy-two and going blind, was fading from life as they knew it.

For a while, reassuring bulletins about the King's condition were issued, but Perceval and his closest colleagues knew they would have to face up to the facts. The King was lost to them, at a time, with a danger threatening from abroad, when they needed a clear executive authority.

Perceval was shrewd enough to suspect undue optimism among the King's physicians. He appointed a Committee of Peers to inquire into the sovereign's mental condition. Their highly secret report to him confirmed his worst fears. There was no real prospect of the King recovering his faculties, and the government was going to be obliged to face up to another Regency crisis.

While this behind-the-scenes activity was going on, Perceval stood up in the House of Commons to assure the nation that news of the King's recovery was expected at any time.

At the same time, he wrote to Prince George with the news that he proposed introducing a Regency Bill into Parliament in the last days of 1810. The only possible acceptable candidate as Regent was George, and he was content to sit back and await the call to power. He sent for the leaders of the Whig party, notably Lords Grey and Grenville, to discuss with them the future administration of Parliament and the governance of the country. They were polite and agreeable, but it was clear to him they would not be malleable to his will. He wished that his old friend Charles Fox was still alive.

However, when George heard the details of the Regency Bill, he flew into one of his rages. The restrictions on the Regent contained in it were exactly on the lines of those proposed by William Pitt over twenty years before. They included the imposition of restraints for twelve months upon the Regent's prerogatives. A fettered Regency. He would be barred from creating peers, the pensions and appointments to public office he ordered would last only as long as the Regency. The power over the royal household was also to be left in the hands of the Queen.

George was understandably irritated. At the time of the earlier Regency crisis he had been a comparatively young man. Now he was nearly fifty, and it was humiliating to be told by Parliament that for a year he could take no measures of a lasting character.

He summoned his brothers to Carlton House and they signed a joint letter to the Prime Minister protesting at limitations which, they claimed, ran counter to 'principles which seated our family on the throne of these realms'.

Perceval, who like the others in the government felt that the passing years had not given George a wise head or discretion, insisted on the limited Regency because of George's proven unreliability. He wrote to the Prince, making this point in the most delicate terms possible in the circumstances.

George pointed out to him in a responding letter that he

had already had this long argument out with William Pitt many years before. All the points he had made then still stood, he felt.

The parliamentary opposition, led by the redoubtable Lord Grey, argued that the limited Regency should have been imposed on George when he was in his early twenties and the wildness of youth had not then left him. Now the position was different. George, the Whigs stressed, was now a responsible man who would undertake his duties with all the seriousness they demanded.

Lord Grey, who himself must have been hoping that George as Regent would be more than willing to assist him into government, declared that Perceval was using the pretext of a possibility of the King's return to health to cling to power.

There was a lot of support for an unfettered Regency in both Houses of Parliament, but Perceval's spirited fight against it won the day.

Early in January of 1811 a Regency Bill which restricted the powers of the Regent had passed through Parliament. Now all George had to wait for was the final deterioration of the King's health.

The Prince busied himself with political negotiations. The Whigs were sharpening their claws at the prospect of power with the effective sovereign behind them. But George was already slipping provisos into their plans. There would have to be a strong administration and he realised this might not be possible if some Tory ministers were not included. All believed that they could not guarantee the support of Parliament if George Canning were left out of the government. George recoiled at the thought of the man who had been so closely associated with his hated wife being granted an important portfolio, but the choice appeared inevitable.

The arguments over the various possible permutations of the Cabinet dragged on, and George wondered if he could ever resolve them. Powerful politicians wanted to help their friends into the government, George had friends of his own he wanted to show favour to. He wanted Richard Sheridan made Secretary of State for Ireland, but Lord Grey compared this to 'sending a man with a lighted torch into a magazine of gunpowder'. George also wanted his brother Frederick reinstated to his post as Commander-in-Chief of the Horse Guards, despite the fact that he had so recently been toppled by scandal. There were brothers, brothers-in-law, and numerous friends to be accommodated, and all their claims were put forward with equal enthusiasm.

A roll of ministers was finally agreed upon and presented to George, but he suddenly recoiled. There was still a possibility that the King could recover, and he did not like the idea of facing another bout of parental fury for dismissing the ministers the King had supported.

This hesitation on George's part was caused by new medical reports which suggested that the King might, indeed, be throwing off his illness. The King was even well enough to have a formal audience with Perceval, and told the Prime Minister that he felt well enough to return to his duties if he was needed. Perceval demurred, saying that the physicians considered that he was not well enough yet, but hoped that the day would not be too far off. This meeting with Perceval was detailed to George by the Queen, who wrote, 'You will be glad to hear, my dearest son, that Mr Perceval has seen the King and communicated the state of public business pending in the two Houses of Parliament. His Majesty gave perfect attention to his report, and was particularly desirous to know how you had conducted yourself, which Mr Perceval answered to have been in the most respectful, most prudent, and affectionate manner.'

This was a shot across George's bows, warning him that he would have to attend to his behaviour, and that the Regency was by no means his for the asking. What he saw as the collusion between his mother and Perceval he called 'too gross to escape detection'.

He did not know which way to step, and he seemed to change his mind from day to day. A jibe that he would not back his Whig friends because he lacked the necessary nerve led him to launch a ferocious attack on the Whigs, claiming that when they had been in office before they had treated him like an enemy. Then he would announce that in due time he would appoint his Whig associates to government. It was very confusing for the politicians, for the country, and also for the Prince.

The answer to the conundrum, George felt, might lie in finding out with certainty the course the King's illness was going to take. So he consulted one of the physicians, Dr Robert Willis, who first said he could not look with any degree of confidence towards the King's complete recovery within any limited time. Dr Willis then added a note of optimism asserting that in recent days hopes of a recovery had risen. Another doctor, though lacking confidence about the claim, believed the King would probably recover within three months.

George wavered more than ever, until Lord and Lady Hertford stepped in with some solid advice. There must be no change in government, they told him, while there was a possibility that the King would recover.

So the Prince wrote to Perceval at the beginning of February to inform him that he did not intend to remove any of the King's ministers from office. He continued, 'At the same time the Prince owes it to the truth and sincerity of character which he trusts will appear in every action of his life, in whatever situation placed, explicitly to declare that the irresistible impulses of filial duty and affection to his beloved and afflicted father leads him to dread that any act of the Regent might in the smallest degree have the effect of interfering with the progress of his Majesty's recovery. This consideration alone dictates the decision now communicated to Mr Perceval.'

It was a haughty and verbose letter, which reflected George's fears that if the King heard his son had dismissed his government, it might be the final blow to his reason.

The Whigs felt cheated by George's decision and a crowd of demonstrators formed outside Carlton House to jeer him. The Tories felt no more secure, believing their future was balanced on the thin line of the King's health.

George had managed to alienate both sides of the political spectrum in one blow. It was a clouded prospect for his Regency, which was now only a matter of days away.

8

PRINCE REGENT

When it became clear that the King's recovery was impossible in the foreseeable future Spencer Perceval enacted the necessary legislation which took Britain into the Regency Age.

The era, which has always been seen to epitomise great taste and elegance, began in typical style at noon on February 5, 1811, when bandsmen of the Grenadier Guards, their regimental colours flying, marched into the courtyard of Carlton House. Inside the house, the grand staircase and hall were lined by Yeomen of the Guard and soldiers of the Life Guards.

As the first members of the Privy Council arrived for the ceremonial swearing in of George as Regent, the band struck up *God Save the King*. When they thought of the grossly fat and self-indulgent Prince, an overgrown schoolboy with little knowledge of the world, it was an anthem dear to many of their hearts.

The Prince, with his royal brothers lined up alongside him, sat at the end of a vast table in the grand saloon to await the Privy Councillors, who entered in full dress. Leading the procession were the Archbishop of Canterbury, the Lord Chancellor, and the Lord Privy Seal, the rest following in order of precedence.

Then the Prince stood to swear the oath of loyalty to the King, and that he would 'truly and faithfully execute the office of Regent of the United Kingdom of Great Britain and Ireland'.

Afterwards, the Councillors each knelt before George to kiss his hand. The Tories among them could not fail to notice that a bust of Charles Fox, which had previously stood in George's private chambers, now had pride of place in the saloon.

George wanted to hold a grand celebration fête immediately after the swearing-in ceremony, but the plans had to be shelved because the condition of the King kept everybody on tenterhooks. Either the King was going to die, or he would suddenly recover. In either case, such a celebration would have been out of the question.

Though George had retained Perceval as Prime Minister, no one expected the Regent to lose his antipathy towards him and the Whigs remained confident of moving into office when his 'probationary' year expired. The change, they believed, would come even sooner if George III died, which was what many really expected. Yet, as George became accustomed to the pleasures of authority, the doubts began to creep in. He grew aloof, and avoided discussions with the politicians who turned up at the small Carlton House gatherings.

He gave his first small party of the Regency at Carlton House a few days after being sworn in. Strangers who had not been inside the building before were overwhelmed by its splendour, and saw that the piety of days at Kew and Buckingham House were at an end. The novelist Robert Plumer Ward compared the house to Versailles, and a visiting diplomat considered its elegance and richness surpassed anything in Europe. Others assessed its rich opulence as vulgar in the extreme.

But the serious-minded Lady Hertford was certainly having an effect on George. Friends shook their heads in disbelief when one of his physicians reported that 'he was supposed to be engaged with religion, and read a daily chapter or two of the Bible with Lady Hertford'. The Prince was forty-eight, and looking a few years older. Certainly at some time he was likely to slow down, his former carousing colleagues realised, but not like this.

He moved, a portentous figure, through the first weeks of the Regency. Dinner at a society home here. Supper at a friend's mansion there. 'An enormous assembly' at the home of Lady Hertford, who was, of course, showing him off and advertising her influence. He inspected the Royal Academy, and after dinner impressed the gathering with what the listeners considered the best King's speech they had ever heard. Soon afterwards, George offered the Royal Academy a bronze lamp to illuminate the Great Room, and commissioned a design. When the massive lamp was installed, and lit up on lecture nights and at annual dinners, it was a reminder of princely patronage. His royal interest in the arts, his enthusiasm for and firm belief in the aesthetic sense and artistic achievement, were to be characteristic of the Regency.

George's long-awaited and twice postponed fête to celebrate the inauguration of his Regency exploded on to society in June of 1811. He declared that it was in honour of the exiled Bourbons of France, so that he might be seen to be thumbing his nose at Britain's greatest enemy, the Emperor Napoleon. Guest of honour among the two thousand invited was Louis XVIII, the uncrowned King of France.

The fête was to last for a whole day, and cost George £120,000. It was little wonder that his debts, which he was still struggling to pay off, were soon over half a million pounds.

Centrepiece of the fête was a two-hundred-foot-long supper-table, where endless dishes of food were served. An artificial stream flowed between banks of flowers down the middle of the table. Covered walks, decorated with painted trellises, flowers, and looking-glasses, had been specially constructed as promenades and supper galleries.

George presided over the fête like Apollo, resplendent in a scarlet and richly embroidered uniform of a Field Marshal, a rank he had an automatic right to as Regent and Commander-in-Chief of the British armies. His corsets, however, could not disguise his obesity, and the sagging flesh of his chins had to be hidden behind the voluminous folds of a high cravat. But he was graciousness personified as he strolled amongst his guests, all charm and courtesy. One guest was so impressed he felt obliged to write, 'That so large a number should have been served in such a style was extraordinary. Tureens, dishes, plates, even soup plates, were everywhere of silver with as many changes as were wanted. There were hot soups and roasts, all besides cold, but of excellent and fresh cookery. Peaches, grapes, pineapples, and every other minor fruit in and out of season were in profusion. Iced champagne at every three or four persons, all the other wines also excellent. There was no crowding, hurry or bustle in waiting; everything was done as in a private house.' Another recorded the 'assemblage of beauty, splendour, and profuse magnificence. Women out-blazing each other in the richness of their dress. I sat for three-quarters of an hour in the Prince's room after supper, silently looking at the spectacle. The Prince spoke to me, as he always does, with the cordial familiarity of an old acquaintance.'

George sat down to dinner at the mammoth table, set beneath ornate lanterns in the fan-vaulted Gothic conservatory. Above his head was a crown illuminated with the letters GR. Sixty attendants served the dinner.

His mother was noticeably absent. She had told George she considered it disgraceful that he should hold such a party when the King was so ill. Princess Caroline, his hated wife, had not expected to be invited and she was not. But she raised no objections to the invited members of her Household attending. She even bought them new dresses for the occasion. However, she was upset that their daughter Princess Charlotte had also been left off the invitation list. Now fifteen, Charlotte had said she was looking forward to the fête. Though she was heir to the throne, George wanted to keep her out of the public eye, and, instead of inviting her, he had her packed off to Windsor to stay with the Queen.

Also striking by her absence was Mrs Fitzherbert. She had, in fact, received an invitation but had declined it when she found that Lady Hertford was listed for a seat at the royal supper-table. If Lady Hertford was to sit at George's table, she reasoned, then so should she. Mrs Fitzherbert wrote a personal letter to the Prince requesting a place at his table. She had gone through many humiliations at Brighton while Lady Hertford usurped her position in George's life, and she was at pains to make sure she did not suffer any more. She pointed out that previously, 'to avoid etiquette in circumstances of such delicacy as regards my own position with reference to the Prince, it had been customary to sit at table regardless of rank'. She wanted to know if the same rule was still in effect.

George's brother Frederick tried to persuade him to change his mind and allow Mrs Fitzherbert to sit at his table. George, however, was strongly under the influence of the domineering Lady Hertford, and had barred Mrs Fitzherbert at her insistence. To Frederick he said that certain rules had applied when he was Prince of Wales. Now that he was Regent he was obliged to act in a different way, as dictated by his position.

The reply George sent was formal and very cold: 'You know, Madam, you have no such place.' Mrs Fitzherbert's terse response was, 'None, Sir, but such as you choose to give me.'

This exchange of letters was the end between them. Mrs Fitzherbert declined to go to the fête, and they never spoke to each other again.

She did write to the Prince, but he never bothered to reply to her letters. This hurt her very much, for she was to carry her love for him to the grave.

After this stinging rebuff, Mrs Fitzherbert realized there was no future in their relationship and knew it had to fade. But she felt she had given so many years of her life to George that it was his due to make good the promises he had made time and time again since their secret wedding in the drawing-room of her home. The Prince had vowed to formally establish her position in society when it came within his power. She felt that, as Regent, he now had that power. But under the watchful eye of Lady Hertford he was to be precluded from fulfilling any debt to Mrs Fitzherbert.

So Mrs Fitzherbert demanded that George grant her a formal separation, which he willingly gave her. This was all carried out through emissaries of the Prince, though how a couple who had never been legally married could have a legal separation would be difficult to explain. However, the terminology suited them both, and Mrs Fitzherbert proceeded to negotiate over her alimony. George agreed to her request that her £6,000 yearly allowance should be continued. Mrs Fitzherbert could not bring herself to accept this politely, because she felt it was something George owed her for dismissing her so ignominiously, in full view of a most interested society. But it was not long before she was writing to George, asking that the allowance should be increased by £2,000 because she found it difficult to live on the £6,000. Her angry letter underlined her claim that all her financial problems 'originated from the old debts of former times and the very scanty allowance' which she had been given. Inflation, she said, had halved the value of it. George, who wanted no trouble from Mrs Fitzherbert's direction, agreed to the increase, and a later one, which brought her yearly allowance up to £10,000. He was motivated by concern for her welfare, certainly, but his mind must have conjured up nightmare images of Mrs Fitzherbert producing the marriage certificate written out in his own hand. He knew that public exposure of the wedding could end in a very uncomfortable exile, something he was most anxious to avoid. Whether she was aware of the blackmail element which was contained in their dealings does not come through in her letters, for she never mentioned the certificate. But its existence must have hung over George's head like a dark cloud.

Perhaps Mrs Fitzherbert, at fifty-five, was beyond George's lingering interest. At any event, he shed no tears at her going out of his life. And, though she kept in intermittent touch through her unanswered letters, Mrs Fitzherbert must have felt a certain amount of relief that she would no longer have to contend with his selfishness, his affairs, and, worst of all, his insults.

The grand entertainment at Carlton House proclaimed the social brilliance of the era. It also brought a burst of radical indignation because of the money the already deeply in debt Prince squandered on his party. The poet Shelley snorted, 'What think you of the bubbling brooks and mossy banks at Carlton House? It is said that this entertainment will cost £120,000. Nor will it be the last bauble which the nation must buy to amuse this overgrown bantling of Regency.'

Shelley's opinion was echoed by many others who objected to the cost effectively incurred by a nation struggling to raise the money to wage a life-or-death struggle against the rampant power of Napoleon.

They also railed about the vast cost of George's palace and the army of staff needed to run it. At the time of the fête, his Household included a Treasurer, a Private Secretary, an Assistant Private Secretary, a Vice-Treasurer, a Vice-Chamberlain, a Keeper of the Wardrobe, a Gentleman Porter, two Clerks, five Pages of the Presence, five Pages of the Backstairs, a Housekeeper, an Inspector of the Household, a Maître d'Hotel, a Butler, a Table-Decker, two Surgeons of the Household, and forty-three indoor servants, including a laundress, two cellarmen, three confectioners, four watchmen, six cooks, and ten housemaids.

The staggering opulence of the interior of Carlton House was put on public display for three days after the fête, when members of the public were admitted, by ticket, to inspect the apartments. Everybody who could wanted to view the splendour and, on the third day of viewing, thirty thousand people clamoured to get in. It degenerated into a stampede in which dozens of hysterical women were almost stripped of their clothes. One unfortunate visitor wrote to a friend that many ladies could not leave Carlton House 'until furnished with a fresh supply of clothes. They were to be seen all round the gardens, most of them without shoes or gowns; and many completely undressed, and their hair hanging about their shoulders.'

The shambles his extravaganza slipped into appalled George. It was as though he realised that behind all the show of wealth and graciousness there was nothing but turmoil. Once again, he became withdrawn and silent, keeping away from others whether at house parties or public events. As the year passed, his preoccupation increased and many who saw him commented on his permanently worried countenance. The state papers he was obliged to attend to as Regent were of monumental proportions. One day at Carlton House he was observed to sign as many as fourteen thousand papers, with his Secretary and Assistant Secretary seated at each side of him, running the papers past as if on a conveyor belt. At the end of the session, George looked up wearily and said, 'Playing at King is no sinecure.'

He was clearly under strain from all this unaccustomed responsibility, and started drinking large amounts of alcohol again in an attempt to calm his nerves. But it did not help, for the more he drank the less decisive he became. Friends noticed with unconcealed distress that George was easily able to sink three bottles of wine at dinner, and wondered how much he would have to get under his belt when he was forced to face up to the crises of government which certainly lay ahead.

Throughout the summer, the King was assailed by wilder delusions than ever. His physicians became convinced that he would never recover, and were so pessimistic about his health they expected to him to die any day.

George realised that kingship would impose political demands on him, and started a series of consultations with the leading parliamentarians of the day. Whig members who hoped for George's patronage in the not-too-distant future were dismayed to hear that he had dined with Spencer Perceval. If he had buried the hatchet with the Tory leader, then past loyalties would count for little, they suspected.

His brother, the Duke of Cumberland, was a well-known Tory supporter, and whenever he got the opportunity bored George by preaching against Whigs, against reform, and against Catholic emancipation.

Brighton was still an escape hatch for the Prince and when he went there in the autumn his relaxed happiness and charm flowed back. He drank, but not too much, and delighted his guests at the end of each day by bidding them good night with a gracious, 'God bless you all!' Thomas Creevey, the Whig Member of Parliament for Thetford, a Pavilion regular, noted in his journal, 'He was in the best humour, bowed and spoke to us all, and looked uncommonly well, though very fat. He was in his full field marshal's uniform. He remained quite as cheerful and full of fun to the last, asked after Mrs Creevey's health, and nodded and spoke when he passed us. He looked much happier and more unembarrassed by care than I have seen him since this time six years. This time five years ago, when he was first in love with Lady Hertford, I have seen the tears run down his cheeks at dinner, and he has been dumb for hours, but now that he has the weight of the Empire upon him, he is quite alive.' George's good humour continued, and he would participate jovially in the musical entertainments, beating his hand on his thigh and even joining in the singing.

But what Creevey and the other Whigs really wanted to hear was how long George proposed to keep the ministry he had inherited from his father in power. They hoped that George's dinners with Perceval meant nothing more than his wish to keep the boat on an even keel until he felt ready to oust the Tory administration. The Tories, for their part, were also apprehensive of George's intention and prepared themselves for his expected decision to remove them from office. However, they did realise that one major point was in their favour: the Prince's indolence. A radical change of government would mean a lot of lobbying work to ensure firm support. George, they reasoned, was probably too lazy to orchestrate it. Even a partial change of government, bringing in some of George's Whig friends, seemed out of the question. For many of them were known to be reluctant to serve with members of the present Tory administration. This was something George, with his underlying authoritarian spirit, could not understand. He thought his friends should step forward when it took his fancy to call for them, whoever their colleagues in government might be. Another problem for the Whigs was that they realised George's word could not be relied on from one day to the next. Firm arrangements could be done away with in hours, and they were wary of the close link between his promise and retraction.

George, however, showed no indolence when it came to handing out the patronage his Regency allowed him, even if it involved him in disagreements with Perceval. At a time when Parliament wanted to abolish the sinecure post of Paymaster of the Royal Bounty of Officers' Widows, which wasted a salary of £2,700 a year, George stepped in to demand that the non-existent job be given to his Secretary, Colonel John McMahon. He got his way over this. Another storm blew up when he insisted that his brother Frederick should be reinstated as Commander-in-Chief of the Household Cavalry, a post which Parliament had deprived him of just two years before. He engineered other military and naval appointments to please friends, and persuaded Perceval that a Dr William Jackson, the brother of his old tutor, should be appointed Bishop of Oxford. George himself related the story of how 'Perceval then put on one of his little cynical smiles and observed, "Your Royal Highness perhaps does not know Dr William Jackson's character. He is a notorious bon vivant."' George recorded that he responded, 'Oh, as to that, I know him very well. I have known him all my life. He has drunk a bottle of port in this house before now and I hope that, when he has got his mitre on, he will drink another.'

All political discussions were, however, banned at Brighton, and George saw to it that members of the government were kept clear of the Pavilion. But his refuge from decision-taking on the crucial matter of government could not be put off for ever. For the restrictions on his executive powers, which stopped him from throwing the whole of his father's government overboard, were to end in February, 1812. The Whigs were prepared to be indulgent and to wait until George felt able to use his full powers. But they grew more impatient when the news from Windsor seemed to indicate that the King's recovery became more and more unlikely by the day. The Duke of Cumberland wrote after visiting his father, 'The King is totally lost as to mind, conversing with imaginary persons, and he is constantly addressing himself to Eliza.' His doctors reported that, 'His Majesty showed clearly his incapability of maintaining any steadiness in his ideas and conversation for more than an instant. He never failed to decline into some wild unnatural frame of thought after a sentence or two.' They recounted 'hearing him speak of new arrangements which the late King was making now, and detail accounts of strange and horrible events which he himself was convinced had occurred in the course of the last night'. He imagined his sons had died or been despatched to some distant part of the globe. His wild fantasies knew no bounds. He believed he could call on people from the world of the dead, and, at times, thought he was an animal in Noah's Ark. They concluded that he was living in another world, the world of his delusions, and had lost his grasp on the real one.

But still George could not bring himself to make the political decision to change the government. For one thing, he did not believe the Whigs of the day carried too well the mantle of his hero, Charles Fox. The number of Whigs who had spoken out in support of the French Revolution worried him. Was their loyalty to the British crown suspect? Were their plans for reform and emancipation too outrageous for society to withstand and remain intact? Were they too much at odds with each other in a fractious battle over leadership and policy to provide a united and firm management of the country?

Perhaps his easiest course would have been to send for the Whigs, consolidate his popularity with his early friends, and win the affection of the great mass of Englishmen. But there was one further important objection to a Whig government which unquestionably weighed with him. After twenty years of war with France, Napoleon's hold on Europe had visibly weakened and the first faint signs of eventual victory had appeared. The Whigs were unlikely to enforce the heavy taxation which was necessary to fight the war, for a number of them were known to oppose it, and were in favour of concluding a peace treaty with Napoleon. George rightly saw the struggle with Napoleon as of life-or-death importance to Britain, and did not want to see the direction of it passed over to people he suspected might urge an effective surrender. Thomas Creevey, for one, had openly expressed the hope that the high British casualties being sustained in Wellington's campaign in the Iberian Peninsula would encourage a move to call it off. George was unconcerned when he was told that support for the Peninsula campaign was waning, and it was now considered 'out of fashion'. He reasoned that a negotiated settlement was a ridiculous aim after all the years of sacrifice and struggle, especially when the hinge of fate was turning the fortunes of war in Britain's favour. Wellington had proved his abilities and, after the early reverses in Portugal, seemed to be heading for victory. And, perhaps most important, news had come through that Napoleon had shown himself unable to resist the ultimate folly and was pouring troops into the crazed dream of a conquest of Russia.

George took time off from the worries of state to go to Prince Frederick's country house, where a ball was being held in honour of his daughter, Princess Charlotte. In his enthusiasm to show her how a Highland fling should be executed, he came down so heavily on an ankle that he was forced to retire to bed, groaning in agony and heavily dosed with an opium pain-killer. He stayed in bed for a fortnight, and this inspired the wildest stories about the true nature of his condition. He complained of violent pains which could only be relieved by lying on his stomach for hours on end.

There was talk that he had gout, but word was circulating from the people around him that the condition was something far more serious. There was a constant fear that George, especially after his earlier emotional illnesses, would go the same way as his father.

Walter Scott wrote from Edinburgh, 'We are here alarmed and stunned with unauthenticated rumours concerning the state of the Prince Regent's health. God forbid any one of them is founded in truth.'

Lady Bessborough recounted, again in a letter to her lover, 'The Prince is, I believe, extremely ill.' She confided that one of the Prince's doctors 'says he suffers such agony of pain all over him it produces a degree of irritation on his nerves nearly approaching to delirium. What will become of us, if as well as our King our Regent goes mad? It will be a new case in the annals of history.'

George, despite his illness, had an explosive argument with the Duke of Cumberland when he heard what his troublesome brother had been saying. Cumberland had not minced words. He said outright that the supposed ankle injury was nothing but a fraud and that George was mad. A better treatment than a poultice on the ankle would have been one on the head, he suggested. Cumberland denied he had made any such statements, but many people he had conversed with said otherwise.

Medical historians who have examined the various symptoms shown by George during this illness and others believe he may have been afflicted with a milder form of the porphyria which destroyed his father's contact with reality. He was never subject to the extreme mental derangement of his father, but the occasional symptoms he displayed led to newspaper stories at the time suggesting a link between his condition and the rambling mind of the King. He was desperate to suppress any account of illness if he felt it would lead to assumptions of this kind, which is why he was so furious with Cumberland. On one occasion, he urged the Attorney-General to launch litigation against *The Sunday Times* for such a suggestion. As a penalty he wanted newspaper taxes trebled. He forbade the issue of any bulletins by his doctors during his illness and all subsequent ones. He feared that they might lead to unnecessary and damaging speculation about his mental condition. The bulletins did not fuel such speculation, but the absence of news from royal sources was to give the gossipmongers *carte blanche*, which may have been even more damaging.

The Duke of Cumberland's irresponsible declarations imposed a strain on the Christmas festivities in the royal circle of 1811. The doctors would have preferred that George had not been told about his brother's comments, for they feared that the Prince Regent's brain was affected. They considered the worries over the Regency had harassed 'his mind and rendered him totally incapable, for want of nerves, of doing anything'.

The illness continued, keeping him out of action for weeks, and was punctuated alternately by loss of feeling in his arms and hands and excruciating pain in them. Massive doses of opium-based sedative could put him to sleep for only three hours a night, such was his distress.

In a letter to Lady Hertford he talked of the pain permeating every part of his body. He said he had passed the worst night of his life, when he had been kept awake by pain which was beyond description.

Princess Charlotte, extremely concerned that the Highland fling demonstration should have reduced her father to his present condition, spent a lot of time at his bedside. She recounted that he was 'suffering a great deal of pain still' and 'for two hours talked entirely of the King and gave a most distressing and lamentable account'. She did, however, detect that he was easier in his manner, which she hoped was a step in the right direction.

Shortly before Christmas he appeared unexpectedly at Carlton House, but was still showing signs of extreme nervous tension. Princess Charlotte told worried members of the royal circle that her father could only be put to sleep with great quantities of hemlock, such was his state of agitation. One of the Prince Regent's physicians felt able to assure her that the worst was past, but pointed out that George's insistence on prescribing for himself large doses of drugs and bleeding himself against medical advice had damaged his constitution as much as the illness.

A worrying glimpse of paranoia showed itself when George heard of a series of murders many miles from London. He ordered that the doors of Carlton House should be bolted at eight in the evening and no strangers admitted. This caused a murmur of dissent among the Household, who were thus precluded from bringing friends and relatives into the house to celebrate Christmas.

When George was sufficiently recovered to discuss his illness with those around him, he offered the opinion that the trouble with his arms and hands had been caused by a temporary paralysis. One physician thought he might be suffering from palsy, and for a while after his apparent recovery George complained he could not write because 'of his three fingers being completely numbed and useless'. As much as a year later, he found it difficult to hold a pen, and moaned about 'my poor right paw'.

As George slowly recovered his health, it became clear

that there could be no avoiding the coming political crisis, which would coincide with the anniversary of his assuming the powers of Regent. He hoped the delicate negotiations, which were continuing all the time, would produce a government which united as many of the talented men available as possible, moderates from both sides, and, of course, a sprinkling of his personal friends. The object of the administration would be to see the Peninsular War against Napoleon brought to a successful conclusion. The question of Catholic emancipation, the burning issue of the home front, would have to be put aside. Before he became Prince Regent George had seen that the emancipation of Catholics would have to come, to calm opinion in England and forestall a possible insurrection in Ireland. He had often spoken out privately for it. Now he was Regent, and could have done something to force the issue, he backed off. The King, it was very well known, had been as strongly opposed to the concept as he had been to anything. He was convinced that to grant the rights Catholics wanted, and to see Catholic members in the Houses of Parliament, would be a breach of his coronation oath. True, the King would doubtless not be aware of what was happening, but George was, after all, acting only in the King's name. His feelings had still to be respected and the Catholic question would have to be put on one side, probably until George III died.

Early in 1812 the Prince Regent called Perceval to Carlton House and asked the Prime Minister to draft a letter suggesting the formation of a coalition to the Whig leaders. George was most unimpressed by it. When he read the letter he remarked, 'It is a great misfortune to Mr Perceval to write in a style which would disgrace a respectable washerwoman.'

So he turned to his old friend Richard Sheridan to help him compose a letter to Prince Frederick, which was really meant to be read by his brother's close confidant, the leading Whig, Earl Grey. In the letter, he suggested that a broadfront coalition, which was to include many of the Whig politicians he had got to know well in his halcyon days as Prince of Wales, could provide the necessary strength at home to see the war through. He wrote, 'In the critical situation of the War in the Peninsula, I shall be most anxious to avoid any measure that can lead my allies to suppose that I mean to depart from the present system. Perseverance alone can achieve the great object in question. ... I have no predilections to indulge, no resentments to gratify, no objects to attain but such as are common to the whole Empire. ... I cannot conclude without expressing the gratification I could feel, if some of those persons with whom the early habits of my public life were formed would strengthen my hands and constitute a part of my Government.'

George hoped for a coalition composed of close friends like Lord Moira and Richard Sheridan, moderate Whigs like Lord Erskine and the Duke of Norfolk, with Lord Wellesley, Perceval's Foreign Secretary, who he described as 'a Spanish grandee grafted on an Irish potato', as Prime Minister. Wellesley agreed wholeheartedly with George's sentiments, and resigned on the spurious grounds that the war was not being prosecuted with sufficient tenacity. But he retained his post at the behest of George, who told him to hold himself in readiness for the highest office.

When Lord Grey learned the contents of the Prince Regent's letter, he conferred with Lord Grenville. Both agreed George was after the best of both worlds. He wanted to keep the Tories in office while preserving his favourable links with the Whigs by tossing them the crumbs of a handful of minor ministries.

They dispatched a frigid and immediate refusal of his proposals, emphasising haughtily that there was a large rift between their own position and that of the existing government on 'almost all the leading features of the present policy of the empire'. They also stressed that they were appalled at the attitude to the problem in Ireland, and would never consider entering an administration which did not state clearly that a major plank of its platform would be to grant Catholic relief.

The Prince Regent may have intended the result of this manoeuvring, which was to throw him onto the arms of the

Tories, for the only option now open to him was to keep Perceval's government in office.

But there were other problems waiting. The frustrated Wellesley urged George to bring Lord Castlereagh and George Canning into the government. George put these suggestions to the Cabinet, who not only refused them out of hand but announced they would resign *en masse* unless Wellesley quit. It was an embarrassing and emotional moment when Wellesley was forced to hand over his seals of office to the Prince Regent in a full dress ceremony at Carlton House. George was so disturbed by it that he could not speak.

George was, however, to gain a certain amount of comfort with the news from the Peninsula campaign that Wellington's men had successfully stormed Ciudad Rodrigo, a strategically important town on the Portuguese and Spanish frontier. Undeterred by the deep January snow, the army was preparing further battles which were to sweep French troops back over the Pyrenees.

The Peninsular War had started to fire the Prince Regent's imagination. As soon as he received the power to create peerages, he granted Wellington an earldom and backed this up by encouraging Parliament to show solidarity with the fighting men by voting the army commander an annuity of £2,000.

The Prince Regent's honeymoon with the Whigs was over, though Richard Sheridan tried to keep the flame alight when he declared at a freemasons' dinner that he would willingly lay down his life for the Prince's principles. George's name was booed and Sheridan, who was unfortunately drunk, was greeted with long and sustained hisses.

Few other Whigs had the courage of Sheridan, or the will to support a man they regarded as a deserter to the cause. Even his aide-de-camp, Lord Forbes, wanted to resign from his Household in protest.

While there had still been a prospect of obtaining office when the Prince of Wales came into his own, the Whigs had been prepared to look benevolently on his many follies. Hardly a word had been raised by them against the outrageous extravagance of the Carlton House fête. Now, a year later, it was different. They turned on him with a fury only possible from former friends who believed they had been let down. Lord Grey, referring to Lady Hertford as 'the old Lady of Manchester Square', told the House of Lords he would not serve in the Regent's government until her destructive influence over George was ended. He talked of 'an unseen and separate influence which lurked behind the throne, an influence of an odious character, leading to consequences the most pestilent and disgusting'. Thomas Creevey, who had earlier been a solid supporter, railed against 'this madman, this most singular man, doomed, from his personal character alone, to shake the throne'. The lawyer Harry Brougham, and Samuel Whitbread, the brewer, championed the wronged Princess of Wales, Caroline, with all the zeal they had shown the worthier causes of reform. Brougham compared the conduct of the Prince Regent with 'the later days of Tiberius'. Understandably frustrated by George's shifting of position, which left them marooned, they allowed it to sway their emotions. George, of course, could not see he had brought these problems on himself, and, in an address to a Carlton House banquet, he furiously attacked his former political allies and accused them of abusing his patronage.

The personal battle waged against the Prince Regent by the Whigs was typical of them. There was certainly a good case to be made against Perceval's government, but their opposition failed to spotlight the mistaken policies. Outside London and the comfortable towns of southern England, morale reached a lower point in the winter of 1811 to 1812 than at any other moment of the Napoleonic Wars. The industrialisation of recent decades, which had promised so much prosperity, was throwing up problems of uncertainty. While the Whigs were charging George with abandoning his principles, a grim mood of disillusionment was growing in the midlands and the north. Angry mobs smashed machines in desperate revulsion at their changed way of life. Everywhere, food was scarce and expensive, with wheat soaring to three times its pre-war price. Napoleon had closed European ports to British exports, and the consequent lack of markets was hitting the great textile centres. Unemployment was rife in the burgeoning new towns of Yorkshire and Lancashire. In one month five major firms in Manchester went into liquidation. This was almost unnoticed in London, but the shock-waves of bankruptcy reverberated across the northern counties.

The anger of this ignored and desperate world exploded on the government on the afternoon of May 11, 1812, when a commercial agent named John Bellingham, who had been bankrupted by the effects of the war, assassinated Spencer Perceval, shooting him through the heart in the lobby of the House of Commons.

There was an ugly mood in the northern towns that spring, and in Nottingham there was so much rejoicing in the streets at the news of Perceval's murder that troops were called out and magistrates read the Riot Act.

But to the Prince Regent the assassination was tiresome, because it once again saddled him with the task of finding an acceptable government. For two months he negotiated with each of the political factions, once again seeking to create a broad coalition of patriotic endeavour which he believed would win the war quickly, and also thereby ease the trade slump imposed by the closure of Europe's markets. Commendably, he refused to let his recent bitterness with the Whigs blind his judgment. He wanted a government headed by Wellesley which would enjoy both Tory and Whig support. But he again found that the suspicions which separated the politicians were too great for a comprehensive administration. Finally, with Parliament's approval, he settled on a compromise candidate, Lord Liverpool, to lead a continuing Tory government. Liverpool was in no way charismatic, and displayed no rare qualities of mind. But he was a skilled debater with an unruffled temperament, and he had always made a capable chairman of committees. The reaction in Parliament was at first one of incredulity. Thomas Creevey wrote in his journal, 'Well, this is beyond anything.' Yet Liverpool showed himself capable of holding together Cabinets containing strong and often conflicting personalities. He surprised everyone by staying in office as Prime Minister for approaching fifteen years, a continuous period of power which had previously only been exceeded twice. However, his ministry had little to offer the rapidly growing population of Britain in terms of solving its problems at home. It never resolved the conflict of workers and manufacturers, and it sought to strengthen authority in the troubled areas of the midlands and the north by imposing ferocious penalties, cowing the workers by threats of hanging or transportation. But in foreign affairs the administration, backed solidly by Wellington's victories against Napoleon, achieved a success denied to any British government for more than a century. This success reflected on the Prince Regent, whose prestige in Europe rose almost to the towering estimate he held of his own stature.

At home, however, his popularity remained low.

Shortly after Perceval was shot, the country's discontent with George was expressed in a letter which threatened the Prince Regent with the same fate unless the price of bread was brought down.

This was followed by a spate of posters on doors in northern towns, proclaiming a bounty of a thousand guineas for George's head.

In contrast to the increasing poverty of so many of his subjects, George continued to live like an eastern potentate, splashing money on fabulous dinners and furnishings at Carlton House. By the beginning of 1812 his debts had reached the heady figure of £552,000, helped in no small part by the continuous refurnishing of Carlton House, which had thus far cost £260,000. Upholstery charges in the previous year had amounted to an incredible £49,000.

George tried to persuade the Cabinet to foist the responsibility for paying all the debts off in one go on to the nation. He also asked that he should be paid £150,000 a year for Regency services. The government allowed him £100,000 as his yearly fee for standing in for the King, and advised him that Parliament could never agree to clearing up the debts as he had suggested. He would have to pay them off through a display of personal frugality.

Public reaction to his arrogant extravagance was expressed when he drove along Pall Mall through a crowd of over ten thousand people and was greeted by a stony silence. That was an eerie experience, but perhaps preferable to the occasions when the crowds would hiss at him and shout, 'Where's your wife?'

In an attempt to stifle newspaper criticism of his lifestyle, George bought the *Morning Post*, one of the most vitriolic of his adversaries. Overnight, the newspaper's tune changed and gave George adulatory titles like 'the Glory of the People', and 'Adonis of Loveliness'. The still independent *Examiner* retorted in more honest vein that 'this Adonis of Loveliness was a corpulent gentleman of fifty! In short, that this delightful, blissful, wise, pleasurable, honourable, virtuous, true and immortal PRINCE was a violator of his words, a libertine over head and ears in debt and disgrace, a despiser of domestic ties, the companion of gamblers and demi-reps, a man who has just closed half a century without one single claim on the gratitude of his country or the respect of posterity'.

George reacted ferociously. Both the author of the article, Leigh Hunt, and the editor of the *Examiner*, his brother John Hunt, were charged before the Court of the King's Bench 'with intention to traduce and vilify his Royal Highness the Prince of Wales, Regent of the United Kingdom'.

They were defended by Harry Brougham, who had decided, that in the absence of royal patronage to smooth his way to government office, he would make a name for himself opposing the Prince Regent. He was a brilliant advocate, but could make no dent in the charge. The brothers were fined £500 each and sentenced to two years' imprisonment.

A public outcry greeted what people saw as a display of vindictiveness on the part of 'Prinny', as George had become indelibly described in the cartoons and satirical lampoons. Leigh Hunt protested that he had been imprisoned 'for not thinking the Prince Regent slender and laudable'. The poet, Percy Shelley, launched a fund for the brothers and damned George as greedy, and a 'crowned coward and villain'. Other noted writers like John Keats, Charles Lamb, and Lord Byron, thumbing their noses at the possible consequences, hurled themselves into the dangerous fray to question the Prince Regent's motivation. George was most outraged by a verse, purporting to be anonymous, but which he knew had been penned by Charles Lamb, entitled *The Prince of Whales*. This eloquent tirade against him read:

> Not a fatter fish than he
> Flounders round the polar sea.
> See his blubbers – at his gills
> What a world of drink he swills. . . .
> Every fish of generous kind
> Scuds aside or shrinks behind;
> But with his presence keep
> All the monsters of the deep. . . .
> Name or title what has he? . . .
> Is he Regent of the sea?
> By his bulk and by his size,
> By his oily qualities,
> This (or else my eyesight fails),
> This should be the Prince of Whales.

Writers considered the debauched Prince Regent thoroughly deserved the lashings he was getting in print, but the libel action did much to quell the flood.

These were nervous days for George and the other members of the royal family. The Cato Street Conspiracy, a plan to murder the whole Cabinet, was uncovered. Street riots were a daily event. The establishment was fighting its last battle to resist political reform in the shape of the enfranchisement which was eventually to lead to Britain's modern democracy. The inherent dangers of this type of conflict had been clearly demonstrated just a few years before in the bloodbath of the French Revolution.

George lurched into one of his spells of heavy drinking in an attempt to hide from the problems of the day. This endeared him to no one. When he imagined that his close friend, Beau Brummell, had insulted the Bishop of Winchester, he reacted petulantly, for he felt that Brummell had already imposed on their friendship by treating him too informally in front of other guests. The next time they encountered each other, George spoke to a companion of Brummell's, but studiously ignored the Beau. Brummell, the master of the acid put-down, asked the companion, 'Who's your fat friend?' It devastated George, who was painfully conscious of his swelling girth, and marked the end of their friendship. George could never bring himself to forgive Brummell.

Even the string of victories in Spain, which continued through 1812 and 1813, could do nothing to repair George's image at home. He was, as always, well and roundly hated, obliged to hide in the corner of his carriage seat to shield himself from the abuse of his subjects. Princess Caroline, on the other hand, was greeted heartily whenever she ventured out in public. George had his wife barred from all public functions, but could not stop her going to the theatre. He was mightily embarrassed one evening at Covent Garden when the whole audience rose as one to clap and cheer Caroline. 'Three hearty cheers for an injured woman,' they chanted. The acclamation was even louder outside, where members of the crowd called out, 'Do you want us to set fire to Carlton House?'

Princess Caroline could never really consider herself lonely. As the symbol of opposition to the defiance of the Prince Regent, she found radical writers and politicians eager to enjoy her company at Kensington Palace. She had become quite an eccentric, walking out on guests at the drop of a hat, or telling them outright how dull she thought they were. At parties, she was always the one leading a lined-up troupe around the floor. She took to going around town, knocking on the doors of private houses to ask if there were any rooms to let. A diarist of the time wrote, 'The poor Princess is going on headlong to her ruin. Every day she becomes more imprudent in her conduct, more heedless of society. The society she is now surrounded by is disgraceful.' The Princess was reputed to be pregnant, then going mad. Talk of her affairs started again.

George was aghast to see his wife becoming the new darling of the Whigs. When he announced to Princess Caroline that she would be allowed to see their daughter no more than once every two weeks, Harry Brougham led the phalanx of Whigs who leaped to her defence. The Prince Regent genuinely felt that the scandalous behaviour of his wife and risqué dinner-table conversations provided an unsuitable atmosphere in which to bring up an impressionable sixteen-year-old, but Brougham and the others ignored this. In any event, they could not see how the Prince Regent's own mode of life could be commended.

The Prince Regent successfully argued that seeing her mother's lovers flaunted before her could only have a bad influence on the realm's future monarch. In fact, he was merely using his daughter as a weapon with which to punish his wife.

Princess Caroline was not overburdened with affection for her daughter either, but loudly protested that Princess Charlotte was 'the only happiness left to me to enjoy upon this earthly world'. She sent a flood of pleading and recriminating letters to the Prince Regent, which he correctly surmised were dictated by her spiritual ally, Brougham. Both enjoyed the opportunity to harass George.

When Caroline complained to the Queen, she refused to intervene. George commended his mother on foiling Caroline's new attempt to use the ploy of love for their daughter to create discord and confusion among the family.

The royal domestic troubles became painfully public when Princess Caroline addressed a letter of remonstrance to her husband and received a formal acknowledgment from the Prime Minister. At the instigation of Brougham she sent her letter to the *Morning Chronicle*, who published it. George's response was to have all the evidence from the 1806 investigation pulled out of the file and placed before the Privy Council. He posed the question 'whether it is fit and proper that the intercourse between her Royal Highness, the Princess Charlotte, and the Princess of Wales should continue under restriction and regulation'.

The Prince Regent first told his daughter that much of the family's dirty linen was about to be washed in public, and assured her he would not hold the consequences of her mother's behaviour against her. Charlotte was stunned by the news, and didn't know what to say to her father.

The Privy Council re-examined the evidence and came to the conclusion that the Prince Regent had the right to regulate the amount of time his daughter spent with Princess Caroline. This decision produced a howl of protest, for the Cabinet had, after all, virtually cleared her of the charges. George then published the evidence given by the Princess's servants. This prompted Brougham to re-publish a pamphlet called *The Book*, which highlighted the biased and inquisition-type approach of the commissioners.

The newspapers printed columns on the case. Some supported Princess Caroline, some the Prince Regent. But it was a campaign of smear and innuendo which did nothing to enhance the public appeal of George or any of his family.

His conflict with his wife was not going well. His country's war against Napoleon was heading for a different conclusion. After the winter débâcle in Russia, Napoleon's days were numbered. New allies tipped the scales against him and at the end of March, 1814, Paris had fallen. Within days the Emperor had abdicated and was on his way to exile in Elba.

The Prince Regent wanted to be sure to stake his claim to at least some sprigs of the laurel wreath in the hour of triumph. Writing 'in a very trembling and hardly intelligible hand', he declared to the Queen, 'I trust, my dearest mother, that you will think I have fulfilled and done my duty at least, and perhaps I may be vain enough to hope that you feel a little proud of your son'.

As the news of France's defeat filtered in, he was to talk of his regret that he had never once seen action, or even set foot outside England. Yet had he not given his confidences to Wellington's army in the Peninsular War when the dusty hills of Portugal seemed so terribly distant from Paris?

In subsequent years, people were to remember 1814 as a year of revelry. The festivities began in London many weeks before the final victory in Europe. The winter was so cold that the River Thames froze solid from Blackfriars to London Bridge, and the capital's population turned out for a fair on the ice. Youngsters who were there were to tell their grandchildren about the whole ox they saw roasted on the ice.

When news came of Napoleon's abdication, London was illuminated for three successive nights. People from every level of society vied with each other to show their relief that the long wars had at last ended.

In residence at a flag-bedecked Carlton House, the Prince Regent felt proud to symbolise the coming of peace, and was determined to celebrate it in appropriate style.

He planned to honour Louis XVIII, about to be recalled to Paris and the Bourbon throne after years of gout and obscurity in his Buckinghamshire exile at Hartwell. Then he wanted to invite the Allied rulers and generals to cross over from Europe, so they might share with him the pleasures of victory. Perhaps he hoped that the dignity and charm of parades, galas, and banquets would silence the critics at home.

On April 20, the very day that Napoleon set out for Elba, the gargantuan figure of King Louis was crammed into a carriage and driven along a route lined by cheering crowds towards London. At Stanmore the Prince Regent greeted him warmly, and their procession of seven carriages, escorted by a troop of Life Guards, trundled down the Edgeware Road for the state entry into Piccadilly.

Lord Byron refused to walk the few yards from his flat in the Albany to watch the procession. 'Louis the Gouty is wheeling into Piccadilly in triumph,' he wrote to a friend. 'I had an offer of seats to see them pass, but they have no attractions for me.' Those who did venture into Piccadilly to watch the parade gave the Prince Regent a distinctly frosty reception. The cheers were spasmodic, and he was as often booed.

King Louis stayed for three nights at Grillon's Hotel in Albemarle Street, where he and George exchanged orders of chivalry. The Prince Regent invested the new Bourbon monarch with the Order of the Garter, and himself buckled the Garter round Louis's leg. It was, he said later, like fastening a sash round a young man's waist. The King responded by taking off his own insignia of the Order of the Saint Esprit and bestowing it upon George.

The Times declared, somewhat grandly, that both the Regent of England and the King of France had done their duty and 'have merited and have obtained the applause of mankind'. The citizens of London, however, did not regard the two portly gentlemen as heroes. As one diarist observed, 'Nothing can equal the execration of the people who recognise Prinny.'

The Prince Regent must have noticed the current of feeling against him, but he did not let that affect his starring role in the victory celebrations. He gave one of his ostentatious dinners at Carlton House for Louis, and a courtier noted, 'Our Prince Regent is never so happy as in show and state, and there he shines incomparably.'

When Louis sailed from Dover on the royal yacht, with eight ships of the Royal Navy to escort him to Calais, George was on the quayside to wave goodbye and lead the cheering. Louis, well fortified for the crossing, had retired to his cabin by the time the *Royal Sovereign* reached the pierhead. The Prince Regent seemed not to have noticed, and waved enthusiastically to the trimmer figures of the royal entourage who stayed on deck.

George returned to London immediately to start preparations for the summer state visit of Tsar Alexander I, King Frederick William III of Prussia, and Prince Metternich, the personal representative of the Emperor of Austria. He looked forward to the visit with all the expectant excitement of a child awaiting Christmas, but it was to prove a sad disappointment. The London crowds took affectionately to the visitors, but none of this goodwill rubbed off on to the Prince Regent. The Tsar stayed at the Pulteney Hotel in Piccadilly, where he was greeted rapturously by the crowds. But George could not visit him there because of the fear of hostile demonstrations against him by supporters of Princess Caroline. King Frederick William also received the enthusiastic salutations of the crowds at Clarence House. But those same crowds chose to ignore the illuminated Carlton House, just down the road. George had to be satisfied with basking in the reflected glory of his visitors on the occasions that they all ventured out together.

The Prince Regent found it difficult to remain calm in the face of this embarrassment, and his liking for the visitors cooled distinctly. In fact, he came to dislike Tsar Alexander intensely. Both were exhibitionists, and there was an inevitable personality clash. The relationship was not helped when the Tsar took an obvious fancy to Lady Jersey, George's cast-off and troublesome mistress, at a ball. Then Alexander capped this at the opera, where Princess Caroline staged her entrance at exactly the moment when the applause for the Prince Regent and his guests had died down. George gritted his teeth amidst shouts of 'God save the King, our good King, the protector of outraged innocence' as the entire audience turned to Caroline and cheered her. The Tsar peered at Caroline through his binoculars, and announced that, whether George liked it or not, he wanted to call on her. Caroline was delighted at this news and waited all the next day, but wiser counsel must have prevailed on the Tsar, who did not appear.

No effort or expense was spared for the visit, which the Prince Regent soldiered disconsolately through. There was a Guildhall banquet for seven hundred guests, which the Annual Register hailed as 'sumptuous as expense or skill could make it'. The army was drawn up for review in Hyde Park, and the fleet assembled off Spithead.

The overall visual effect was striking, but George's patience with his guests was running out. He fumed at the tactlessness of the Tsar and soon they stopped even pretending to make small talk together.

George did, however, commission Thomas Lawrence, the most gifted of English portrait painters, to capture the likenesses of his guests, thereby paying hundreds of pounds for images of people he had grown to dislike heartily.

He breathed a sigh of relief when his royal visitors left, but the summer festivities were far from over for the Prince Regent. The next day Wellington arrived in England for the first time since his triumphs in the Peninsula War. And, once again, George was obliged to exercise his skills as an impresario of victory. His personal tribute to Wellington was a grand ball at Carlton House which was more elaborate than any celebration before or afterwards. Architect John Nash was called in to build a brick polygon in the grounds, covering an area as big as Westminster Hall. It was draped with white muslin and hung with mirrors, so that it appeared to be a huge tented pavilion. In the centre a bank of flowers concealed two bands, which played from midnight until six in the morning. A giant bust of Wellington overlooked the proceedings, and all the walls were studded with so many Ws that the tribute embarrassed the guest of honour. To complete the grandness of the occasion, the walls of the supper marquees were decorated with paintings bearing titles like *Military Glory*, and *The Overthrow of Tyranny by the Allied Powers*.

That was not the end. A few days later Hyde Park, St James's Park, and Green Park were given over to an enormous people's festival, celebrating both peace and the centenary of Hanoverian rule in Britain. There were fireworks, a Chinese pagoda, Japanese lanterns, and a Temple of Concord. And a mock Battle of Trafalgar was fought with model boats on the Serpentine.

Londoners enjoyed their festival, but it seemed George could not win, whatever he did. For *The Times*, while expressing itself pleased that so many people could rejoice at an historic event, questioned the propriety of the celebrations, and deplored the expense.

Princess Caroline had been banned from all the festivities of the summer, and refused a seat at the thanksgiving service for peace at St Paul's Cathedral. Ignored as the legal wife of the Regent, she had a lonely season, for many friends who had been compelled to choose between husband and wife prudently abandoned her. She was reported to have passed the time making wax effigies of the corpulent Prince Regent and sticking pins in them. When she was ignored by the visiting heads of state, it was the last straw for her. Her brazenness in the face of insult had been demonstrated when she encouraged acclamation from her box at the opera. But even she could not allow herself to be ostracised any longer. She determined to 'leave this vile country' and go to live abroad. The cheering in the streets and at public events was directed, she felt, more against the Prince Regent than for her.

Harry Brougham, the brilliant and ruthless barrister who had become adviser to Princess Caroline, warned her of the potential danger of her plan. He told her, 'Depend on it, Madam, there are many persons who now begin to see a chance of divorcing your Royal Highness from the Prince. As long as you remain in this country I will answer for it that no plot can succeed against you. But if you are living abroad, and surrounded by the base spies and tools who will be always planted about you, ready to invent and swear as they may be directed, who can pretend to say what may happen?' When Caroline did not respond to his reasoning, Brougham spoke to Princess Charlotte, pointing out that George might divorce her mother, marry again, and produce a son, in which case Charlotte would lose her position as heir to the throne.

But Princess Caroline, who felt she had suffered beyond endurance, stubbornly refused to be swayed by the pleas of Brougham or her daughter. She had had enough, and she was determined to turn her back on the misery of the past years.

The Prince Regent could hardly believe his ears or his good fortune when he heard the news. He knew that the Whigs had been pressing the government to increase Caroline's allowance, and urged that her income of £22,000 a year should be swept aside in favour of an annuity of £50,000. The price was worth it, he said, to encourage her yearning for travel.

Brougham immediately wrote Caroline a letter, urging her not to accept the money offered because it would appear that she was letting George buy his way out of her claims and grievances. But before she received the letter Caroline had accepted the offer, saying she had done so 'in order to prove to Parliament that she was never averse to any proposal coming from the Crown to replace her in the proper splendour adequate to her situation, and to throw no unnecessary obstacles in the way to obstruct the tranquillity or impair the peace of mind of the Prince Regent'. Brougham was exasperated at her impulsive acceptance, but managed to persuade her to turn the episode into a resounding public relations victory with a letter to the government asserting that, so as to ease the taxpayers' burden, she was prepared to accept the lesser figure of £35,000 per year. Her apparent act of generosity was trumpeted by partisans both inside and outside Parliament.

Princess Caroline's decision to leave England was, however, irrevocable. In the first week of August, 1814, she travelled down to Worthing where the frigate HMS *Jason* had been put at her disposal, and embarked on it for Germany. She declared to those around her that, as the English Court would not give her the honours due to a Princess of Wales, she was content to remain 'Caroline, a happy, merry soul'. For the next six years she was to spare no effort to live up to her promise.

George ignored the criticism of his wildly expensive festivities, and rather fancied that he could claim personal credit for the military and naval victories being celebrated. His vanity did not allow him to realise the full extent of his unpopularity, engendered by his lavish spending and cruel harassment of his wife. He was even known to remark that no other prince had been idolised by the British people as much as he had.

Perhaps the Prince Regent was referring to his reputation as a patron of the arts. He liked to think of himself in this role, and expressed the hope 'that this country may be as distinguished for its excellence in art, as it is for its other eminent advantages'.

His patronage ensured the fortune and the lasting reputations of many painters. He bought *The Blue Boy* from Gainsborough, and both he and Mrs Mary Robinson sat for him, as both did for Joshua Reynolds. He was a consistent supporter of the Royal Academy and his art collection rivalled any in the country, possibly any in Europe. He genuinely wished to encourage pride in artistic achievement and tried to combat the mildly philistine taste of the English aristocracy. His aesthetic sense permeated his time, giving the Regency era an atmosphere of great taste and elegance.

Of course, the fortune he spent in the pursuit of artistic splendour had to be provided by the middle-class taxpayers, who were not necessarily happy at the use to which their money was being put. Carlton House became a bottomless pit of his artistic ambitions. It was continually being refurbished and redecorated. The additions were endless: a Gothic dining-room, a Gothic library, a golden drawing-room. The fact that his Pall Mall version of Versailles cost the nation hundreds of thousands of pounds seems not to have bothered him in the least.

George needed an architect to help him fulfil his grandiose dreams. He found such a man in John Nash, the son of a poor London tradesman, who had designed the building for the Wellington fête.

He had known Nash since the young architect won a prize for his plan for the redevelopment of Marylebone Park, then an expanse of open land north of Portland Place which had recently reverted to the Crown. Nash saw the land – naturally renamed Regent's Park – as a succession of wooden groves separating clusters of villas from a grand double circus surrounding a pleasure pavilion. Only eight villas were constructed in Regent's Park, and most of Nash's vision remained a fantasy in his sketch-book. Yet, even in its limited form, the project was the most dramatic attempt made by an architect to create a sense of space and symmetry in London. It urbanised the characteristically eighteenth-century feeling for landscape, yet retained the self-assured naturalness of the English country house.

There was a long and sympathetic partnership between the Prince Regent and Nash, whose greatest years of achievement coincided with the peak of the Regency decade. Their 'Regency-style' architecture is a byword for grace and elegance which has lived until today.

The best-known example of their co-operation is the Oriental extravaganza of the Brighton Pavilion, which Nash rebuilt between 1812 and 1820, after the Prince Regent had decided the earlier building was too ordinary for his taste. Nash was also called in to design the ornate Gothic fantasy of the Royal Lodge in Windsor Great Park, a magnificent thatched edifice which George rather disparagingly called The Cottage.

But their most ambitious project was London itself. For the Prince Regent and Nash conceived the plan which would give the West End of London an impressive and orderly system of streets, squares, and open places. Nash proposed the construction of a line of elegant buildings which would stretch for over two miles southwards from Regent's Park. Then he envisaged a 'Royal Mile' of classically arcaded terraces to be called Regent Street – stretching from Portland Place to end in a final flourish of Ionic columns at the approach to Carlton House. None of this project could have been achieved without the patronage and encouragement of the Prince, whose name and dignity it so frequently commemorates. For ultimately it was the Regent's authority which enabled Nash to cut through the legal tangles of the Crown Commissioners and to confound the timidity of men less lavish in their style.

Not that Nash's work, particularly the stucco and cast-iron terraces, was immediately appreciated by all who beheld it. The grandiose, extravagant, showy exuberance took a lot of assimilation. But eventually its influence was to spread all over England. It can still be seen today, a noble witness to a man of panache and extraordinary vision.

There was a high degree of criticism of the Prince Regent's fanciful taste and extravagant expenditure, but many conceded that his patronage of the arts and artists was to be commended as perhaps some compensation for his many faults.

George's attention was diverted by matters of a more urgent nature early in March, 1815, when serious rioting broke out in London against the Corn Bill, which prohibited the importation of foreign corn if the cost of home produce fell below a certain level. He considered the Bill, designed to restore agricultural prosperity at the expense of the consumer, a political error. But he also regarded any violent demonstration as proof of a will to revolution. Members of Parliament known to support the Bill were attacked in the streets, and, because they believed the Prince Regent to be actively in favour of the measure, a crowd of demonstrators planted a blood-stained loaf on the parapet of Carlton House.

His home had to be protected by troops, and George, who shared the common fear of revolution, and could never blot the memory of the French refugees flocking to Brighton in 1792 from his mind, felt he had to support a firm stand. The riots climaxed in a mob attack on a Tory Minister's home less than half a mile from Carlton House, when two men were shot dead by soldiers.

These events paled into comparative insignificance as news came in that Napoleon, weary of being Emperor of Elba, had landed in France. For the next hundred days the world would hold its breath.

Napoleon entered Paris in triumph and Louis XVIII trundled off into exile once again. The previous year's peace celebrations had, it seemed, been premature.

The Prince Regent sent a message to both Houses of Parliament, declaring his intention to join the Allies. England, Austria, Russia and Prussia bound themselves by treaty not to lay down their arms until Napoleon was finally vanquished. Wellington was appointed Commander-in-Chief of the Allied forces and started gathering the army which would seal Napoleon's fate at Waterloo.

On the evening of June 21, Major Henry Percy, who had travelled straight from the battlefield of Waterloo to announce the victory to the Prince Regent, found him at a house party in St James's Square. He laid the eagle insignia of the French army at George's feet and Lord Liverpool read aloud the dispatch Major Percy had brought with him. Afterwards, George turned to the courier and said, 'I congratulate you, Colonel Percy.' Later, the Prince was to cry at the loss of life in the battle. He said, 'It is a glorious victory and we must rejoice at it, but the loss of life has been fearful, and I have lost many friends.' He took a vicarious pride in the news that his own Tenth Hussars had distinguished themselves in the final action of Waterloo.

There was to be a strange epilogue to the Waterloo campaign for the Prince Regent. Napoleon, seeking refuge in the French Atlantic port of Rochefort, surrendered to the Captain of HMS *Bellerophon*, handing over a carefully worded request for asylum addressed to the Prince Regent. It read,

'Pursued by the factions which divide my country and by the hostility of the greatest European powers I have ended my political career and I come, as Themistocles did, to seat myself at the hearth of the British people. I put myself under the protection of its laws, which I claim from your Royal Highness as the strongest, most consistent and most generous of my foes.'

Napoleon correctly guessed that George would be flattered by the tone of respect, for when the Regent read the request he said, 'Upon my soul a very proper letter – much more so, I must say, than any I ever received from Louis XVIII.'

There was a surprising amount of sympathy in Britain for the fallen Emperor, and Napoleon in defeat exercised a curious fascination over the British public. A government less frightened by popular demonstrations might well have shown magnanimity. Even Lord Castlereagh seriously considered the possibility of keeping Napoleon under some sort of dignified restraint in Scotland rather than transporting him to a distant exile. But Lord Liverpool was not prepared to take the risk of confining the Emperor within the British Isles lest his presence might encourage those who despaired of the existing order.

Accordingly, the Prince Regent did not reply to Napoleon's request, and, taken aboard HMS *Northumberland*, General Bonaparte sailed into legend on the South Atlantic island of St Helena.

Problems much closer to home were in the offing as the Regent's daughter, Charlotte, grew towards womanhood. Her exhibitionist tendencies and liking for men confirmed for George the similarities between the girl and her mother. The Queen's comment that young Charlotte was more consciously her mother's daughter than her father's did nothing to endear him to her. Nor did the shouts of 'God bless you! Never forsake your mother!' which greeted Charlotte's carriage.

Then Charlotte told her father a story which shocked him. The Princess said she had met a dashing young Captain, Charles Hesse of the 18th Hussars, while out riding at

Windsor. The girl's aunt, Princess Mary, was present at the interview, and later wrote, 'The Princess Charlotte confessed to her father that she always met him at her mother's at Kensington and had private interviews with him with the Princess of Wales's knowledge and connivance. The Princess of Wales used to let him into her own apartment by a door that opens into Kensington Gardens, and then left them together in her own bedroom, and turned the key upon them saying, "I will leave you now. Amuse yourselves." '

George was thunderstruck to hear that his wife had actually encouraged their daughter, who was then sixteen, to make love to the Captain. He was also worried to learn that so far Captain Hesse had not returned indiscreet letters the Princess had sent him, though he had promised to do so. His mind must have drifted back to the compromising correspondence which had caused him so much trouble in his own youth.

He saw there was only one solution for his flighty daughter. She would have to be married off to a suitable young prince, and quickly. He authorised Foreign Secretary Castlereagh to make the necessary arrangements for a marriage between Princess Charlotte and Prince William of Orange, the heir to the Dutch throne, a dynastic union of considerable political importance because it would link Britain with the projected new kingdom of a United Netherlands, made up of Belgium, Holland, and Luxembourg.

Prince William was tiny, and not at all good-looking. He drank too much, and if the Prince Regent had not heard that he was 'a dissolute, untidy, and stupid young man', he was the only one. But William had spent two years at Oxford, and served on Wellington's staff in the Peninsula War.

George had William brought over to London and introduced the couple. Charlotte knew her father wanted her to marry him, and was prepared to acquiesce from a sense of duty.

However, the sight of William appalled her, and she was to say shortly afterwards, 'I think him so ugly that I am sometimes obliged to turn my head away in disgust when he is speaking to me. Marry I will, and that directly, in order to enjoy my liberty, but not the Prince of Orange.'

The Princess consulted Lord Grey, who advised her that the Prince Regent had no power to force her into a marriage she did not want, but said she must avoid a public confrontation with him.

George piled the pressure on, sending emissaries around almost daily to talk to her, and later arranging a party at Carlton House where both his daughter and Prince William were guests. He talked with the couple in the conservatory, and he began to realise that perhaps the match was a mistake. Taking Charlotte aside, he said to her, 'Well, it will not do, I suppose.' Her reply surprised him. She said, 'I do not say that. I like his manner very well, as much as I have ever seen of it.' The Prince Regent was delighted. He led her to Prince William and joined their hands. George considered this an acceptance of the proposal of marriage, and Charlotte later talked of herself as being engaged.

But within a few days she was starting to have second thoughts about the betrothal. It was clear that she and Prince William would have to live abroad, and she began to wonder if this, as much as any of the other benefits of the match, had appealed to her father. When the contract of marriage was being negotiated, Charlotte protested that she could not countenance living the whole year out of England. A compromise on this question was being worked out when she announced that, whatever happened, she would break the engagement. Lord Grey wrote to a friend, 'The connection is much approved of by the country. It's failure would create general disappointment, and if it could be presented as arising from levity or capriciousness in the Princess it would injure her in the public estimation.' The Prince Regent was of the same opinion, and furious about her change of mind. For Princess Charlotte had already met a representative of the Dutch government, accepted the formal proposal of marriage, and ordered jewellery paid for by Prince William.

The young Prince tried to resolve the dilemma with a personal visit to Charlotte, but she declined at first to see him.

So he wrote out a note which a lady-in-waiting took up to her bedroom. It read, 'Dearest Charlotte, I am extremely disturbed at your not wishing to see me; but I ask it once more as a particular favour that you will allow me to wait till you are up. If you insist upon a refusal I must follow your wish and return at two o'clock. I am most desirous and anxious to be able to speak to you freely.' This appeal raised Charlotte from her bed, and she assured William the only problem was over the question of where they should live. Told about this, the Prince Regent tried to talk her round. The discussions went round and round, and kept returning to the question of living in England or abroad. Whatever compromise was offered up, Princess Charlotte found a way round it. Finally, Prince William told her that his father and the government had agreed that she would never be required to leave England without her consent, and she accepted the promise. At this point the Prince Regent stepped in, demanding that she drop her stipulations as a mark of respect for the House of Orange. The situation was not aided by the fact that every time she saw Prince William, Charlotte found him even less appealing than before. Stories of his drunkenness added to her apprehension, especially one about him returning to London from the races at Ascot hanging onto the roof of a stagecoach.

So, with the Queen busy arranging her trousseau and the preparations for the wedding going ahead, Princess Charlotte dropped her bombshell. She asked Prince William to come round to see her, and told him the marriage was off. Her decision was confirmed in letters to William and to her father. The young Prince was said to have left England looking miserable, and with tears in his eyes. The Regent's fury was predictable and explosive, for he had suffered a public humiliation at the hands of his insubordinate daughter. He tried to bully her into changing her mind, then switched to a gentler form of persuasion, pleading with her to think of the good of the family. Charlotte was unlikely to be persuaded by this, because she was weary of the hatred between her parents. She felt she was the pawn of each in turn in the ruthless family politics. Her father spoke sentimentally of her and lavished expensive gifts on her, but he rarely showed her any affection. It is little wonder that when she reached adolescence she often appeared to be sulking. Charlotte was a tragic and often lonely figure. Her mother naturally wanted her, and her father had responded by claiming that Caroline was not fit to look after her. He then determined to control Charlotte's upbringing, but it had been an appalling mess. Her governesses and ladies-in-waiting had been frequently changed, and for years she had no friends of her own age. She had lived in growing isolation in a harsh adult world. It would be hard to imagine a childhood more disturbed than that of this girl, who needed so much emotional stability.

The Prince Regent heard that his volatile daughter had shown a definite attraction to some German princes she had come into contact with and decided to have her sent to Cranbourne Lodge, a royal home in the Windsor Forest. There she was virtually a prisoner, under the watchful eye of four newly-appointed and loyal ladies-in-waiting.

News of all this got out, of course, and the Prince Regent became the subject of more abuse. Harry Brougham called his treatment of Charlotte barbarous, and a Whig Member of Parliament compared his behaviour to that of a Prussian corporal. Popular feeling reflected this, regarding him as a heartless bully.

George persisted in his campaign on behalf of the Prince of Orange, and pointed out that if she were left unmarried too long it might become impossible to arrange a suitable match. Charlotte, while agreeing that she should marry before too many years had passed, made it clear she was upset that her father still wanted her to marry Prince William, who was so obviously an unsuitable match. In a letter, she told her father, 'There is no act of obedience, no sacrifice you could wish me to make that I am not ready for, if it is necessary to prove my sense of duty. But where the future and the whole happiness of my life is concerned I think I cannot be too plain in humbly stating my strong and fixed aversion to a match with a man for whom I can never feel those sentiments of regard which surely are so necessary in a matrimonial connection. I hope you will not love me less for thus laying open the sentiments of my heart, and you told me you would never urge any union that would make me miserable.'

He finally capitulated, and assured his daughter that he would not press the matter any further. A thankful Charlotte went off on holiday to Weymouth, where her companions noticed a regeneration of her old exuberance, and an air of happiness.

The reason for Princess Charlotte's renewed zest for life was to electrify her royal circle. She was in love.

The catalyst who was to transform Charlotte's view of the world was the Grand Duchess Catherine, a sister of the Tsar of Russia, who had settled in London and become a friend and confidante of the Princess. She had seen how wretched Charlotte had become over the attempt to force her into marriage with the Prince of Orange, and decided the best hope of making her happy was to conjure up a handsome and attentive prince to conquer her. The Grand Duchess's choice was the blond and charming Prince Leopold, third son of the rulers of the German Duchy of Saxe-Coburg-Saalfield.

The coldly ambitious Prince Leopold accepted the role offered to him by the Grand Duchess, writing to her, 'Perhaps I shall end by getting married in England, and staying here.'

Princess Charlotte was immediately attracted to the Prince, and in no time was declaring her love for him to her companions. Secret letters between them were carried by the Regent's brother, the Duke of Kent, and the romance blossomed. Soon Princess Charlotte was talking in terms of marrying Prince Leopold and approached her father for his blessing. The Prince Regent was not pleased with the news, for Leopold offered no political advantage and came from a penurious family. In fact, the young man was so short of money that he had taken lodgings over a grocer's shop in Marylebone High Street. But the happiness radiating from Princess Charlotte was there for all to see, and at the beginning of 1816 George invited the couple down to the Pavilion at Brighton, where he was in residence with the Queen and other members of the royal family, and in the constant company of Lady Hertford.

Lord Castlereagh, who had been favourably impressed by Prince Leopold at the Congress of Vienna which followed the defeat of Napoleon, backed the match, and the Prince Regent allowed himself to be persuaded.

The wedding took place on May 2, 1816, amidst the splendour of Carlton House. There was one embarrassing moment, when Charlotte laughed as her husband intoned, 'With all my worldly goods I thee endow.' But it was a happy family occasion, and after the ceremony the Princess knelt before her father to get his blessing. He gave it, then raised her to give her a warm, paternal hug which delighted the guests.

Princess Charlotte and her husband, granted an allowance of £60,000 a year, settled down to a quiet, retiring, and very happy life at Claremont Park, a house near Esher which had been bought for them.

It was a love-match which the public heartily approved of, and Charlotte's popularity was beyond doubt. None of this acclaim however, was transferred to her father. He had recurring attacks of gout, which the cartoonists rejoiced in. Even *The Times* printed a detailed account of how the Prince Regent had to be hoisted into the saddle of his horse after being wheeled up an inclined ramp to a platform which was then raised high enough to allow the horse to pass under it. Such a ludicrous operation was irresistible to cartoonists, especially when they could set it against the backdrop of the mock-Oriental design of the Brighton Pavilion. These shafts of wit troubled the Regent personally, but they were not as serious as the renewed attacks being mounted against his continued extravagance. The contrast between his reckless quest for luxurious living and the poverty of the labouring masses inevitably bred resentment. About the time of Charlotte's wedding, a Whig Member of Parliament was so indignant at reports of life at the Brighton Pavilion that he told the Commons he wished to hear 'no more of that squanderous and lavish profusion which in a certain quarter resembled more the pomp and magnificence of a Persian satrap seated in all the splendour of Oriental state, than the sober dignity of a British Prince, seated in the bosom of his subjects'. The government found it impossible to ignore the loud protests from back-benchers of both parties, and a joint plea was sent to the Prince Regent in the names of the Prime Minister, the Leader of the Commons, and the Chancellor of the Exchequer. They begged him to ensure 'that all new expenses or additions or alterations at Brighton or elsewhere will, under the present circumstances, be abandoned'. George made another gesture of economy, a momentary pause in his royal spending spree which had been aided by a £50,000 gift from the Queen towards what she considered the 'splendid improvements' at the Pavilion. In reality, he barely checked the extravagant flow. The band at Brighton, kept for the entertainment of his guests, cost £6,000 a year. And when the Music Room in the Pavilion was redecorated and furnished by Nash the total cost amounted to no less than £45,125.

It was disturbingly reminiscent of Marie Antoinette's notorious sentiments that, while the new Corn Laws made starvation a real threat in many country districts of Britain, the Prince Regent employed the finest of all French chefs, Marie-Antoine Careme, to prepare the dinners at Carlton House and Brighton. Most of the Prince Regent's subjects believed both houses to be dens of iniquity where the wealthier landowners abandoned themselves to orgies. With unemployment and repression stalking the land, Lord Liverpool's government genuinely feared a wave of resentment which could be the prelude to revolution. At a demonstration in Spa Fields, a working-class area of London, in November, 1816, tricolour flags were waved and a 'cap of liberty' was mounted on a pike. Gloomy observers, thinking of Carlton House on one side of the capital and Spa Fields on the other, were reminded of Paris in the year 1789. The seething discontent dramatically surfaced again in January, 1817, when George, returning down the Mall to Carlton House after formally opening a new session of Parliament, was greeted by a seething crowd of demonstrators who hurled stones at his coach. Later a round hole, believed to have been caused by a shot from an air-gun, was found in a window of the carriage. George declared that it had been an assassination attempt and the following Sunday a solemn prayer was offered in churches throughout the country for the 'protection of his Royal Person', and that he might be shielded 'from the arrow that flieth by day and from the pestilence that walketh in darkness'.

Princess Charlotte had meanwhile been experiencing difficulty in fulfilling her royal duty to produce an heir who would be the custodian of the Hanoverian line. She miscarried twice, and for her third pregnancy she was put in the care of Sir Richard Croft, the most esteemed obstetrician of the day. Early in October of 1817, it was announced that the royal birth was expected within a few days.

The Prince Regent visited his daughter at Claremont Park in mid October and, finding her in the best of health, went on to Lord and Lady Hertford's country estate at Sudbourne, Suffolk, where he had been invited to shoot.

There was a ripple of public concern about the delayed birth, but the bulletins betrayed no problems, and Sir Richard Croft expected none.

All this suddenly changed for the Prince Regent on November 5th when the tone of a letter sent from Claremont at ten the previous night so alarmed him that he drove back to London as fast as tired horses would carry him. His fears were justified. Princess Charlotte had gone into labour on the 3rd, and it had continued for two days. At nine on the evening of the 5th she gave birth to a stillborn son.

George got back to Carlton House in the early hours of the next morning to be given the news, but, on hearing that his daughter was extremely well, he collapsed exhausted into bed.

However, at midnight Princess Charlotte had complained of pains and feeling suddenly cold. When she was given some soup, she was sick. The pain spread through her stomach and her chest and she started having convulsions. Then she passed into a coma and, with a gentle sigh, died.

The tragic news was broken to the Prince Regent by his brother Frederick less than two hours later. George struck his forehead violently with both hands and fell into Frederick's arms.

Harry Brougham recorded that the country was stricken by Charlotte's death 'as if by an earthquake at dead of night. It really was as if every household throughout Great Britain had lost a favourite child.'

Walter Scott lamented, 'What a cruel blow for this poor country death has lately dealt us! The loss of the dear Princess Charlotte to us is irreparable!'

Conversely, the Duke of Wellington, who had never liked Princess Charlotte, said privately that 'her death is a blessing to the country, for she would have turned out quite as her mother'.

Though totally overcome with grief, the Prince Regent insisted on being driven out to Claremont Park to view the bodies of Princess Charlotte and his stillborn grandson before they were laid in their coffins. There was a scene of terrible emotion, and his companions found it impossible to calm him. When he was escorted back to Carlton House, he insisted that the blinds of his carriage should be drawn so as to shelter his grief from inquisitive eyes.

He had not recovered his composure by the time of the funeral, and could not bring himself to attend it. He remained in shattered seclusion, weeping for the daughter he had lost, and for the grandchild he had hoped would determine the succession.

The country at large shared deeply in his loss, for Princess Charlotte, especially since her marriage, had been the darling of the people, a talisman of a happier future, embodying hopes for the nineteenth century.

Inevitably, amidst the painful sense of bereavement, people started pointing accusing fingers at those whom they considered responsible for the tragedy. The competence of Sir Richard Croft was unfairly brought into question. Both the Prince Regent and Prince Leopold publicly cleared him from blame, but Sir Richard felt so reviled that just over a year later he committed suicide.

Sir Richard was not the only target. Many people wondered why the Prince Regent himself should have been enjoying himself in the company of Lady Hertford at such a critical moment in his daughter's life.

Within days of the funeral, George went to the Pavilion in Brighton, where he was to spend three months in deep mourning, unable to see anybody, unable to talk about anything but the tragic deaths, and unable to sleep. He appears to have suffered a physical and nervous breakdown. He let himself go, abandoning the corsets which had valiantly restricted his girth. Lord Folkestone, informed of what was going on by members of George's Household, wrote to a friend, 'Prinny has let loose his belly, which now reaches to his knees.'

The effect of the deaths on the Prince Regent's three younger and unmarried brothers was somewhat different. They realised that the honour of siring the next heir to the throne could fall to them. So, with a haste bordering on the distasteful, they started jettisoning their mistresses and seeking out dynastic marriages, which also held out the prospect of increased allowances from Parliament and the settlement of debts. Within the space of a couple of months in 1818, the Duke of Cambridge married Princess Augusta of Hesse-Cassel, the Duke of Kent wed Prince Leopold's sister, Princess Victoria of Leiningen, and the Duke of Clarence was joined to Princess Adelaide of Saxe-Meiningen.

Another personal blow was awaiting the Prince Regent in November of 1818, when his mother died in his arms at Kew. His spirits battered again, he became a recluse in Carlton House for weeks, venturing out only for her funeral.

A month after the Queen's death, he was back in his favoured refuge at Brighton, where the Pavilion had been completely transformed from the house of Henry Holland's design. During a visit there in the autumn of 1814 George had decided the building was too cramped, and he authorised John Nash to undertake a major project which would give him more rooms while stamping the external appearance of his favourite home with individual genius. Inspiration came to Nash from Sezincote, a country house near Moreton-in-Marsh, built in Hindu style for a retired administrator of the East India Company. The work had been periodically interrupted, usually when Parliament was making angry noises about George's extravagant mode of life, but slowly his and Nash's vision of an Indian palace had gradually taken shape. Wings sprouted at each end, with oriental windows, and topped by tall pagodas and minarets. In the summer of 1818, the famous Oriental dome built on a cast-iron frame was lifted into position. Around it grew other smaller domes, screens of Indian columns, and battlements. His contemporaries were astounded, and to us the Brighton Pavilion is synonymous with the Prince Regent. The cost of seeing his dream fulfilled did nothing to endear him to his subjects. In seven years he spent over £150,000 on the external fabric alone.

While the work was progressing, the wife of the Russian ambassador was shown over the Pavilion. She wrote to a friend, 'We were shown a chandelier which cost eleven thousand pounds sterling. I write it out in full because it is really incredible. The chandelier is in the form of a tulip held by a dragon. How can one describe such a piece of architecture as this palace? The style is a mixture of Moorish, Gothic, Tartar, and Chinese, and all in stone and iron. It is a whim which has already cost £700,000, and it is still not fit to live in.'

The Reverend Sydney Smith eyed the Oriental dome and observed, 'The dome of St Paul's must have come down to Brighton and pupped.'

Another observer noted that the outside design was said to be taken from the Kremlin at Moscow, adding caustically that perhaps it was 'copied from its own stables, which perhaps were borrowed from the Kremlin'. He concluded it was 'an absurd waste of money, which would be a ruin in half a century or sooner'.

Life was now more sedate at the Pavilion. Dinner-parties were given twice a week for twenty or so guests, and some visitors complained of their dullness. Lady Hertford was ever in attendance, and most mornings the couple could be seen out riding in the Pavilion grounds.

The Prince Regent was obliged to turn from this tranquil existence to face a new threat from the Continent. The menace was not posed this time by an army. It was his detested wife, Caroline, who, since leaving England in 1814, had flitted from scandal to scandal, and shocked European society. All-night parties, topless outfits, and blatant seductions of men of her choice were commonplace.

Her friend, Harry Brougham, had predicted that everything she did would be reported back to London immediately. Caroline, in her hatred for her husband, probably revelled in such humiliating publicity.

The Prime Minister, Lord Liverpool, wrote to Caroline, urging her not to go to Naples. It was like an invitation to her. The ruler of Naples, Napoleon's brother-in-law Joachim Murat, prepared a palace for her reception. He led her into the capital in splendour. She was captivated by the bearded Murat, and promptly induced him to make love to her. They spent the next four months together in a whirlwind round of masquerades, balls, boar-hunts, and processions. At one ball she was observed 'in the most indecent manner, her breast and her arms being entirely naked', as one of the Prince Regent's spies recounted. Murat was just the theatrical sort of figure to appeal to Caroline, and she realised she could hardly humiliate her husband more than by giving herself to the brother-in-law of Napoleon.

In Genoa she rode through the streets in a carriage, displaying her ample bosom to the populace. In Athens she wore fewer clothes while she danced with her servants. In Milan, she gave orgiastic balls at her villa and had murals of the ecstatic scenes daubed on the walls.

She was said to be acting like a madwoman. But she was not mad. Her behaviour was brought on by the blight she felt on her affections, her sense of loneliness and isolation, and the contempt she felt for the Prince Regent.

The English servants who had travelled to Europe with her left her one by one, to be replaced by Frenchmen and Frenchwomen, Austrians, and Arabs. And on the way she picked up a darkly handsome and virile Italian, Bartolomeo Pergami, whom she appointed as her Chamberlain. Pergami swiftly progressed to a place at Caroline's table, then in her bed. Her vigorous and attentive companion was a former quartermaster in the First Italian Regiment of Hussars, who had served on a general's personal staff during the Napoleonic Wars. His bold, bewhiskered face proclaimed his coarse, uninhibited nature. Caroline was delighted with her find. After the repression and humiliation of the Court in London, she had at her command an energetic, enthusiastic, and swaggering Italian, who was there only to do her will.

Princess Caroline and Pergami consorted openly, and made no real attempt to hide the fact that they shared the same bed. Pergami behaved like a gentleman in public, but he had no conventional education or talent. The Princess helped him to purchase a country estate near Milan, and he took the title of Baron della Francina. When they visited Malta together, Caroline created Pergami a Knight of Malta.

She could not resist an ostentatious pilgrimage to the house where Napoleon had lived on Elba, cocking a snook at her husband by accepting the gift of Napoleon's billiard cue and a book from his library.

The couple explored Sicily, Algiers, Syria, and the Greek islands together before sailing to Palestine. There, the Princess astounded the pilgrims by riding at the head of her two-hundred-strong entourage into Jerusalem – on an ass. There she founded the Order of St Caroline of Jerusalem. Grand master of her order was, of course, 'Colonel Bartholomew Pergami, Baron of Francina, Knight of Malta, and of the Holy Sepulchre of Jerusalem.' The first Knight of the Order was William Austin, the boy whose parentage had been inquired into by the men who conducted the investigation of Caroline's conduct at Blackheath. His motto was the same as the British monarch's – *Honi soit qui mal y pense.*

Back in Europe, Caroline set herself up in the Villa d'Este on Lake Como, then moved on, with Pergami constantly in tow, to the Villa Cassielli, near Pesaro on the Adriatic coast.

At Pesaro she was brought a letter by a King's Messenger which informed her that her daughter Charlotte had died. Now she knew that the Prince Regent would renew his efforts to remove her from his life, and would hold no reservations about dragging her name through the mud.

The Prince Regent was thinking exactly along those lines. Reports from diplomats all over Europe had confirmed Caroline's outrageous and uninhibited behaviour. Everyone talked of her obvious intimacy with Pergami. By the time George had assessed the reports, he felt he had no alternative other than to demand that the government institute an investigation into her conduct.

In the late summer of 1818, two lawyers and an Italian-speaking army officer were ordered by Vice-Chancellor Sir John Leach 'to proceed forthwith to Milan, and from thence to all other places at your discretion for the purpose of making inquiries into the conduct of Her Royal Highness the Princess of Wales'. The Milan Commission – as the three investigators came to be called – settled down to its distasteful work. A bureau was established for the collection of evidence, a network of spies was organised, and Caroline's discharged servants were invited to inform on their former mistress. The Austrian authorities then ruling Milan were happy to co-operate with the Commission, but they found officials in other parts of Italy, particularly in the Papal States, less forthcoming. However, within three months the Commission reported that it was confident of proving the charges against the Princess, and that already enough evidence had been gathered to warrant a public inquiry. One of the Princess's former equerries, Guiseppe Sacchi, told of seeing her and Pergami often strolling arm in arm and kissing each other. Dances given at Pergami's villa near Milan had invariably been orgies, with the women of the Princess's Household selecting servants to take outside. Princess Caroline was well aware of what was going on, he said, for on one occasion she had said to him, 'I know, you rogue, that you have gone to bed with three of them and how many times you have had intercourse with them.' Sacchi claimed he regularly saw Pergami going to the Princess's room late at night, and heard the affectionate names she called him. The couple shared a carriage when they travelled, and he had found them cuddled up together in the morning, or even fondling each other. Other witnesses confirmed the level of intimacy between Caroline and Pergami. How they took rooms close to each other when they stopped at inns, and were seen wearing the same silk bedgown.

Teodoro Majocchi, a servant who travelled with the couple to Palestine, told of them using the same bedroom, and how one night on the boat it was so hot that the Princess had a tent erected on deck and slept in it with Pergami. When she took a bath in her cabin, he said, Pergami had supplied the water and bathed the Princess.

This particular account of their relationship led to an oft-quoted couplet: 'The Grand Master of St Caroline has found promotion's path. He is made both Night Companion and Commander of the Bath.'

The Commission also heard that the couple sprawled around the deck, kissing, and a servant related how Pergami would always be present while the Princess went about her toilet, almost naked and with her breasts bare. Pergami often walked into her room dressed only in a shirt, and at night the Princess used sometimes to sleep in Pergami's room.

A painting of the Princess depicted her as a penitent Magdalen, naked to the waist. This she gave to Pergami.

During a boat trip on Lake Como, the couple were observed kissing and fondling each other, with Pergami running his hands over her breasts and thighs.

By the summer of 1819, a total of eighty-five witnesses had given evidence and the Commission was able to report: 'From this comparison of evidence and from the cool, clear, and distinct manner in which these persons delivered their testimony, we should give credit to the truth of what they have said. We are under the necessity, therefore, of humbly stating that in our opinion this great body of evidence established the fact of a continued adulterous intercourse.' The Commissioners felt they could conclusively prove the Princess's adultery, and that this proof would satisfy a British court. The Prince Regent was grimly satisfied with their work.

In response to the Milan Commission, Princess Caroline's adviser Harry Brougham had despatched his brother James to Italy, supposedly to assist in resolving her financial problems. His true mission was to provide first-hand information on her behaviour.

He reported that Caroline was furious about some of the evidence given to the Milan Commission, especially that by servants she believed she could trust. But with paintings of Pergami on the walls in every room of the Princess's villa, and the evidence of his own eyes, James Brougham wrote to his brother, 'In fact, they are to all appearances man and wife, never was anything so obvious. His room is close to hers, and his bedroom the only one in that part of the house. The whole thing is apparent to everyone, though perhaps there might be difficulty in proving the fact to find her guilty of high treason, yet I should think all the circumstances being stated would completely ruin her in the opinion of the people of England, that once done, the Prince might get a divorce, or at any rate prevent her being Queen of England if he wished it.' He urged that, at all costs, a public enquiry into Caroline's conduct should be avoided. He continued, 'I should propose that she write a letter to the Prince stating her reasons for wishing a divorce or Parliamentary separation. She should begin by asserting innocence, high-toned in the style of Mary Queen of Scots, accusing the Regent of plaguing her by those inquisitions, and concluding by saying as her daughter is dead, and there is no hope of her having any pleasure in England, she thinks it better for both to separate. I am quite convinced that it is the very best thing that can be done on every account, and the sooner the better, before she loses more character, or in fact before England knows more of the matter.'

Harry Brougham believed Princess Caroline would accept a divorce and had given up all her ambitions of being Queen. He thought she could be paid off by the Prince Regent, as long as the amount was satisfactory.

Both Brougham and the Prince Regent wanted a formula agreed which would prevent Caroline becoming Queen. But this raised a Constitutional problem, for Parliament was unable to pass a law agreeing to a separation and a renunciation of Princess Caroline's rights unless she were either proved to have committed adultery, or confessed to it. It was clear that Caroline would admit nothing, for, by some extra-ordinary reasoning process, she had convinced herself that she had not conducted her life in a scandalous way. Should the Prince Regent try to smear her good name, she was prepared to raise a storm of protest throughout England. George's government ministers were obliged to advise him that it would be impossible to rely on back-bench support if a wave of sympathy for Princess Caroline were suddenly to sweep the country.

But the Prince Regent was adamant. He wanted a divorce. Lord Liverpool had to advise him that he would not be able to have a divorce 'except upon proof of adultery, to be substantiated by evidence before some tribunal in this country, and such a proceeding could not be instituted without serious hazard to the interests and peace of the Kingdom'. He feared that any apparent persecution of Princess Caroline would lead to a reaction in her favour, and, with the growing number of radical demonstrations in the country, uncertainty over the precise legal form any action might take, for the alleged offences had occurred only on foreign soil, and Pergami had never in his life been subject to British law. Had he been British his conduct might have constituted high treason. Fortunately he was not and less dramatic measures would have to be employed, or, perhaps, none at all. For the government rightly feared that in a contest of airing dirty linen, the Prince Regent would surely lose. The Opposition, and the Princess's supporters, would be sure to raise the question of his secret marriage to Maria Fitzherbert, his many other mistresses, his wild conduct. They decided that, at least for the moment, the question of divorce would have to be shelved. 'We must always recollect,' said Lord Castlereagh, 'that the proceeding, if it be taken, must ultimately be a parliamentary one.'

George was still gloomily contemplating his failure to secure a divorce from his despised wife when news came through that George III, the pathetic, deaf, blind, and mad recluse of Windsor, had decided to give up eating. He still held conversations with his predecessors and strummed tunelessly hour by hour on a harpsichord in the gloom, but within weeks the eighty-two-year-old King was dead. He breathed his last at 8.30 in the evening of January 29, 1820, and two days later King George IV was proclaimed sole and rightful ruler of his British domains by the Garter King of Arms in the forecourt of Carlton House.

9

FECKLESS KING

George was into his fifty-eighth year before he finally came to the throne, and his reign dawned in an era when the earth trembled at the dissent caused by social unrest, poverty, and the pressing need for overdue political reform.

Only months before, there was serious trouble in Birmingham, a growing industrial city still without parliamentary representation. Then the local magistrates in Manchester lost their nerve when fifty thousand people assembled in a reform rally in St Peter's Field, and sent in the local Yeomanry. The subsequent 'Peterloo Massacre' claimed eleven dead and four hundred injured, and it created a legend of popular resistance to government tyranny. The Cato Street Conspiracy had been so full of the menace of revolution that it sent apprehensive shivers through society. When five of the men who had planned a general insurrection in London were publicly executed, it was thought advisable to close each end of the Old Bailey with a troop of Horse Guards lest the spectacle of hanging and subsequent decapitation should provoke the mob to violence.

But George's paramount concern centred around what to do about his wife. He was determined at all costs to prevent her taking the title of Queen and, if possible, to see her hounded from society in disgrace.

First he had any reference to the Queen deleted from the Liturgy, the prayer offered up in each church for royalty's well being. There was no precedent for this, but he browbeat the Archbishop of Canterbury and members of the government into submission, and the Liturgy was duly altered.

Then he demanded that the machinery be set in motion to

procure a divorce. He wanted to go ahead with this, though he conceded that 'recriminations of every kind' might be raked up, because anything was bearable to be rid of his unspeakable wife. His ministers, who had formally resigned to take up office again immediately under the new monarch, blanched at the prospect. He was advised that none of them would agree to take office again if it were contingent on them agreeing to a divorce. George threatened to find other ministers who would agree to bring forward a Bill for Divorce, but it was an empty gesture. He realised that no government openly opposed to Caroline could guarantee its survival. A series of unpleasant arguments with his ministers ensued, for George knew well that they had read the evidence about Caroline's behaviour and were convinced of her guilt. Privately, they assured him that if Caroline were to come back to England, they would be prepared to help him get the divorce he so earnestly desired. However, they only gave the promise because they were certain that Caroline would never dare to return to the risk of a public inquiry into her conduct. George knew her well enough to believe she would come back, especially if the resultant storm were likely to trouble him.

When Princess Caroline had earlier asserted that she did not want to return to England, she meant it. The news of George III's impending death had encouraged her to think of going back to see him for the last time. But when the news of her father-in-law's death reached her she was in Italy, and seemed in no hurry to return to claim her place in the kingdom now ruled by her husband. This all changed when she heard of her deletion from the Liturgy, and foreign courts refused to recognise her at the express wishes of George. She determined to get back to England as speedily as possible and demanded that she be accorded all the rights due to her as Queen. She told her associates she planned to move into the old Queen's residence, Buckingham House.

George became apoplectic at the thought of Caroline being acclaimed Queen, and in a meeting with his ministers which carried all the drama of a council of war he pounded out the message that she must be stopped. The government finally agreed Caroline should be offered £50,000 a year as inducement to relinquish the title of Queen and any other linking her with the British royal family. And, fearing demonstrations in her favour, George insisted that as part of the deal, she must agree to keep out of England, and any of the British dominions.

Harry Brougham intercepted Caroline at St Omer, in northern France, and pleaded, 'I entreat your Majesty once more earnestly and patiently to reflect upon the step about to be taken.' He recommended that she should accept the annuity offered by the government, so long as she did not have to renounce her title. He also warned her of the danger she could put herself in if she went openly to England and was greeted with popular demonstrations.

But there was no stopping Caroline. Her mind was firmly made up. She had already written to the Prime Minister, Lord Liverpool, requesting a royal yacht to take her from Calais to Dover on June 3. The letter ended, 'I desire also to be informed of his Majesty's intentions what residence should be allotted to me, either permanent or temporary.' It was signed, 'Caroline, Queen of England.'

Her request for a royal yacht was ignored, so she boarded a passenger ferry for the crossing to Dover, where a wild reception awaited her. Local fishermen and tradesfolk turned out in their hundreds to cheer her into her hotel. Next day they were out again and her carriage was greeted at intervals along the London road by clusters of enthusiastic people. The crowds grew bigger as she reached the suburbs of the capital. An observer recorded, 'The road thronged with an immense multitude the whole way from Greenwich to Westminster Bridge. Carriages, carts, and horsemen followed, preceded, and surrounded her coach the whole way. She was received everywhere with the greatest enthusiasm. Women waved pocket handkerchiefs, and men shouted wherever she passed.' She triumphantly crossed Westminster Bridge and moved on up through St James's, where people in a torchlight procession shouted, 'Long Live the Queen!' A mob milled around the friend's house in Mayfair where she stayed for two days, cheering her whenever she appeared. They broke off only to hurl stones at carriages and break windows at the nearby house of Lady Hertford. The

City folk had taken to Caroline, and at the same time were expressing the revulsion they felt for their new King. Ale-houses handed out free drinks to soldiers who would toast the health of the Queen. The government was alarmed at the abrasive spirit of the crowds, and Lord Grey warned friends that they were heading for 'a Jacobin Revolution more bloody than that of France'.

George watched this spectacle with helpless rage, and trembled when an angry crowd gathered outside Carlton House, shouting, 'Nero!' He was forced to retreat to the Royal Lodge at Windsor, where he stayed, frightened to show himself in public.

All this only fuelled George's determination to destroy Caroline. Half an hour before Caroline's triumphal arrival in London, Foreign Secretary Lord Castlereagh had entered the House of Commons (he was an Irish peer, and therefore entitled to sit there) with a green bag in his hand. He announced, 'A message from the King.' The message was read, and the bag laid on the table. It contained the evidence of the Milan Commission. The King's message, which was delivered simultaneously to both Houses of Parliament, called for the members' immediate and serious attention to the evidence, and hoped they would 'adopt that course of proceedings which the justice of the case, and the honour and dignity of his Majesty's crown required.'

With her extrovert entry into his realm, Caroline had thrown the gauntlet down at the feet of the King. He had picked it up.

George had the report of the Milan Commission seen by a secret committee of the House of Lords, which held there were grounds for public concern over the licentious conduct of Caroline, and called, though reluctantly, for a 'solemn enquiry'.

He prodded the House of Lords to introduce a Bill of Pains and Penalties, a device whereby Parliament could punish Caroline without being obliged to resort to a law-court trial. It was introduced by the Law Officers as a private Bill on behalf of an unnamed person. There was no secret about who the shadowy figure was.

The Bill accused Caroline of adultery with Pergami and sought to 'deprive her Majesty Caroline Amelia Elizabeth of the title, prerogatives, rights, privileges, and pretensions of Queen Consort of this realm, and to dissolve the marriage between his Majesty and the said Queen'.

The attention of the whole country was riveted to what became known as the Queen's Affair for the summer and autumn of 1820.

Concerned parliamentarians attempted a compromise which would let the King, the Queen, and the government off the hook. A deputation begged Caroline to withdraw her claims, suggesting she should do so not because she feared a public enquiry, but for the good of the country. Every attempted compromise was brought to nothing by the Queen's continued insistence on her name being reinstated in the nation's prayers.

There was a very real fear of civil war over the issue. The populace at large and much of society supported the Queen, who, though clearly not an innocent, was certainly being trampled on by George. Even the army tended to favour Caroline, and a battalion of the Guards showing signs of revolt had to be marched out of London. As they went, they were heard to cry out, 'God save the Queen!' One writer observed, 'The extinguisher is taking fire.' Toasts to Caroline's health were drunk by soldiers all over the country, and stories circulated of George's own regiment, the 10th Light Dragoons, raising its glasses to her health. And the manager of a Brighton theatre was afraid to play *God Save the King* because he thought it would cause a riot.

The hearings in the House of Lords were labelled a public enquiry. In fact, they amounted to a trial, with the evidence of the Milan Commission being laid before the Lords. Though Caroline was not allowed to address the House, she went to the Palace of Westminster each day, and waited in an ante-room, playing backgammon. The evidence was relayed to her.

On every morning of the hearings, noisy crowds gathered outside her rented house in St James's Square, which she had taken for the duration of the 'trial'. Shouts of 'The Queen!

The Queen!' would bring her to the windows, and gain her a ripple of applause. Her progressions to and from the House of Lords were in the grandest style, in a state carriage pulled by six bay horses, with liveried footmen in attendance. When she passed Carlton House the guard presented arms, which never failed to please the crowds of people lining the route.

Almost every peer and bishop, together with most of the judges in the realm, were required to attend the 'trial'. For weeks they listened to the evidence from witnesses assembled by the Milan Commission. Teodoro Majocchi's evidence about the sleeping, bathing, and bedroom arrangements for Caroline and Pergami appeared damaging, until Harry Brougham, acting as the Queen's counsel, dramatically took him to pieces in a brilliant cross-examination. Frightened out of his wits, he ended up answering almost every question with the response 'I don't remember', a phrase which the satirists made great play with.

From crew-members of the boat which had taken the couple to Palestine, the Lords heard the evidence about them sleeping together in their cabins or in the tent on deck. Without a clear refutation of their evidence by independent witnesses, it seemed Caroline's adultery had been clearly established. Even when a Household lady, Louisa Demont, whose evidence had weighed heavily with the Milan Commission, was shaken in the witness box, the case still appeared secure. Then it suffered a blow from which it never recovered. A batch of witnesses from the Continent were abused by the people of Dover, and had stones thrown at them. By the time this story got back to Europe, it had grown out of all proportion. One of the witnesses was supposed to have been murdered, another imprisoned for life, and Caroline, elevated to the throne as Queen, had ordered retribution against all those who gave evidence against her. A government agent was sent to Italy to try to persuade the reluctant and frightened witnesses to come to London, but he had no success. One of these witnesses, who believed his head would be torn from his shoulders by the English mob, apparently had the most damaging evidence against Caroline, for he had seen her making love to Pergami on a sofa during her visit to Sicily. In the absence of further testimony, the prosecution case was closed at the beginning of October. The popular reaction to the hearings was demonstrated that same day when Caroline sailed down the Thames on her state barge, watched by a crowd estimated at two hundred thousand. Deputations, including one from the navy, took messages of support to Caroline. Graffiti carrying invective against George appeared all over town. One giant slogan read, 'The Queen for ever, the King in the river!'

Caroline's defence was brilliantly presented by Harry Brougham, and witnesses on her behalf were able to throw grave doubt on both the testimony of the prosecution witnesses and the methods of the Milan Commission.

The first vote on the Bill of Pains and Penalties gave it a majority of twenty-eight, much smaller than the government expected. They decided that if the next margin fell below ten, the Bill would have to be withdrawn. On the next vote the majority was only nine. George's ministers realised the Bill had no prospects of survival in the Commons, and it was jettisoned to avoid embarrassment.

George was so upset at the demise of the Bill that he considered abdicating the throne in favour of his brother Frederick, and going to live in Hanover. Then he toyed with the idea of sacking the government and bringing in the Whigs in an act of spite. Next he complained to Lord Liverpool that if his government were unable to get the Bill through Parliament, they should not have raised it in the first place. Liverpool responded truthfully that the Bill had only been drafted to satisfy George. The whole affair had been abysmally and clumsily handled. George retired to Windsor to sulk and lick his wounds.

There was widespread rejoicing in London, which celebrated with a three-night 'illumination' of the type which had greeted the end of the Napoleonic Wars. There were fireworks, bonfires, dances, and parades. Ships were lit up on the Thames.

The Queen's name remained excluded from the Liturgy,

she was not to be crowned, and she was not to be given a royal palace to live in. This was all assured by a strongly-supported government motion. But the Queen shed tears of happiness when she knew the Bill of Pains had been rejected, and entered into two weeks of unparalleled popularity. Her supporters requested a solemn service of thanksgiving in St Paul's Cathedral for the deliverance of the Queen from her enemies, but this was turned down by the Church authorities. It did not stop Caroline and a group of her most ardent supporters, including officials of the City of London, riding through London in state a few days afterwards for their own service of thanksgiving. Though the Cathedral was half empty, many thousands turned out on to the streets to cheer her. Her husband, conversely, had to keep off the London streets for weeks to avoid the virulent demonstrations against him.

Some weeks later, George did venture out to a play at Drury Lane. He seems to have been enthusiastically received inside the theatre, though there were shouts from the gallery of 'Where's your wife, Georgie?' And he did consider it advisable to see that his carriage was escorted by a troop of Life Guards.

His anger had cooled sufficiently by the end of the year for him to put a royal residence at Caroline's disposal and to authorise the government to settle the problem of her annuity.

George consoled himself with the attentions of the new lady in his life, the fifty-two-year-old Lady Conyngham. Her maternal nature appealed to George, who now needed that sort of comfort rather than the physical ministrations offered by Lady Hertford. So, as Mrs Fitzherbert's power had faded with the Regency, Lady Hertford's ended with the new reign. Lady Hertford, naturally, was distressed to see her position of power and influence at the new King's side being usurped. At first she affected to be unconcerned about his new interest. Then she would make barbed comments about the foolishness of such a love-match 'in view of the age of the contracting parties'.

Lady Conyngham, the daughter of a City banker of

humble Yorkshire beginnings, had been happily married for twenty-seven years and was mother of four grown-up children. Many years before, she had a couple of lovers, but she had considered that part of her life closed. She was no doubt overwhelmed that, at fifty-two, an age when women were considered elderly, she had enthralled the King himself. She was not noted as being intelligent, and her beauty was fast fading, but, now that his mother had died, George felt a growing need for a comfortable, warmhearted woman in whom he could confide, and with whom he could have a close relationship. This warmth and closeness had always been impossible with Lady Hertford, who was not capable of emotional intimacy. George needed this kind of comfort, and felt that Lady Conyngham could give it to him.

George's association with Lady Conyngham embraced her family as well, and her husband seems to have raised no complaints that the couple whispered together on his sofa while he was in the room. Or when George would raise his wine glass to touch Lady Conyngham's, then drink while holding her hand under the table. The physical side of their relationship was not totally absent, for, as a friend later recalled, at a Carlton House ball George 'was devoted to her the whole night and at last retired to one of the rooms with her and placed a page at the door to prevent anyone going in. Some tried to go in when the page stopped them and, laughing, told them nobody could be allowed to go in. As the King can see Lady Conyngham every day all day long, I really think he might control his passion and not behave so indecently in public.'

Lady Conyngham represented a transformation in his private life. Though considered a trifle vulgar, she was light-hearted and pleasant. Lady Hertford, on the other hand, had tended to be morose, for ever reminding George how people abused him. Perhaps she hoped he would look on her as a true friend by passing the detrimental stories on to him. After all the problems of the past few years, particularly those associated with his wife, he was ready for some gaiety and good humour. Not long after he had taken up with Lady Conyngham, a friend, who travelled in a carriage with the couple, declared, 'I have never seen a man more in love.' George even managed to lose weight for her, and was delighted when she was seen as the mistress of his homes in London, Windsor and Brighton.

There was no public resentment at the affair, and the government ministers were relieved to see him so content. But they felt he overstepped the mark when he tried to have a curate who had been tutor to Lady Conyngham's children promoted to a senior Church post. This provoked a government crisis, and at one time it appeared that Lord Liverpool was about to resign over the issue. But a face-saving compromise was worked out which ended in a different promotion for the curate, who was eventually appointed Bishop of Winchester.

Almost immediately, a second crisis blew up over the job of Lord Chamberlain of the King's Household. While Lady Hertford held sway over George, her husband had retained this post. Now he resigned, and George wanted to replace him with his new mistress's husband, Lord Conyngham. Lord Liverpool, believing that Lady Conyngham was very friendly with the parliamentary opposition, let George know he was opposed to this move. George was furious, for he considered an appointment in his own Household should be entirely his own affair. He wrote to his Prime Minister: 'The King desires Lord Liverpool distinctly to understand that whatever appointments the King may think proper to make in his own family, they are to be considered as quite independent of the control of any minister whatever; and Lord Liverpool must be aware that the present government was framed on that basis alone under him.' But, wishing to avoid another governmental crisis in such inflammable times, George was obliged to climb down again. He would like to have thrown Liverpool and his colleagues out on their ear, but he knew he would then have to invite the Whigs into government. That would mean raising the spectre of Catholic emancipation, which he now felt would be a breach of his oath as King, and possibly lead to the liberal reforms which George feared would mean the end of the monarchy. The King, who had been a Whig in his younger days as

Prince of Wales, was shifting round to the point where he was to become an ultra-Tory.

George's coronation, scheduled originally for the summer of 1820, had been postponed because of the trauma promised, and realised, by the Queen's trial. The new date set was July 19th, 1821, and George immersed himself in the finer details of a ceremony which he wanted to outshine any pageant in living memory.

His one recurring nightmare was that Caroline, who was to be barred from the proceedings, would somehow find a way to upset them for him.

George's incessant hatred for her was demonstrated when a government minister called to tell him, 'Your greatest enemy is dead,' and he replied, 'Is she, by God?' The emissary had, in fact, called to announce Napoleon's death in exile on St Helena.

Caroline did not disappoint her husband's expectations. In the opening months of the coronation year she was to be seen everywhere accepting the adulation of the mobs and helping to stir up dissension. She even made a summer tour of the minor theatres around the country, showing herself off and, as one observer commented, 'preparing a stir at the coronation'. She was assisted by the fact that George's passion for Lady Conyngham was well known, and the satirists had taken to calling his new mistress 'the Vice-Queen'.

Parliament surprisingly voted a quarter of a million pounds for George to lavish on his coronation. He responded in typical style, spending £24,000 on the coronation robes alone. His velvet train was twenty-seven feet long, and his hat surmounted by ostrich feathers and a heron's plume.

Seats in the decorated stands around Westminster Abbey were being sold for up to twenty pounds, but a sour note was sounded when it was reported that some people were reluctant to pay for the seats because they feared a riot in favour of the Queen might take place. For Caroline was playing up her slighted position by riding around in an unnecessarily shabby carriage to gain more sympathy.

George spent the night before the coronation at the Speaker's house at Westminster, so as to be near the Abbey.

In the morning, as the minutes ticked by, the nervousness he felt about Caroline showed in his face. He knew she would try something.

Craftsmen had transformed both Westminster Abbey and Westminster Hall, where the coronation banquet was to be held, building triumphal arches, boxes, and galleries, and draping the scenes in crimson cloth. Spectators were overwhelmed by the splendour of the occasion, as George walked regally before a canopy of gold cloth, preceded by officers of state holding the crown, the orb, the sceptre, and the sword of state, and by three bishops. At the very front of the procession were the King's Herbwoman and her six maids, strewing the way with herbs and heavily scented flowers as a precaution against the plague. Following him, in order of seniority, were the peers of the realm.

George stepped into the Abbey to the stirring strains of the Hallelujah Chorus, for the five-hour-long ceremony. Such was the weight of his cumbersome robes that some of the observers believed he would be dragged down by them, and he appeared so tired and distressed at times they thought he was about to faint.

All the time, he was waiting for a commotion which would announce that Caroline had, after all, managed to get in. For he well knew that she had written to his government ministers saying that it was her right and privilege to attend the coronation. When this letter went unanswered, she had her lawyers look up the rules of precedence in relation to coronations to see if she could demand her rights. Then she had written to Lord Liverpool, stating that she intended to be present at the ceremony, and cheekily concluded, 'The Queen, being particularly anxious to submit to the good taste of his Majesty most earnestly entreats the King to inform the Queen on what dress the King wishes the Queen to appear in, on the day, at the coronation.' This letter also received no reply, and made her more determined than ever to attend the coronation. George, who received information gathered from Caroline's Household, was told that Caroline was going to try to get in whatever happened.

When Caroline's carriage, a coach of state drawn by six

horses, arrived at the Abbey, her reception was mixed. Soldiers presented arms and there were cries of, 'The Queen!' and, 'The Queen for ever!' But from other sections of the crowd there was loud whistling and shouts urging her to leave. She stepped down and walked up to the entrance, which was well guarded. One of the men asked to see her ticket. Lord Hood, one of Caroline's companions, told the guard, 'I present to you your Queen. Surely it is not necessary for her to have a ticket?' The doorkeeper said that, whoever she was, she could not be admitted without a ticket. At the sign of this disturbance, an official moved forward to inform Caroline, 'Madam, it is my duty to inform your Majesty that there is no place for your Majesty in the royal box, or with the royal family.' Caroline saw that she was not going to be allowed in, and got back into her carriage to be driven away. Now there were hisses from the crowd, and cries of 'Shame!' or 'Back to Pergami!'

Inside the Abbey, the ceremony droned on, with the Archbishop of Canterbury preaching a thunderous sermon on the need for the good ruler to preserve his subjects' morals 'from the contagion of vice and irreligion'. George's concentration lapsed from time to time, and his head nodded. Some people believed he actually dropped off to sleep momentarily. Others noticed him sighing and making eyes at Lady Conyngham. When the exhausting service finally ended George walked through crowds who, for a change, were cheering, to Westminster Hall, where a banquet for three hundred had been prepared. The guests devoured vast quantities of salmon, trout, venison, beef, goose, lobster, crayfish, roast fowl, jellies, and creams.

Throughout the ceremony and the banquet, firework displays were given along the River Thames and in Hyde Park, and the population seemed genuinely to want to join in the festivities to mark the coronation. An observer wrote in a letter, 'The people were all in good humour. The King was excitedly and most enthusiastically cheered, and seemed in the highest spirits.'

The public's hatred for the new King had not disappeared overnight. They were just happy to have something to celebrate. It is a little difficult to see what most of his subjects gained from the coronation festivities. But it was a warm night, and a colourful and noisy day for them to remember. It was a remarkable triumph for George's sense of majesty, and as his carriage carried him back to Carlton House, with cheers still ringing out, he must have felt content.

There was a lot of speculation at the time about the state of Caroline's mental health. If she were mad, it would comfortably explain all her behaviour. Whatever the case was, after she had been turned ignominiously away from her husband's coronation, she was a shattered woman, her spirit broken.

The fickle public, who had supported her as a symbol of political opposition to George, allowed its enthusiasm for her to wane. She had been the subject of ridicule in cartoons, and meetings called to celebrate the end of her persecution after the House of Lords trial were very subdued affairs. A man who bellowed that she was a 'damned whore' at the theatre one night was cheered by the audience, much to Caroline's discomfort as she sat in her box. Politicians who believed she still had something to offer visited her secretly, but she was aware that the heady days when she had reached the pinnacle of her public approval were past. George was delighted to receive reports about her depression and disconsolate manner, and the insults offered to her in public.

Her distress at the events of the year made her ill, but she refused the attentions of her doctors and continued living in her usual way. A visit to Drury Lane, where Robert Elliston recreated the magnificence of the coronation on stage, proved to be too much for her. She felt ill during the performance, and went outside. She returned, looking ashen, just in time for the playing of *God Save the King*. A member of the audience recounted, 'When it was over, she got up and curtsied to the manager, to the pit, galleries, and boxes in a manner so marked, so wild, and with a countenance so haggard that I burst into tears to see royalty and pride so broken down and humbled.'

It was her final public appearance. On the way home she was doubled up with abdominal pain and started to vomit.

Her pulse raced and became erratic. Copious doses of opium did nothing to ease the pain, and her doctors announced she had 'an obstruction of the bowels, attended with inflammation'. Caroline, certain that she was going to die, had her last will and testament drafted and called for her loyal friend, Harry Brougham. As he recalled later, she told him, 'I am going to die, Mr Brougham, but it does not signify.' Brougham assured her that the doctors did not believe so, to which she responded, 'I know better than they. I tell you I shall die, but I don't mind it.' She became delirious, then had convulsions. On August 8, just three weeks after being so humiliatingly banned from the coronation, she was dead.

A few days before her husband had embarked at Portsmouth in the yacht *Royal George* for a state visit to Ireland. After sailing slowly down the Channel, it had rounded Land's End and headed northward for the Welsh coast. It had reached Anglesey and anchored off Holyhead, preparatory to crossing the Irish Sea, when news of Caroline's death arrived. As one of his entourage observed, it would be absurd to think that he was afflicted by her sudden death, but he was certainly affected by the news, and retired to his cabin, where he walked about for the greater part of the night.

Aware that his moves were being closely watched, George ordered that the flags of the squadron accompanying his yacht should be lowered as a sign of mourning. There were to be few other signs. He was to spend the first five days in Ireland in retirement, but in very good spirits among his friends. He also ordered six weeks' mourning at Court, but he did not sanction a more general mourning, or cancel his state visit. He refused to lament the wife he had detested so vehemently for twenty-six years.

There was a burst of public feeling at her passing. *The Times* appeared with black columns and edges, and piously mourned 'the greatest, perhaps the best woman of her day'.

There was no reflection of this feeling on board the *Royal George*. George celebrated his fifty-ninth birthday during the crossing and drank so much that he could barely stand up when he landed at Dublin. One of his companions on the voyage was to recall, 'The passage to Dublin was occupied in eating goose-pie and drinking whisky in which his Majesty took most abundantly, singing many joyous songs, and being in a state, on his arrival, to double in number even the numbers of his gracious subjects assembled on the pier to receive him. The fact was that they were in the last stages of intoxication.'

A problem which weighed on George's mind was the burial of Caroline. He did not want to accord her the honour of internment at Windsor or Westminster Abbey, but, as legal Queen of England, she would be entitled to it. Caroline herself rescued him from this dilemma, for her last testament contained the request that her body should be speedily removed from England for burial in the family tomb in Brunswick. However, the inscription she wanted engraved on her coffin attested to the fact that she had taken her hatred with her into death. It should read, she instructed, 'Caroline of Brunswick, the injured Queen of England.' Lord Liverpool promised that no such inscription would be approved while the coffin was in his government's charge.

George was concerned that demonstrations in favour of Caroline should be avoided by removing the coffin quietly from her house and having it transported down the Thames to a warship which would take it to the Elbe. He ordained that the coffin should not be moved through London, or any part of the country. Somehow, these orders were changed and an army detachment was instructed to move the coffin through Chelmsford to Harwich. Police and troops were told to stand by in case of trouble and Caroline began her last journey. It was not to be a smooth one. When word got around that the cortège was not to pass through the City of London, whose merchants had cheered her opposition to George, a mob of people turned out to lay obstacles on the route to force the procession to detour through Temple Bar. Sir Robert Baker, the Chief Magistrate of Bow Street, had been placed in charge of arrangements for the coffin's transportation, and told to avoid popular demonstrations. But he realised there would be a serious riot if he had the obstacles removed and tried to bring the cortège back on to its prescribed route. So the triumphant crowd, joined by the Lord Mayor and members of the City's Common Council, escorted Caroline's coffin across the City as far as the Essex Road. Church bells tolled in each town the cortège passed through, and at a stop in a Chelmsford church, a City alderman who had remained in the procession produced a silver plate on which were written the words, 'Caroline of Brunswick, the injured Queen of England.' A cabinet-maker screwed it on to the coffin, but it was removed at the request of a King's official, only to be put back on later before the coffin was placed in the Brunswick royal vault.

The tumultuous scene at Harwich was recorded by Harry Brougham: 'We found everything ready prepared for immediate embarkation. The scene was such as I never can forget or reflect upon without emotion. The multitudes assembled from all parts of the country were immense, and the pier crowded with them as the sea was covered with boats of every size and kind, and the colours of the vessels were half-masted high, as on days of mourning. The contrast of a bright sun and the gloom on every face was striking, and the guns firing at intervals made a solemn impression. The crimson coffin slowly descended from the pier.'

Caroline's will left everything to William Austin, the boy who had been at the centre of the Delicate Investigation. However, apart from a small trust, he received nothing, for Caroline's combined assets in England and Italy were not enough to pay off her debts. Even members of the household who had been promised pensions had to look to King George for settlement.

Meanwhile, King George was enjoying himself in Ireland as he had not felt able to for years. He endeared himself to a crowd of thousands of Irish men and women by inviting them into the grounds of the Viceregal Lodge in Phoenix Park, and telling them how Irish in spirit he had felt all his life. They, like so many people during this visit, appreciated that George was the first reigning monarch to make a state visit since Richard II. One old man echoed the sentiment felt by many of his countryfolk when he said, 'I was a rebel to old King George in '98, but by God I'd die a hundred deaths for his son, because he's a real King, and asks us how we are.'

For George, it was a complete turn round in terms of popularity amongst his subjects, and he revelled in it. In the euphoria engendered by his presence, the evils of absentee landlords, oppression of farmers, and lack of Catholic freedoms seem to have been forgotten. Even Lord Cloncurry, an Irish rebel who had been incarcerated in the Tower of London, saw a 'strange madness' descend on Irishmen during the visit, and declared himself infected by it. He invited King George to his house, and gave him a 'pledge of sincerity'.

A tumultuous crowd greeted George's public entry into Dublin. He wore the Order of St Patrick, and was delighted at the warmth of the welcome. But he later called an attendant to his room for a serious discussion. The attendant subsequently wrote, 'He was walking about greatly agitated between pleasure at his reception in Ireland and dissatisfaction at what has occurred in London when the Queen's coffin was taken across town. He kept me a full half an hour, and talked the whole time, alternately at the triumph of Dublin and the horrors of London. Bloomfield tells me that the King sat up the greater part of the night fretting about this latter affair; it affects him certainly more deeply than I should have expected.'

George's continuing torment over his wife led him to demand an inquiry into why her coffin was taken to Harwich instead of shipping along the River Thames as he had directed. He was told that two considerations had enforced the change. First, the difficulties of getting a frigate along the Thames in time. Second, the authorities in London feared that the trouble caused by the mob could have been even worse if the coffin had gone by river and passed under London Bridge, where a demonstration could have been mounted. George accepted the explanation, but saw to it that the magistrate, Sir Robert Baker, was fired for not handling the emergency situation more effectively.

In marked contrast to his relaxed progress, King George hurried through an open-air breakfast given by the Dublin

Society, spending less than five minutes on the lawns where the tents were laid out. The reason for this haste was that he was finally getting round to his real motive for visiting Ireland: to spend three days at the Conyngham family home, Slane Castle in County Meath. There, he was once again in the midst of a family, as he liked to be. The three days he stayed with them were the brightest of the tour, and at least one companion considered they were possibly the happiest of his life. Lady Conyngham ministered to his needs while the domestic life continued around him. He danced a jig at a ball which was given in his honour, and he attended matins at Slane church. When two advisers arrived for dinner a couple of days later they found him in the best of spirits. Another asserted that he had 'not heard an unpleasant word nor seen a sullen look'.

Protestants and Catholics alike delighted in George's visit, and hoped that it might mark a happier time ahead for their country. George proclaimed the belief that poverty and disaffection would disappear in the presence of a resident gentry, encouraged to live on their Irish estates.

Shortly before he left Dublin to return to England, George was presented with a laurel crown. He accepted it, and told the crowd gathered to see him off, 'My friends! When I arrived in this beautiful country my heart overflowed with joy. It is now depressed with sincere sorrow. I never felt sensations of more delight than since I came to Ireland. I cannot expect to feel any superior nor many equal till I have the happiness of seeing you again. Whenever an opportunity offers wherein I can serve Ireland, I shall seize on it with eagerness. I am a man of few words. Short adieux are the best. God bless you, my friends. God bless you all.'

King George's visit to Ireland had been an unprecedented triumph, and spectators lined the shore for miles to see him off. Cannons thundered and bands played. George was rowed out to his yacht, where he stood on deck till darkness fell, waving his hat to the gathered masses ashore. It was a euphoric moment, but George was never to fulfil his promise to Ireland.

He arrived back in London just in time to set off on another trip he had promised himself, a visit to Hanover, the German state of which he was also sovereign. His one and only Continental visit lasted for seven weeks. It began with a one-night stay in Calais, where his now bankrupt and destitute former friend Beau Brummell had fled, one step in front of his creditors. George took care to avoid Brummell and continued on to Brussels, where he dined with the King and Queen of the Netherlands, and to Waterloo, where the Duke of Wellington gave him a conducted tour of the battlefield. There, George ordered a tree cut down and the wood from it used to make a chair which he installed at Carlton House, inscribed with the legend *Georgio Augusto Europae, Liberatori*. Since the famous victory at Waterloo, the immodest George had managed to convince himself that he was the genius and the driving force behind the defeat of Napoleon. If any of his contemporaries knew better, they did not try to contradict him. The journey on to Hanover was a rigorous one, for road conditions were so bad that the exhausted horses had to be changed every five miles. As in Ireland, the absentee King was welcomed enthusiastically, with illuminated buildings, flags and streamers, cheering crowds, and a hundred-and-one-gun salute. In the Cathedral he was crowned for the second time, and he plunged into a round of hunting, presentations, and ceremonials. But soon he was very bored. Though deeply touched by the obvious loyalty of his German subjects, he found their solemn and conventional way of life tedious. He was pleased to get back to England, and headed immediately for the Pavilion at Brighton, where he proceeded to bore everybody to tears with endless stories about his travels and his views on international politics, on which he now considered himself a leading expert. But he was cheerful and relaxed, a state no doubt enhanced by the presence once again of Lady Conyngham. Friends noticed their intimacy was such that he had started taking snuff from her shoulder. George's gout still troubled him, and he often had to rest his leg up on a chair, but the wild debauchery of his younger days was past. There were no more accounts like the ones that had continued throughout the Regency days, of him getting so drunk with friends that they ended the evening slumped on the floor beneath the table. An intriguing picture of a Pavilion gathering of this time is given by Charles Greville, a Privy Council clerk: 'The gaudy splendour of the place amused me for a little then bored me. The dinner was cold and the evening dull beyond all dullness. They say the King is anxious that form and ceremony should be banished, and if so it only proves how impossible it is that form and ceremony should not always inhabit a palace. The King was in good looks and spirits, and after dinner cut his jokes with all the coarse merriment which is his characteristic. Lord Wellesley did not seem to like it, but of course he bowed and smiled like the rest.' George was pleased to reach a satisfactory compromise over a royal job for Lord Conyngham, who was sworn in as a Privy Councillor and Constable of Windsor Castle, and made Lord Steward of the Household. This contentment was reflected in the pleasant mood in which he passed the first weeks of 1822 at Brighton, where he walked across each afternoon to Lady Conyngham's house. When Lord Liverpool refused to sanction a government job for a relative of Lady Conyngham, an element of bitterness crept into their relationship, but it did not last for long.

George felt in his element again when he immersed himself in the planning for a trip to Scotland, the first by a British monarch since Stuart times, that summer. His orders for clothes, hats, and gowns showed he had not lost the taste for flamboyant dress and spending which marked his youth. The *Royal George* took him up the east coast of England to Edinburgh, where Sir Walter Scott had overlorded the arrangements for the visit. George's welcome was as ecstatic as the one he had received in Ireland, much to the disappointment of a number of leading Scotsmen, who had urged people to ignore him. He appeared in full highland costume at a Holyroodhouse party, and further endeared himself to his Scottish subjects at the Caledonian Hunt Ball, where he insisted, 'No foreign dances. I dislike seeing anything in Scotland that is not purely national and characteristic.' He did, however, have to suffer the annoying indignity of seeing distributed in the city a cartoon depicting his inflated self entitled *Landing of the Old Amorous Dandy*! Scott felt the good effects of the King's visit would last, and wrote in sycophantic tone, 'The people's delight was extreme at seeing a portly handsome man looking and moving every inch a King.'

George returned to England to the news that his trusted confidant and adviser, Foreign Secretary Lord Castlereagh, had killed himself by cutting his throat with a penknife. The burden of handling Britain's intricate foreign affairs for many years had proved too much for him.

The obvious choice as successor to Castlereagh was George Canning, but there were two things against him. The first was that he had opted out of government at the time of the Queen's trial – a move which convinced George that he had been Caroline's lover. The second was the personal animosity that Lady Conyngham felt for the veteran politician. Though George made his reluctance abundantly plain, Canning ignored it and took office. The King's antipathy towards him was to continue, but Canning overcame it later to become Prime Minister.

Canning was to offer the King an olive branch in the form of a vacant Under-Secretaryship of State for one of Lady Conyngham's sons. It was accepted, but the gesture did not heal the rift. George seemed to take exception to almost everything Canning did. He was particularly incensed when Canning suggested he should dine with two visitors from the South Seas. George stormed to the Duke of Wellington, 'Think of that damn fellow wanting me to have the King and Queen of the Sandwich Islands to dinner. As if I would sit at table with such a pair of damned cannibals.'

Early in 1823, a friend observed that George had aged considerably in the recent months, and soon he was struck down with an attack of gout which made it impossible for him to move without a great deal of pain. He retired to his bed, refusing to see anybody except his doctors, and newspapers speculated that he might be going the same way as his father. The Duke of Wellington believed he was going to die within months, and Lady Conyngham, eyeing the jewels and splendour her association with George had brought her, told a friend, 'What a pity now if all this were to end. For you must admit that it is charming.' To her great relief, George recovered, though for a while he had to hobble around on crutches to ease the pain of the gout.

George directed his energies to his chosen role as a noble patron of the arts and literature. He founded the Royal Society of Literature, hoping to encourage the emergence of writers to follow those of his day like Shelley, Wordsworth, and Coleridge. He encouraged the formation of a national collection of paintings to rival that of Italy or France, and his efforts eventually led to the establishment of a permanent art exhibition in London. It is appropriate that the colonnade which formerly stood outside Carlton House should today still form the principal entrance to the National Gallery. He renewed his efforts and financial contributions to the Royal Academy, and presented to the British Museum a splendid library of almost seventy thousand volumes which his father had collected over the course of half a century. This collection was to form the basis of the British Museum Library.

At the same time, he seemed to have lost interest in his own artistic extravaganza, the Pavilion at Brighton. He lost his affection for the place, perhaps because the growth of the town destroyed its mood of privacy. Lady Conyngham was certainly never at ease there, for she must often have felt the presence of Mrs Fitzherbert, in spirit at least. Now that he was King, George seems to have thought that the exposed position of the Pavilion offered a temptation to any would-be assassin. He continued to pay short visits, but now the entertainment was more likely to be a musical party than the interminable banquets of earlier years. His last visit there was in the spring of 1827, and the house remained unoccupied until his brother's accession in 1830.

George also decided that Carlton House was not a suitable residence for the King of England. The rooms, he complained, were too small for large receptions, and despite the fortune that had been spent on the house, he declared it was now antiquated and decrepit. He had, in fact, gradually tired of the place, particularly after it was damaged by fire in

1825. He planned to have Carlton House pulled down stone by stone, and have a terrace of elegant private houses built on the site. He trusted that the rents from these would compensate the crown for some of the fortune lavished on his home in the past.

He wanted to build a London palace with enough grandeur to be the royal home. After considering the merits of a new residence in Green Park, he commissioned John Nash to convert Buckingham House into a palace. Lord Liverpool advised him that the highest amount the government would sanction for the new home was £150,000. George estimated it would cost £500,000, but still gave the go-ahead. It ended up costing £700,000 by the time Nash had finished, and George was faced with another battle royal over finances with his ministers. In typical grandiose style, Nash had five hundred blocks of marble delivered for the new palace. Wings were built, and then torn down again if they did not match his visualisation. The work went on and on, and was to remain unfinished when King George died.

His all-absorbing interest in rebuilding Buckingham House and other royal residences left him little energy for anything else in life. The Duke of Wellington declared that the King's attention was diverted to such a degree 'that he appears not to be the least interested in public affairs'.

When George turned his attention, it was to Windsor, the wreck of a medieval stronghold, an uncomfortable building, overcast by associations with the old, mad King George III. He stayed in the castle for two months in 1823 to judge whether he would like to live there, and took care to avoid the gloomy ground-floor rooms in which his father had passed his last years. He decided to transform it into the most royal of the royal palaces, into a proper symbol of English sovreignty. A competition was held to decide which architect should be entrusted with the job. The winner was Jeffry Wyatt, who swept away the last traces of the mediaeval fortress and changed the whole character of the castle. Working in the four years between 1824 and 1828, Wyatt raised the Round Tower by thirty feet, and a series of state apartments replaced the small drawing-rooms and dark music-rooms which contained so many hollow memories. The Waterloo Chamber was built as a final tribute to the victory over Napoleon, and it became a fitting home for the portraits of Allied sovereigns, statesmen, and soldiers which George had commissioned from Sir Thomas Lawrence as soon as the wars were over. Between five hundred and seven hundred men were employed full time on the work over the four years. The £150,000 which represented the first estimate soon disappeared, and costs mounted steadily. When they topped £800,000, Parliament was informed that another £100,000 was still needed. A select committee was set up to investigate the expenditure, but this time George really had his government over a barrel. If the castle were left uncompleted, it would fall into disrepair and become a symbol of national disgrace. It was now a matter of national concern, and the money had to be produced. George spent a lot of time at Windsor, supervising the decorations which reflect his taste for the baroque and gilt. Doors and fireplaces from the dismantled Carlton House were fitted in, and George delighted in the comparison to French palaces.

However, when Windsor Castle was completely transformed, he did not move in. He still preferred the thatched comfort of the Royal Lodge, the building a few miles away in Windsor Great Park which he had dubbed The Cottage.

It was in the privacy of this house that George formed what became known as the 'Cottage Clique', consisting of eight or nine members. These were the Russian ambassador and his wife, Prince and Princess Lieven; the Hanoverian minister, Count Munster; the Austrian ambassador, Paul Esterhazy, and his wife; Polignac, the French ambassador; Lady Conyngham; the Duke of Wellington; and Sir William Knighton, the King's physician and unofficial secretary. Creation of the clique seems to have been a rash political move on George's part, but it may have been accidental. He always maintained that his constitutional functions as ruler of Hanover were distinct from his obligations as King of England. He believed himself entitled, as sovereign of Hanover, to correspond directly with the rulers of Austria, Russia, and France through their representatives accredited to him in London and without informing the British government of what he said or did. If he had restricted himself in this correspondence to Hanoverian affairs, all might have been well. But he made it clear to the foreign rulers that he did not approve wholeheartedly of Canning's conduct of British foreign affairs. Canning put a warning shot over George's bows when he threatened to apprise the House of Commons about the plot by a cabal of foreigners to undermine his authority and force him from office. And when von Metternich, the Austrian Foreign Minister, was invited to circumvent the government at Westminster and discuss European affairs with the King at Windsor, Canning stepped in. He wrote, 'I wonder whether he is aware that the private communication of Foreign Ministers with the King of England is wholly at variance with the spirit, and practice too, of the British Constitution.' The letter, sent to the British ambassador in Paris, where Metternich was staying en route to Windsor, was shown to the Austrian and stopped him in his tracks. It also marked the end of George's political intrigues. He lost virtually all interest in politics, and consulted Parliament only to raise the money for his grandiose building schemes.

Canning's popularity, helped by his stand against George's attempted interference, soared. George realised that if he openly backed Canning's policies, some of that popularity might come to him. And before long he realised that Canning's resolute and independent stand in the face of foreign powers raised his own royal prestige. He even came to like Canning, inviting him for weekends to the Royal Lodge. George found he enjoyed Canning's natural wit, and the parliamentary reports he delivered to his sovereign, a chore of his post as Leader of the House, were entertaining. A bonus for George was when Canning realised George's desire to remove a tiresome rival for the interest of Lady Conyngham and had him shipped out to a vacant diplomatic post in Buenos Aires.

The gatherings of the clique at the Royal Lodge were not exhilarating. Princess Lieven recalled that George would sit gazing soulfully at Lady Conyngham, who showed more interest in her jewels than her lover. George certainly realised that Lady Conyngham was an opportunist who was not in love with him. He tolerated her presence because he was so used to it he found it comforting. In any event, he was far too lazy now to face up to a change in habits. Princess Lieven was so bored with these soporific surroundings that she sometimes felt close to screaming. But the King's spirits were occasionally raised sufficiently for him to play cards, or even entertain his guests by skilfully mimicking past and present government ministers. However, most of the time he seemed to spend either reading or dozing in bed. From 1824 onwards he was frequently in pain, from gout or troubles with his bladder. To relieve the discomfort, he took larger and larger doses of opium pain-killer, which inevitably made him drowsier still. It was not unknown for ministers to travel from London to Windsor at his request, only to find the King too weary to give them an audience.

George continued to be unpopular with his English subjects and he was well aware of it. As if to remind him, a cartoon depicted him fishing on a lake near Windsor with Lady Conyngham. It was entitled *A King-Fisher*. His reaction was to spend more and more time in seclusion, away from the public gaze. Occasionally his subjects would hear of him moving from Brighton to Windsor, or from The Cottage to the castle, but they would hardly ever see him in person. It reached a point where, when he held a party, people were barred from waiting to see him pass on his way in. For he had also become obsessively self-conscious about his rapidly spreading girth.

The Duke of Wellington remained a member of George's clique, and he was able to save George from a potential disaster when Lady Conyngham wanted to go abroad to her son, who was supposedly dying on the Continent. George, who was still besotted with her, or so Wellington believed, insisted that if she went, then he would accompany her. Wellington had always considered Lady Conyngham vulgar, and could not understand what his King saw in her. But he was also certain that George would create a furore of protest if he went to Europe with her. People would believe, he said, that he put Lady Conyngham above his duty as King. Wellington continued to be aware of the importance of Lady Conyngham in George's life, and took care not to raise anything with the King that he had not first mentioned to her. On this occasion she resolved the crisis by allowing an emissary of the King to go abroad on her behalf and escort her sick son to Italy.

George's niece Princess Victoria, daughter of the deceased Duke of Kent and later to reign as Queen Victoria, years afterwards remembered an encounter with the King when she was seven. He picked her up and placed her on his knee. She recalled, 'It was too disgusting because his face was covered in grease-paint. He wore the wig which was so much worn in those days. Then he said he would give me something to wear, and that was his picture set in diamonds, which was worn by the Princesses as an order to a blue ribbon on the left shoulder. Lady Conyngham pinned it on my shoulder.'

The cruel jibes about his stout body, swollen legs, hobbling gait, and wrinkled features which the grease-paint could scarcely hide hurt George so much that he became paranoid about it. He always believed the servants were staring at him, and gave strict instructions that any caught doing so should be dismissed. Visitors to Windsor Castle were forbidden to look out of the window, in case George was passing nearby. He also excused himself from attending the previews of exhibitions at the Royal Academy because he found the stairs difficult owing to his crippling attacks of gout. When his legs and ankles swelled up so much he had to be wheeled or carried everywhere, he became more of a recluse than ever. Shortly afterwards, the gates of St James's Palace were boarded up so people could not see him being carried to and from his carriage. A rare visitor from the outside world recorded, 'It is unpleasant for him to see a strange face, or indeed a human being of any kind whatsoever, within his domain. The Park is consequently a perfect solitude. The King's favourite spots are, for further security, thickly surrounded by screens of wood, and plantations are daily laid out to add to the privacy and concealment. In places, where the lie of the ground would enable you to get a glimpse of the sanctuary within, three stages of fences are planted one behind the other.'

George was brought back into the political arena briefly and for the last time over the issue of Catholic emancipation. Canning took over briefly as Prime Minister when Lord Liverpool died, and George made it plain to him that, come what may, he could never agree to a law which would allow Catholics to sit in Parliament, because he was convinced it would represent a breach of his coronation oath. Death removed Canning from Parliament, and the formidable figure of the Duke of Wellington, the hero of Waterloo, stepped forward to claim the seals of office of Prime Minister. George, who knew the Duke well from the 'Cottage Clique', reaffirmed his determination never to allow the laws which would grant Catholic relief. At first, Wellington agreed with the King, but before long he came to realise that unless the Catholic repression were lifted, the country would have to face civil war in Ireland. When Daniel O'Connell, a Roman Catholic and thus disqualified from a seat in Parliament, was elected as the member for Clare, Wellington knew the issue could not be put off any longer. The battle for parliamentary acceptance got under way, and was won. George did not want to sign the resultant Catholic Emancipation Bill into law, but was obliged to do so when he realised that if he did not he would be without a government and that no other would serve. The stubborn King gave his formal assent to the Bill on April 10, 1829. He had learned where the true power lay in his constitutional monarchy. He commented bitterly, 'Arthur is King of England, O'Connell King of Ireland, and I am Canon of Windsor.'

George's eyesight began to fail, and physically his condition was clearly waning during 1829. Yet he still travelled up to London for a ball given for the sons and daughters of his friends. He genuinely liked children, and seemed not to fear being seen by them as much as by his other subjects. He probably was still grieving for Charlotte and his stillborn grandson.

His behaviour became erratic, and he would retreat to the

sanctuary of his bedroom, pleading illness to avoid simple duties like the signing of documents. He started keeping ministers waiting unnecessarily. Wellington wrote, 'When one goes to Windsor no person can answer for the hour of return.' Others noted that when visitors turned up with business to transact or with papers for him, he would delight in keeping them waiting for hours while he discussed or went about trivial matters. A visitor noted, 'A more contemptible, cowardly, selfish, unfeeling dog does not exist than the King. There never was such a man or behaviour so atrocious.' Ministers sometimes arrived to find him drunk or anaesthetised by opium pain-killers. They would wait, but when he came round, they would be told he was in no condition to see them.

The summer of that year passed, with George making occasional trips to his private zoo, where he showed concern for a giraffe which was sick and soon to die. The cartoonists found sport even in this, depicting the King and Lady Conyngham weeping over the animal. A large part of his day was spent in bed, but he had the newspapers brought to him at dawn each morning. There were so many that some believed he must have read every newspaper published. He seemed to have enjoyed this occupation of his time, though the carping comments still appeared. He also read a lot of history and travel books, and retained the ability to remember much of the information. And sometimes he would call in a favourite actor or actress to entertain him with the reading of a play.

Each evening, George would visit Lady Conyngham in her room for an hour's light conversation, something which she looked forward to less and less. For, as he rambled on about his youth, about his father, and about the army, she became increasingly bored. She considered leaving The Cottage and George and going to live abroad, but was persuaded by his friends not to. They pointed out that, unpleasant as she may find him at times, she had gone along with the relationship for all these years, and the King needed her. This, they said, was no time to walk out on him. She agreed to stay, but only on condition that she could dine on her own whenever she wanted to. A friend of the King who frequently visited the Royal Lodge noted, 'Considering the King's extreme kindness to her, she really does make him a most ungrateful return. She detests him, shows it plainly, yet continues to accept all his presents which are of enormous value.'

When Lady Conyngham was herself ill in the autumn of 1829, with a fever and fainting fits, George showed himself much more concerned than she had been about him. She, like others at the Lodge, grumbled that George seemed to enjoy being ill. The gout and failing eyesight he certainly had, she conceded, but asserted that she believed a lot of his other illness was imagined, and was his method of trying to gain sympathy from those around him.

But George had become a doddering old man, his flabby and wrinkled body betraying the damage done over the years by lack of exercise, by prolonged and excessive eating and drinking. He had also been suffering for some time from arteriosclerosis and when, early in 1830, he started having attacks of breathlessness, he could only get to sleep propped up by a pile of pillows in a bed-chair. The abuse of his system had transformed him into the bloated, grotesque caricature of his former self which the cartoonists had anticipated. His sister Mary said he looked 'enormous, like a feather bed'. He still ate vast meals, and the Duke of Wellington observed one breakfast which consisted of two pigeons, three steaks, three-quarters of a bottle of wine, a glass of champagne, two glasses of port, and a glass of brandy.

A few days after this gargantuan breakfast, George, driving his pony-chair in Windsor Great Park, got out to look at his hounds. As he tried to climb in again, he was overcome by a severe breathlessness. That night his doctors, who knew the weakness of his battered body, were alarmed. They felt obliged to issue a bulletin, but made it as innocuous as possible. It said, 'We regret to state that the King has had a bilious attack. His Majesty, although free from fever, is languid and weak.' There were to be a series of bulletins over the next weeks, all posted up at St James's Palace, and all suitably vague. They did not reflect the true concern of the doctors, who observed how the attacks of breathlessness debilitated the King. It even reached the stage where George wanted Parliament to authorise stamping the royal papers to save him the wearying effort of actually signing them. He was persuaded against this because his advisers pointed out that such a move would cause gossip about his health.

When George told Lady Conyngham he was about to die, Wellington believed he did it just to try to upset her. Mrs Fitzherbert, when she heard of his illness, showed a similar reaction. She remarked, 'The King always liked to make himself out worse to excite compassion, and he always wished everyone to think him dangerously ill when little was the matter with him.' But the word soon spread that George's illness was more than a plea for attention. His appetite finally disappeared, and during attacks his face and the ends of his fingers would go black. Assured that the King was very gravely ill, Mrs Fitzherbert decided to forget the insults of the past and her resolve never to communicate with him again, and sent him a letter. It read, 'After many repeated struggles with myself, from the apprehension of appearing troublesome or intruding upon Your Majesty, after so many years of continual silence, my anxiety respecting your Majesty has got the better of my scruples, and I trust Your Majesty will believe me most sincere, when I assure you how truly I have grieved to hear of your sufferings. From the late account, I trust your Majesty's health is daily improving, and no one can feel more rejoiced to learn Your Majesty is restored to complete convalescence, which I pray to God you may long enjoy, accompanied with every degree of happiness you can wish for or desire.'

Mrs Fitzherbert was now seventy-four, and she still loved the man she had married in the clandestine ceremony forty-five years before. She moved from Brighton to London, so that she might be closer to George if he called for her. He did not, although his surgeon, Sir Henry Halford, who conveyed the letter to the King, noted he 'seized it with eagerness and placed it immediately under his pillow'. Mrs Fitzherbert was devastated that he did not bother to reply, but must have gained some consolation from the fact that George ordered her annuity should be raised to £10,000 a year and continued for the rest of her life.

George alternated between planning a convalescence in France, calling for copies of the Racing Calendar, and morosely predicting his death. When Home Secretary Robert Peel returned from his father's funeral George told him, 'You will soon have to pay the like ceremony to me.'

Parliament finally had to pass the King's Signature Bill, whereby state papers could be stamped at the King's verbal direction. His doctors, who had drawn copious amounts of water from his legs, closed the wounds for fear of causing gangrene and the liquid spread all over his body, swelling him up even more. The public was asked to pray for the King, but had little idea of the true nature of his illness. The medical magazine *The Lancet* complained about the vague and ambiguous bulletins, stressing, 'His Majesty is in as alarming a state as ever. The integuments have been again punctured, but his body and his extremities from the immense collection of water, are still enormously swollen. In the management of the royal sufferer, the attendants experienced considerable difficulty in inducing him to take proper medicines, food, and drink. The King does not consider that his case is hopeless. From private information, however, we can only say that although in our opinion ultimate recovery is impossible, immediate dissolution is not inevitable.'

As the month of June passed, the remaining strength in the King faded. His doctors, who had been astonished at his resilience, prepared for the inevitable.

George's physician, Sir Wathen Waller, sat up with him on the night of June 25. The King dropped off to sleep in his chair, with his head resting on a table set in front of him. In the middle of the night, when his breathing became laboured, George woke and asked for some water. He could not swallow it, then, as Sir Wathen recorded, 'as usual took my hand in his and I felt him instantly press it harder than usual and he looked at me with an eager eye and exclaimed, "My dear boy, this is Death!" ' King George lay back in his chair and closed his eyes. He died within minutes, as the clock chimed a quarter past three on the morning of June 26, 1830.

The diarist Thomas Creevey noted, 'Poor Prinny is really dead – on a Saturday too!' Sir Wathen Waller said that over-excitement and high living had, not surprisingly, contributed to George's death. He wrote, 'I am truly broken-hearted and have lost one of the most affectionate friends man ever possessed.'

Few others mourned the King's passing. When the funeral took place at Windsor, *The Times* reported that, though there were many people in the town, the only sign of mourning visible was in their dress. It added that among the congregation gathered in St George's Chapel at the castle, which included the Duke of Clarence, George's oldest surviving brother, now King William IV, there was 'not a single mark of sympathy. It seemed as if the servants of the household, the friends of the carpenters and upholsterers, the petty tradesmen of the town had been admitted to the exclusion of all those who, for public character or official situation, ought to have been allowed free access to the funeral of the Sovereign. We never saw so motley, so rude, so ill-managed a body of persons.'

The new King was clearly impatient to get away from the funeral service. For, while the anthem was still being sung at the end, he rose and walked out of the chapel.

At the first meeting of the Privy Council after George's death, as one of the members recalled, 'There was no grief in the room. It was like an ordinary levee.'

It is true that the Duke of Wellington, addressing a tribute to the House of Lords, declared that King George 'acquired a degree of cultivation, almost unknown in any individual, and he was admitted by all to be the most accomplished man of his age'. But this was only the courtesy of eulogy, as was the adulation heaped on the dead King from pulpits around the country, associating him with the reforms and victories of his time. There was praise for his role as a patron of the arts, which was deserved. But sycophantic newspapers built on this to trumpet the triumphs of Britain which, in reality, had little to do with him. The *Morning Post*, incredibly, referred to him as 'one of the best and most popular monarchs that ever swayed the sceptre of Britain', and mourned 'the loss of a monarch so conspicuously endowed with all the qualities calculated to endear him to the hearts of his subjects'. *The Times* reflected the true feelings of the country by slamming George's 'indifference to the feelings of others ... his most reckless, unceasing and unbounded prodigality'. That newspaper's caustic obituary declared, 'In the tawdry childishness of Carlton House and the mountebank Pavilion, or cluster of pagodas at Brighton, His Royal Highness afforded an infallible earnest of what might one day be expected from His Majesty when the appetite for profusion and the contempt for all that deserves the name of architecture, should have reached their full maturity. Princess Caroline's reception in her husband's house was a stain to manhood. A fashionable strumpet usurped the apartments of the Princess, her rights, the honours due to her, everything but the name she bore. The heroine has now at least nothing to fear from her destroyer.' Determined not to allow the unrevered King to rest in peace, *The Times* carried an editorial three weeks later, reading, 'There never was an individual less regretted by his fellow-creatures than this deceased King. What eye has wept for him? What heart has heaved one throb of unmercenary sorrow for that Leviathan, George IV? If he ever had a friend – a devoted friend in any rank of life – we protest that the name of him or her never reached us. An inveterate voluptuary, especially if he be an artificial person, is of all known beings the most selfish. Selfishness is the true repellent of human sympathy. Selfishness feels no attachment, and invites none; it is the charnel house of the affections. Nothing more remains to be said about George IV but to pay – as pay we must – for his profusion; and to turn his bad conduct to some account by tying up the hands of those who come after him in what concerns the public money.'

Lord Grey made an incisive assessment of George's character when he said, 'He was, indeed, the most extraordinary compound of talent, wit, buffoonery, obstinacy, and good feeling. In short, a medley of the most opposite qualities that I ever saw in any character in my life.'

The public showed their feelings, which followed George into death. Champagne parties were given in Windsor, and observers considered that London showed more signs of rejoicing than mourning.

A tussle threatened over George's will. For the one he signed shortly before his death, which left the residue after family bequests to Lady Conyngham, was declared invalid. The only legal one in existence was the will made out years before for Mrs Fitzherbert. She, however, graciously signed away her rights, and was content with her annuity. Lady Conyngham, deprived of the wealth she had waited years for, raided George's private apartments to make off with boxes of his jewellery. She felt she had earned the reward, which would see her securely into old age.

Such was the paucity of affection for George, even at the moment of his death. He gave us the Regency years, for which he is remembered, and posterity has viewed the era as a glorious age in English history. In fact, his overpowering attachment to buildings and things artistic may have been an unconscious quest for a monument which would bury the horrors of his private life.

There is no doubt that the handsome and charming Prince wasted his gifts and abilities. But if he had led a quiet, domestic life like his father, instead of remorselessly devoting himself to pleasure, he may have been forgiven his extravagances and his lukewarm interest in economic and political conditions.

As it was, his nation found little to regret in his passing. But we do know of one person who genuinely and unselfishly mourned him. George had instructed his executors that he was to be buried 'with whatever ornaments might be upon my person at the time of death'. When the body was lowered into the grave at Windsor, Wellington, one of the executors, spotted a black ribbon round George's neck. On that ribbon was a glittering locket containing a miniature portrait of Maria Fitzherbert. George had worn the locket in expectation of death, thereby making sure it would be buried with him. When Mrs Fitzherbert heard this, she wept.